Arcana Arcanorum:

Cosmic Evolution and Initiation

Libers Trigrammaton and Arcanorum of the Atus of Tahuti

by
Robert C Stein

Incorporating

ARCANA231 Art

by
Barry William Hale

Keep Silence

Winter Solstice 2023 e. v.
An. Vix: ☉ in 0° ♑; ☽ in 27° ♈

Buffalo, New York
42°59'59"N; 78°50'24"W

Publiblished by
Keep Silence
Seattle, WA
keepsilence.org

ISBN: 979-8-218367-46-6

All Rights Reserved
Copyright © 2023 R. C. Stein
ARCANA231 Artwork © Barry William Hale

Aleister Crowley Material Public domain
Scans of texts available at keepsilence.org/the-equinox

This first edition is an unlimited run
of which 22 copies hand are hand numbered א – ת

Do what thou wilt shall be the whole of the Law.

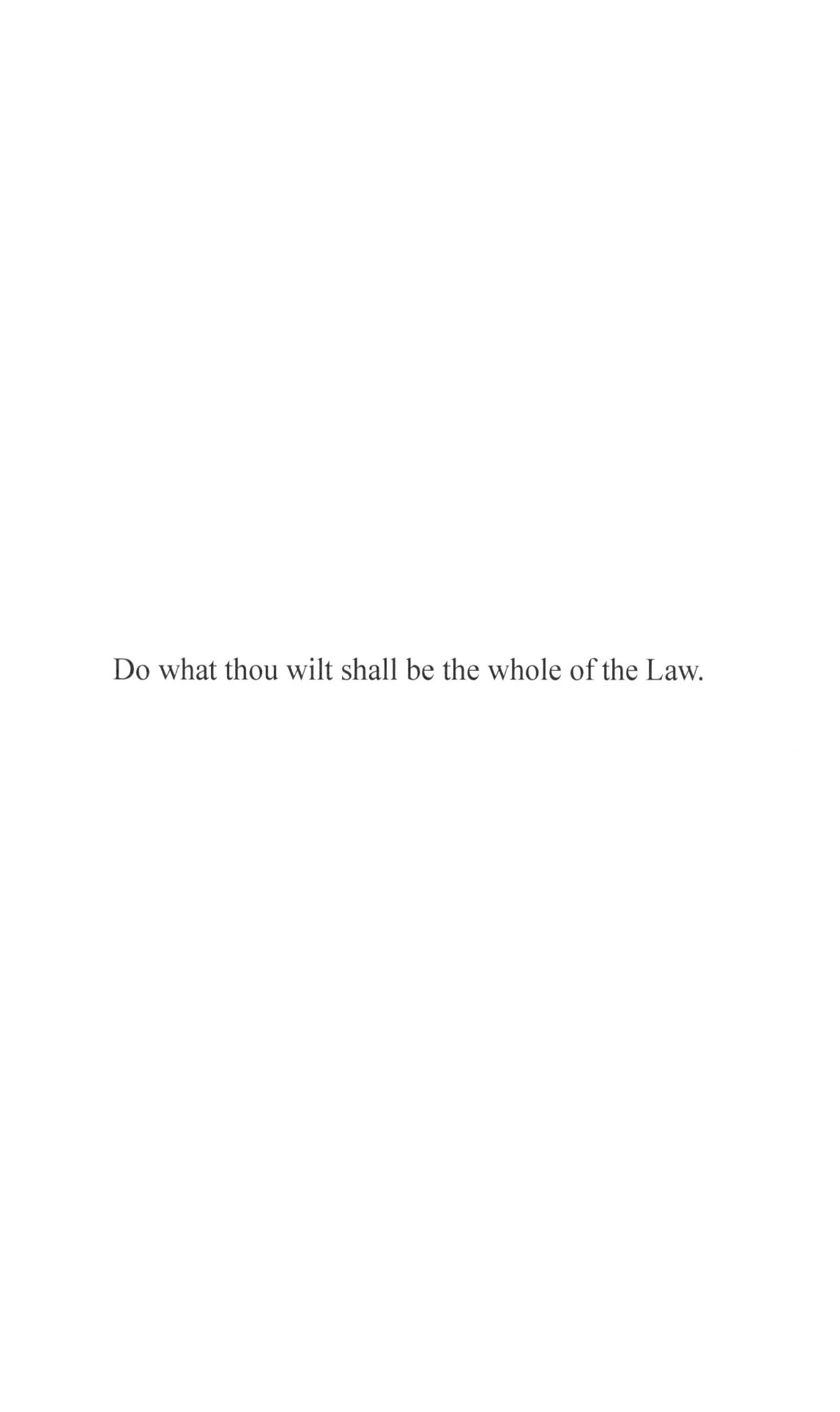

Table of Contents

Acknowledgments	VII
Preface	VIII
Chapter One — Introduction	1
Traditional Tree of Life (TL)	
Sepher Yetzirah and Hebrew Alphabet	
Thelema Class A	
Trigrammaton and the Quantum Tree of Life (QTL)	
Chapter Two — ARCANA 231 - Art by Barry William Hale	9
Chapter Three — Tarot and Tree of Life Models	15
Tarot History	
Hebrew Alphabet Symbolism	
The Glyph in Liber XXXI is a Path Label	
Tarot Trump History	
Tarot Trump Order	
Cosmic Process	
Formula of Initiation	
Chapter Four — Path Messages, Descent from Aleph	27
Air — Man of Earth — Aleph to Kaph	
Water — Adept, Esoteric Self — Mem to Resh	
Fire — Hermit — Shin, Tau	
Chapter Five — Arcana 231 — Tarot Path Accounts	35
Chapter Six — Summary	169
Literature Cited	173
Appendices	
One — Liber CCXXXI vel Arcanorum facsimile	177
Two — Liber XXVII vel Trigrammaton facsimile	185
Three — ARCANA231	195

Acknowledgments

The author of the text first wishes to acknowledge the creative art of Barry William Hale. His interpretation of the Class A material exemplifies a universal message. He is experienced with a wide spectrum of occult models, magical and religious interpretations and applies them here.

To August LaScola for his continual reading, support and suggestions about the text.

The many members of Pyramid Lodge in Buffalo, New York have reviewed and discussed the text. Their comments and suggestions have been very informative. They have helped clarify the message. Especially, the author acknowledges the contributions of Norman Fleck.

To my daughter, Marian, for developing the Word Style that systematized the typographic presentation. Any failure of consistency is strictly mine.

To Scott Wilde for the photography of images and the final editing and preparing the manuscript. I particularly appreciate his skill, tenacity, and support toward publication matters.

To the many individuals who have discussed ideas with me, though not listed individually, I give thanks for many formal and informal discussions during the 40 years that have shaped this summary presentation.

It has been a long journey. I hope the sharing the author's thoughts provides some useful insight and stimulus to follow the reader's path.

RCS
21 DE 2023, e. v.

Preface

Man visualizes Nature (creation) as the emanation of Ineffable. He starts from traditional knowledge and history. He builds on the shoulders of giants of earlier ages. He re-evaluates their tradition, symbols, models, assumptions, and views. He must question all if he seeks knowledge and truth, wisdom, and peace. He faces the unknown. That is initiation in progress.

The prophets of old still have much to say. Their messages, models and traditions are bases for change and growth. Some seem true. There may be justification to modify or reject others. The challenge is to ask questions, take different viewpoints, recognize new facts, and uncover the reality. Judgment sorts them. As experience broadens, knowledge increases. When this happens, some assumptions die, some undergo modification, few survive. Wisdom approaches the perfect knowledge of nature asymptotically. There are always unknown factors. The absolute is unattainable, but the race for it must go on.

Ineffable is not known, not communicable, non-dimensional, and not defined. Omnipresent, omniscient, and omnipotent all fail as descriptions. Even proposing a name for Ineffable destroys its ineffability. Man perceives the implications only by **contrast** to a manifest universe, analogous to the event horizon of a black hole. The universe of nature or the nature of the universe is his limit. It is beyond the mind of man. Man has no idea what he does not know.

Because of hubris and perception, man perceives and can describe truth in human terms. Alchemists sought truth through nature and consciousness. Scientists seek truth through experiment and observation. Artists and poets seek truth through sensory expression and imagery. Magicians seek truth through ritual and symbol. Each approaches his gnosis differently and individually.

The formula of universal operation, *Solve et Coagula*, is Nature's *modus operandi*, whose laws are never broken. Yet, man in his hubris tries to measure everything. But his understanding of the laws of nature is incomplete and may be erroneous. Miracles appear as exceptions to "known" Natural laws, but they are just labels to assuage the ignorance of man. Rather, they expose fallibility. Miracles apply to unexplainable occurrence in Nature. Truth comes when reality replaces mystery and miracle.

Many consider magic a supplement to or subversion of Natural Law. The initiate recognizes the label, but the meaning behind is not fully understood. Lifting the veil between unknown and known exposes truth.

Aristotle has been said to say that the mark of an educated mind to be able to entertain a thought without accepting it. Properly entertaining a thought means to consider its place relative to current experience. Man may then propose changes and challenge limits for approaching reality. This is growth.

Crowley carried his Golden Dawn background about the Tarot into the New Æon in the Class B Liber 78, A Description of the Cards of the Tarot (Equinox I (8): 143ff). He later explored the esoteric meaning further in the Class B Book of Thoth (1944). He expanded the message.

Liber CCXXXI vel Arcanorum applies number symbolism to the New Æon. As Class A it is not subject to change. However, it is subject to interpretation. Crowley wrote little about it.

Arcanorum and the Tarot paths are instructive thoughts about life for an initiate in the New Æon. They provide subjects and outlines for meditation. Each individual path has a message for the initiate to explore. The paths use new words, sigils, and genii and viewpoints to express gnosis. Contrast is necessary to gain knowledge, understanding and interpretation. The initiate must challenge each encounter and evaluate its results. The totality of the paths represents is the universe. The paths are individual studies for meditation and enlightenment. They direct individual study. In all cases of doubt, he can only rely on himself. Every man and every woman is a star.

Arcanorum uses the sequence of Hebrew letters as an index to tarot paths and cognate symbols. It is one model sequence for organizing aspects of life but requires experience to expose the meaning. The liber includes qliphothic and mercuric aspects, negative and positive existence. The book models cosmic evolution and initiation. The cosmic aspects encompass the universe and manifestation. The paths correlate to the tarot paths to life.

Many models of the universe exist — I Ching, Qabalah, Tree of Life, and Cube of Space. Each model the others in some ways. Each has a specific viewpoint, Arcana Arcanorum is a commentary on Liber CCXXXI interpreting the Tarot message revealed through Aleister Crowley. Its result, hopefully, helps others to meditate about and understand essence of life. It presents text and artistic interpretations to explain the underlying message of each path. Specifically, it is designed to assist an initiate to understand Thelema and its primary revelation, Liber XXXI vel AL, whose basic principles are universal.

Know thyself and join the universe!

Chapter One
Introduction

The Book of the Law, *Liber XXXI vel AL*, I: page 17 (verse 56) warns about revelations by prophets: All words are sacred and all prophets true; save only that they understand a little. Learn first and evaluate the reality for yourself. *Liber CCXXXI vel Arcanorum* is one approach to Thelemic understanding.

Aristotle advocated an open, receptive mind and a willingness to experience and challenge truth. He is reported to have said:

> **It is the mark of an educated man to be able to entertain a thought without accepting it.**

Schopenhauer, in Studies in Pessimism, continues that:

> **Each prophet characterizes truth from his limited experience.** Each professes knowledge as he understands it. But his description is either false, incomplete, or both.

> **Every man takes the limits of his own field of vision for the limits of the world.** This is an error of the intellect as inevitable as that error of the eye which lets us fancy that on the horizon heaven and earth meet.

> The discovery of truth is prevented more effectively, not by the false appearance of things present and which mislead into error, **not directly by weakness of the reasoning powers, but by preconceived opinion, by prejudice**.

> The oriental story of the blind men and elephant illustrates the conundrum. The first blind man, holding the leg of an elephant, calls it a tree trunk. The second, feeling the trunk, says it is a snake. The third, pushing against its side, imagines a wall.

Each man is true to his perception. Behind each blind man operates the omnipresent and unbreakable laws of Nature — in TRUTH. No one owns the first mortgage on heaven, wisdom, or truth. All human labels, interpretations and comparisons are necessarily internal, fallible, and subject to challenge. Different models may have commonality but are not necessarily congruent. Revelation, belief, and truth are interpreted variously according to context and culture. Distinguishing between outward objective fact, labels and underlying meaning is critical! To grow requires a challenging, open, and receptive mind. The principle of Occam's Razor applies. When this happens, assumptions often die and labels change, few survive. Truth and meaning shine through. Even so, all perception is not likely true, but just the best for the times.

Traditional Tree of Life

Diagrams of the traditional Tree of Life occur in many formats. The origins go back to Hebrew qabalah as early as the 13th Century. The most familiar form follows Kircher (*Oedipus Aegyptiacus*, 1652-4) and the Golden Dawn of the late 19th Century. They precede Thelema. The diagrams show an arrangement of sephiroth in three triads and three columns, plus Kether and Malkuth. The sephiroth are static in columns and triads. Their names derive from the Bible (I Chron. 13: 34).

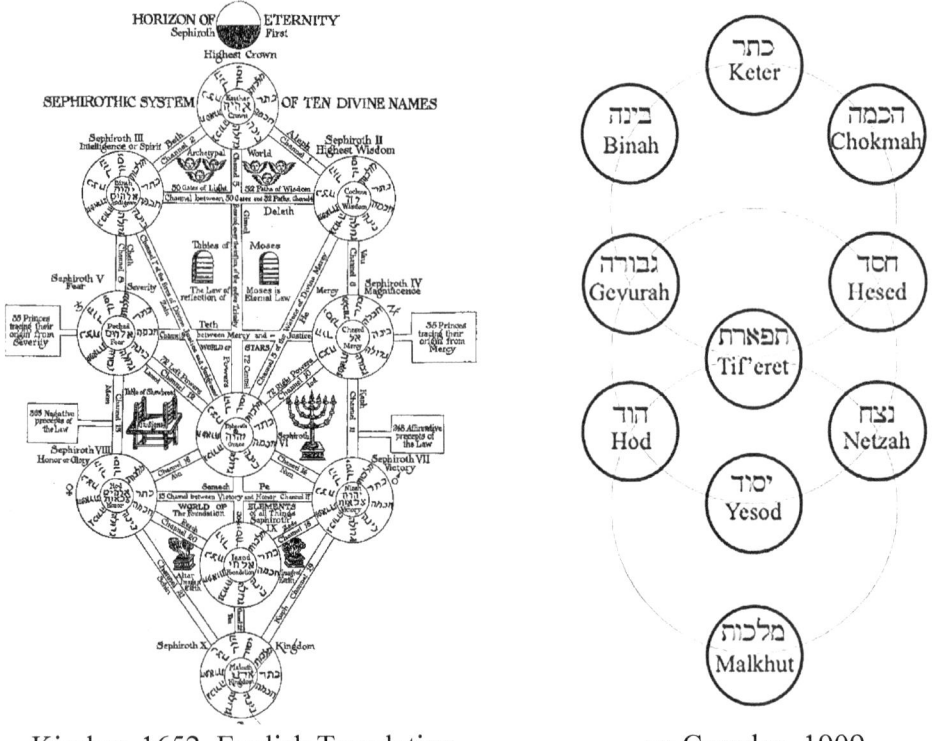

Kircher, 1652, English Translation   ex Crowley, 1909

The traditional 2-d Tree of Life model has suggestion of 3-d indicated by crossing paths. These are artefacts of the projection. The 3-d model has the path of Samech (Tiphareth to Yesod) pulled forward and upward, leaving Kether and Malkuth connected to Da'ath as a central axis, and three peripheral triads around the axis.

Sepher Yetzirah and Hebrew Alphabet

The Hebrew alphabet is alpha / numeric, where each letter has a numerical value. Each has been a numeral for thousands of years. Even though the numerical function has often been replaced by Arabic numerals, base 10, in modern times for easier calculation, the Hebrew alpha / numeric system has been retained. The corresponding equivalents are as follows:

Aleph	1	Yod	10	Qoph	100
Beth	2	Kaph	20	Resh	200
Gimel	3	Lamed	30	Shin	300
Daleth	4	Mem	40	Tau	400
Heh	5	Nun	50	Kaph Final	500
Vau	6	Samech	60	Mem Final	600
Zain	7	Ayin	70	Nun Final	700
Cheth	8	Peh	80	Peh Final	800
Teth	9	Tzaddi	90	Tzaddi Final	900

The sequence of the 22 letters from Aleph to Tau indicate the eight verse groups in Psalms 119: 1 to 176. This alphabet is inherent to Hebrew qabalah.

The final letterforms are not as ancient as the base 22 letters. They first appear after the Babylonian Captivity of the Jews under Cyrus. There is no zero in the Hebrew system. Changing the number value equivalents of the letters would change the sequence of the Hebrew alphabet or possibly their numerical value.

Kaplan (1990) has a thorough discussion of the *Sepher Yetzirah*. He discusses the history and symbolism of this *Book of Creation*. That has commentaries from the 10th Century, and the text quoted as early as the Sixth Century It is an early source, one of the classic bases of qabalah. The correlations are classic.

His Chapter 1 discusses the 32 mystical paths of Wisdom, relates them to the Biblical story of creation and the sephiroth. The commentary reinforces the relationship between letter, number, symbolism, and the sephiroth and qabalistic worlds.

Kaplan assembles several Trees of Life interpreted by classic Hebrew authorities. Their common view assigns the mother letters on the three horizontal paths (from Kether toward Malkuth) as Aleph, Mem, and Shin. The other paths are assigned different Hebrew letters, according to the authority quoted. Each tree has three horizontal triads and three vertical columns.

In mystical symbolism the three mother letters have symbolic elemental assignment. The seven planets, using their occurrence now match the first hour of the day. The single letters follow in zodiacal order, beginning with the Spring Equinox in the Northern Hemisphere. At this point the sun, traveling north, crosses the equator.

These correlations of symbols carry through the mystical tradition to the present time.

Thelema Class A

In 1904, Aiwass, the minister of Hoor-paar-kraat, revealed the New Æon to Crowley as The Book of the Law, *Liber XXXI vel L [now AL]*. This is the original authority for Thelema. Crowley put this liber in Class A. As such, it is not subject to change or alteration, though he made some. Verses I: (page 18) 57, II: 76, and III: 47 refer to paths on the Tree of Life.

Other Class A texts have references to Tarot. They include *Liber VII vel Lapidus Lazuli* (V: 5), and *Liber CDXVIII, the Vision and the Voice*, especially the First Æthyr (Equinox I (5): Supplement p. 170-171). In the last, the voice of the Angel (interpreted as Class A within AB) describes the tarot card sequence in Hebrew alphabetical order within a single paragraph.

Appendix One has a facsimile of Liber CCXXXI. Its units correspond to the 22 Hebrew letter paths and sequence on the 2-d Tree of Life.

Appendix Two is a facsimile of Liber XXVII. The trigrams correspond to vessels and lights of the sephiroth on the 3-d Quantum Tree of Life.

Trigrammaton and the 3-d Quantum Tree of Life

Liber Trigrammaton uses trigrams as a system of numeric labeling. The trigrams use universal number sequence and theory. The text is a Thelemic interpretation of Nature. The Quantum TL is a model derived from Trigrammaton and the Cube of Three. The Cube is usually seen lying on a flat surface. The Quantum Tree uses an apical vector view as with a Cube balanced on a vertex.

Figure 1. The 3-d Quantum Tree of Life, Lower phase, erect, non-helical form.

In Figure 1 the triads deflected slightly downward. The sephiroth appear in the same relationships as in the 2-d Golden Dawn Tree.

The Quantum Tree is a 3-d model. Like Trigrammaton, it uses tri-radial symmetry and base-3 numbers. It is a projection of the Cube of Three. It is a more inclusive model of the traditional Tree of Life. It applies the same consistent definitions of sephira (including complete vessels and lights), paths, triads, and columns. The different models represent the meaning differently.

Trigrammaton reveals the Middle Triad to be double, serving with the Upper Triad, as the lower triad of Briah, and with the Lower Triad as the Upper Triad of Yetzirah. The KCHGA occurs between Yetzirah and Briah. The 2-d TL is rigid. The 'spherical sephiroth' of the QTL form peripheral helices around the erect Central Axis of the Quantum TL because of dense packing. The Central Axis remains erect, with each unit matching a triad.

Figure 2. Lower Phase    *Figure 3. Upper Phase*

Figure 2 shows the 3-d Quantum Tree of Life, Lower Phase helical arrangement. The Central Axis (hidden) is surrounded by the Peripheral Sephiroth. Tiphareth is in the Middle Triad, Yesod in the Lower Triad. The light gray sphere in the upper right represents the space for the Brothers of the Left-hand Path.

Figure 3 shows the 3-d Quantum Tree of Life, Upper Phase, helical arrangement. The Central Axis is surrounded by the Peripheral Sephiroth. Tiphareth is in the Upper Triad.

The light gray sphere in the lower left represents the Black Brothers (see Trigrammaton).

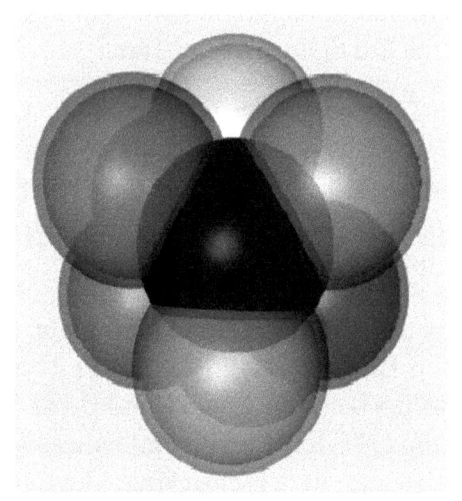

Figure 4 shows the QTL viewed from below Malkuth. Malkuth is at the center. The Lower and Middle Triad sephiroth match Yetzirah of the Holy Hexagram.

The tangent points between the pairs of sephiroth vessels are the path connections on the QTL. Each path pairs two distinct sephiroth. No paths cross. All peripheral paths are the same length. Paths from Da'ath are shorter and equal in length. Most TL paths are the same for the QTL. The QTL has 32. The QTL adds eight connections between Da'ath and the peripheral sephiroth. The path of Samech is duplicate, one path between Tiphareth and Yesod each in Briah and Yetzirah. The tenth path automatically becomes evident between Geburah and Yesod in the model because of dense packing.

Chapter Two
ARCANA 231

Art/Magical engagements with Liber CCXXXI from 1993-2018/19.

Barry William Hale

The catalyst for my artistic inspiration surrounding Liber CCXXXI1 [Book 231] was found in an old edition of an O.T.O. newsletter. It had the Liber 231 manuscript sigils received by Aleister Crowley in 1907, and included instructions and suggestions to JFC Fuller, who redrew the sigils for publication in Crowley's Equinox:

> General Design: Maybe a wheel with 22 compartments on the rim. The wheel has 8 spokes. At the 4 corners are the 4 Kerubim [sketch with Aquarius, Scorpio, Taurus, and Leo clockwise from top left]. But the Pillar Scheme is equally good… These sigils are dangerously automatic and should not be exposed or left lying about.

The 231 Gates found in the Jewish mystical classic, the Sepher Yetzirah, are created by placing the 22 letters of their alphabet in a circle or wheel. It is remarkably reminiscent of Crowley's circular arrangement of sigil ideograms/hieroglyphs found in Liber CCXXXI [Book 231]. Furthermore, the Genius sigil associations of hermetic correspondences, Christianized Kabbalah, and the Sepher Yetzirah, were obvious when constructing a magical hieroglyphic wheel.

Liber 231 contains a series of two registers of Genii/Qliphoth sigils and their associated offices correlated to the 22 letters of the Hebrew alphabet and the 22 Atus of Tahuti, the Major Arcana of Tarot. They imply they are tied to intertwined branches of the Qabalistic Tree of Life as diurnal and nocturnal phases within both the astral and sublunary spheres.

It may also be observed that the two sets of 22 sigils exhibit notably different characteristics. For example, the Domes, or Houses, are generally more geometrical in nature.

The sigils of the Qliphoth are more anthropomorphic, bestial, fantastical or figurative in nature. In the Domes there are only two examples of figurative elements, the Face in the Sun in the sigil for Resh and the Eye of Horus (Wajet) in the sigil for Vau. By comparison in the Qliphoth there are 17 examples where faces appear, made up from various elements or emerging from the sigils. They are strange little monstrosities, blobs with teeth, strange succubi, anthropomorphic, bestial, and abortive creatures.

My research into Liber 231 is extensive. Here is a brief overview to show relationships between an inspired artwork and the Holy Book.

I commenced working art in Wentworth Falls, Blue Mountains, New South Wales, in 1995, using Crowley's notes to Fuller. This was a two-paneled piece, one for each of the two sets of sigils, in a circle girded by the four Cherubim. Each wheel was eight spoked; one warded by a winged foot Mercurial child with caduceus wand for the Houses of Mercury, and one a form of Typhon for the Prison Cells of the Qliphoth. Each wheel was inspired by Crowley's note and by personal oneiric experiences while working with the sigils. They confirmed and clarified Crowley's wheel arrangement.

The circular diagrams were elaborated further during a sojourn in Bundeena, New South Wales in 2001. These were called 'Wheels of Heaven and Hell'. In this series, the two wheels of sigils appeared in my initial artistic arrangements separately, but now merge in most of later paintings.

The four cherubs of the previous artworks gave way to vibrant pictorial fields replete with historical depictions of Heaven and Hell. Their inhabitants are in a liminal carnival, wheels of fortune, anthropomorphic citadels, visions of the Apocalypse, fire-belching hell-mouths, tormenting demons, and choirs of celestial angels. The fantastical creatures and symbolic motifs collapse into a luminous visionary menagerie. The Wheels are overlooked by a primary figure or figures in the form of Angelic/Demonic entities interlocked in a hyperstatic union.

The aesthetic result of bringing the two wheels together resulted in double-sided, reversible compositions so that the paintings might be viewed either way and serve to reinforce the concepts of duality and cosmic juxtaposition. There are also two of the series of large square compositions that have two sets of dual demons and angels. They can be rotated as four different orientations. This series of paintings on average is 1.8 meters in height by 1.3 meters in width and are produced using thin layers of brightly colored acrylic on stretched canvas. Each of these paintings were completed within 3-4 days generally which led to extended periods of sleep deprivation generating a hallucinatory state. It gave rise to most depictions of the genii and chimeric spirits. At one time during praxis, I fell into the pictorial plan and into an immersive lucid vision.

In 2003, I completed a second major series based on Liber 231 which was exhibited at The Hospital, London. Consisting of thirty-six works; twenty-four based around a single Wheel – twelve for the Domes or Houses of Mercury and twelve for the Carcers or 'Prison Cells of the Qliphoth'. Twelve larger works combined the two wheels into one containing the two registers. In this series, the rich backgrounds of the paintings have disappeared completely. The composition focus is on figures contain the Wheels of the Genii sigils themselves — one figure for the twenty-four and two interlocking figures of the twelve. The single and double wheels produce a panoply of different characters, generating from the turning of the wheels of Heaven and Hell. Gargoyles and Heralds are a menagerie of the wonderful and strange. They not only contain the powers of the wheels but constrain and command the forces of the genii within. The 24 are depicted sounding trumpets or blowing horns. This imagery connects directly to Revelations, foreshadowing the immanence of the Eschaton. The eleven double wheel compositions are all reversible or double-sided, later they were published in an art folio titled CODEX 231 in 2014 with the addition of specific color-coded bars, a stylistic nod to the previous series of paintings. The second part of the series is double the size of the twenty-four. They center around twin wheels housing intertwined branches of two trees from which hang the strange fruits of the sigils from Liber 231.

Now we come to the artwork presented in this current volume entitled ARCANA 231. The series began with the production of three artworks for an art show themed around the Tarot in 2015. Admittedly, I had an aversion to the concept of the show, since over the years I have had countless suggestions to produce a complete Tarot deck, especially following the completion of my second series based on Liber 231. However, I felt a fraternal obligation to support my brethren, and therefore I produced three artworks for a Tarot themed exhibition organized by the Art Guild of the Australian Ordo Temple Orientis. The exhibition was held in Rutgers, New Jersey, USA.

The first three pieces of what would become ARCANA 231 were based around the three sets of Genii from the Domes and Cells corresponding with the Hebrew letters, Aleph, Mem and Cheth and were acquired by the present author.

Although I understood that the execution of these three implied the fabrication of the remaining nineteen (to become the artwork present volume), I initially had no intention of embarking upon the rest at that time, being busy with other magical endeavors. As fate would have it, one drawing led to another until Bob Stein came to patronize the entire series of 22 works which drove the project to completion between 2015 and 2016.

It should be noted that the artwork which accompanies the text of ARCANA 231 is directly inspired by Liber 231. It consists solely of my own response to the subject matter and is an aesthetic outgrowth of previous artistic endeavors. ARCANA

231 represents part of my ongoing aesthetic exploration in which different concepts arise. It is, in many respects, an evolution articulating the natural results in previous related series. Polarity and the play of opposites have been an enduring and central motif. The resulting artwork derives from meditations on the mysteries of Liber 231. This typifies my art/magical process. It is reflected throughout my overall output. The investigation and research build upon themselves. New concepts emerge in an organic fashion from intense and long magical working. This is especially true with Liber 231 and my study of the Tarot in general.

The Tarot, Atus, or Major Arcana can be seen as symbolic picture boards, astral doorways or landscapes. They are a catalogue of hermetic hieroglyphs, edusemiotic devices, and memory palaces. They area a blueprint of a Hermetic initiatic process. They are a vast repository of profound occult and esoteric expression. They also can be a divination device.

The Genii represented throughout ARCANA 231 are the embodiment of intelligences specific to different realms of the Atus. The dualism is dynamic and stems from the ancient Egyptian mythology concerning Amennta, the Underworld and the various deities who rule over the nocturnal and diurnal spaces, the Tuats.

The twenty-two primary compositions of ARCANA 231 are a meeting place of the two opposing and complementary Genii, reconciled in a singular composition. Each intelligence is personified and placed in a symmetrically divided picture plane strongly suggestive of the rotational symmetry obtained within the court cards of a generic playing deck. This personification is drawn from the mythological matrix-maze of world culture, religion and folklore, which should be seen easily by a discerning viewer.

The symbolic landscapes of the Tarot trumps contrast the 22 dual Genii expressions of the focus is the Genii. They represent the intelligences of the paths and contrast the symbolic figures in the trumps.

The figures used in ARCANA 231 are taken from myriad contexts and myths, the narrative is a created initiatic journey. They express the idea that the Atus map the unfolding of a New Aeon. The Genii are keys to the gates hiding mysteries. It is their dynamic relationship and their concomitant stories that give life and association to the Genii as a whole — to the Genii on the Tree of Life as light and dark phases of Being.

The figures used in ARCANA 231 are taken from myriad contexts and myths. Conceptualizing the two aspects of Mercurial and Qliphothic personifications as two poles of a narrative arc is an ordeal that tempers the attainment of wisdom through experience.

I have focused on the dual couplings on a more individual relational dynamics rather than on the cosmological or initiatory narrative drawn across the entire arc of the Trumps as a whole.

In this manner, one should see the dual nature of each Path/Letter as an integral component of the whole. Yet, the general focus within ARCANA 231 remains tied to the 22 Hebrew letters and the Tarot.

The interpretation chosen for each of the 22 compositions is in no way exhaustive of the limited possibilities. Artists no doubt will have different representations. ARCANA 231 is my own personal choice. My choices are an emergent quality. Their creation evolves through symbolism of the Tarot. They relate to mythological narratives. In many respects they set parameters for inspiration to take root, but hard to express in words.

For almost thirty years Liber 231 has continued to be an inspiration. Crowley's note to Fuller sparked a possibility that took root in my imagination. It grew from my magical journey and flourished through artistic endeavor. Crowley left an important key. His notes turn relationships among the Genii into a veritable double Ring of Solomon. They constrain and command the Spirits therein. It is a new tool to access knowledge, power, and inspiration. The result of the work is an ornate Brazen Vessel, a repository for the Genii elaborately embellished with artistic result.

Chapter Three
Tarot and the Tree of Life Models

Liber CCXXXI vel Arcanorum is the only Class A document specifically relating to Tarot paths in the New Æon. Its first publication is in the 1912 Equinox I (7): 69-74. Aleister Crowley, prophet of the Æon, noted its cosmic and initiatory aspects. It is didactive, revealing and revolutionary. It provides focus for awareness and meditation. See Appendix One for a facsimile.

Arcanorum presents a model of the cosmos and a process called 'Initiation'. Few have analyzed the approach and message of Arcanorum since it was published in 1912. Crowley, who published it and made a few but significant comments. For the most part, later students have seen it as a puzzle. The sigils seem difficult to interpret. The text requires visualizing symbols. The genii have peculiar names and character. Many published accounts consider only the qliphothic aspects. It has been considered a Crowley joke by some. But Crowley assigned it to Class A!

This liber uses the 22 paths on the traditional Tree of Life. The paths are in linear Hebrew alphabetic order, from Aleph to Tau. Crowley also suggested a circular model, but barely explored it. Fuller did so after World War II. Hale used the linear sequence in the form of a circle.

Arcanorum supplements the message of Liber AL. It presents a broad outline of cosmic evolution. It is also a road map for the journey of the Fool / Initiate. The paths each have a basic message for consideration. They relate to external Light, Law, Love, Life, and Liberty. The Ordeal and development of internal natures are complementary. The combination results in understanding Nature and the Great Work. Uniting Duality with Unity is the goal by crossing the Abyss. The Tarot developed independently and preceded Trigrammaton and the QTL. The three converge around the meaning of their components.

Tarot History

Tarot originated as an Italian card game, Tarocchi, circa 1425. The original cards showed various aspects of life and persons at the time. The trump card sequence was not established. Their design and order varied with location. They evolved into a set of basic images, variously interpreted, redrawn, and expressed in different artistic styles. Platonic or cardinal virtue cards formed a subset among them. They express ethical guidance for life. Later, by association with the Hebrew alphabet and mysticism, the symbolic meaning of the cards increased. Whether the original intent, design, or sequence consciously applied to a life story narrative or archetypes is moot.

Tarot cards are now used as a popular mode of divination (cartomancy). That use is not considered here. Crowley's guide is Liber LXXVIIII. Collectively, the cards provide an outline for organizing the universal aspects of life and Nature.

Vieville and Noblet began the French tarot tradition circa 1650. By 1761, the Conver Marseilles deck had 78 cards in particular order. That order is now widely followed. The sequence follows from The Fool to the Ten of Discs, the man of earth that is also the Fool. However, the Fool card was unnumbered, and variously inserted into the others.

When Tarot became popular for divination, upright and inverse views of each card in a spread came to have different interpretations — contrasting aspects of the message or card. In 1781, le Comte de Mellet first related the 22 Hebrew letters to the 22 tarot trump cards. The letter associations became the confounder for other attributes of the cards. Eliphas Levi (1856) particularly expanded their qabalistic interpretation. He considered the true sequence of the trumps to be secret.

Hebrew Alphabet Symbolism

Class A libers and the *Sepher Yetzirah* use the Hebrew alphabet letter sequence.

In the *Sepher Yetzirah*, the Hebrew alphabet is organized into three groups of letters. The initial three mother letters relate to elements. The twelve single Hebrew letters follow a zodiacal sequence. The seven Hebrew double letters have planetary associations. The intermediate paths explore aspects between mother letters. See Liber 777.

Three mother letters — The Elements

א,	Aleph	🜁	Air
מ,	Mem	🜄	Water
ש,	Shin	🜂	Fire

Seven double letters — The Planets

ב,	Beth	☿	Mercury
ג,	Gimel	☽	Moon
ד,	Daleth	♀	Venus
כ,	Kaph	♃	Jupiter
פ,	Peh	♂	Mars
ר,	Resh	☉	Sun
ת,	Tau	♄	Saturn

Twelve single letters — The Signs of the Zodiac

ה,	Heh	♈	Aries
ו,	Vau	♉	Taurus
ז,	Zain	♊	Gemini
ח,	Cheth	♋	Cancer
ט,	Teth	♌	Leo
י,	Yod	♍	Virgo
ל,	Lamed	♎	Libra
נ,	Nun	♏	Scorpio
ס,	Samech	♐	Sagittarius
ע,	Ayin	♑	Capricorn
צ,	Tzaddi	♒	Aquarius
ק,	Qoph	♓	Pisces

Assignments of other data sets attributed to these letters may not correlate to one another. The correlation between the annual cycle of ice-cream cone sales and the frequency of deaths by drowning is confounded, not relevant or causal. Compare lines among the columns of Liber 777 with care.

The Glyph (☍) in Liber XXXI is a Path Label

The Golden Dawn cipher manuscript is background for Crowley's understanding of the tarot sequence. The facsimiles are folios 35 and 38 in Runyon (2009). They appear as folios 32 and 35 in Kuntz (1996). The earlier folios show the interchange in the Leo / Libra pair from the Marseilles deck. They are changed to zodiacal order in the latter. Crowley must have been aware of both during his progress in the Golden Dawn. The sequence in the Class B Liber LXXVIII in Equinox I (7): 143ff reflects the earlier tradition.

Crowley establishes his distinct tarot trump sequence on the Tree of Life model because of his interpretation of the glyph (☍) in Liber XXXI, I: page 18. His interpretation of the glyph as Tzaddi (צ) first occurs in an unpublished typeset proof for the Collected Works Vol. III, p. 231ff (1907). The earliest publication of the glyph as Tzaddi (צ) is in Thelema Vol. 3 (1909), p. 11. Glyph is a descriptive label used here to avoid any preconceived interpretation. Figure 4 shows a scan of the Class A citation. It does not show in Liber CCXX or Liber CCXXXI. It is not among the 'old letters of my Book".

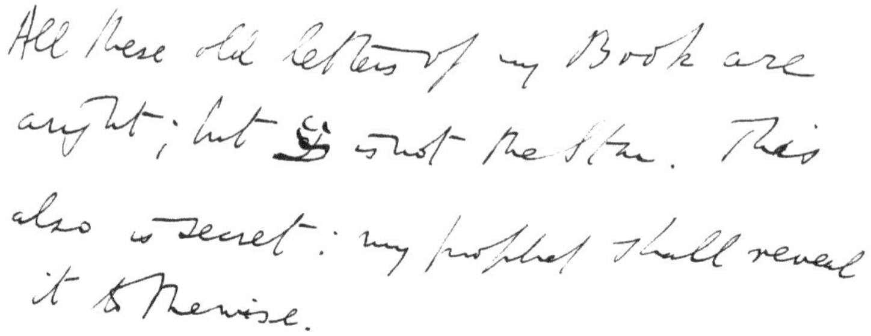

All these old letters of my Book are aright; but ☍ is not the Star. This also is secret: my prophet shall reveal it to the wise.

Figure 4. Liber XXXI, 1: p. 18 (≈ Liber CCXX, Ch. 1, v. 57)

Crowley considered the glyph to be equivalent to a Hebrew letter! To have his ה / צ reciprocal change valid, Crowley ignored the first clause of the sentence, *i.e.*, "All these old letters of my Book are aright". Any exchange in a closed set (*e.g.* the 22-letter Hebrew alphabet) must affect at least two members. If both are aright, reciprocal exchange makes both not aright and out of alphabetic and numerical order. Logically, there must be another interpretation for the whole verse. Instead, the correction seems to suggest an additional path. Then the glyph (☍) is not recognized as an 'aright' letter. The Glyph must be beyond the closed aright set of the old 22-letters that includes traditional Tzaddi assignment to The Star. The manuscript cites no specific assignment for it as a path on the Tree of Life model. The 'but' clause becomes a caveat regarding interpretation!

Tarot Trump History

Circa 1890, the Golden Dawn in England organized tables into columns of correspondences and attributes. It associated tarot paths with the Tree of Life based on the Kircher (1652) model. Its series of other correspondences do not necessarily correlate to one another. In the early 20th Century, member of the Golden Dawn Aleister Crowley brought these tables into the New Æon as Class B Liber 78). His descending tarot trump order correlates to paths on that Tree. He used sephiroth ascending the Tree of Life as his model for the initiatory process.

Liber 777 has many columns of correspondences. The Hebrew alphabet letters and the *Sepher Yetzirah* are a confounding index. The Hebrew final letterforms were not used as labels for separate paths.

Arcanorum reveals aspects of tarot paths as *Carcerorum Qliphoth* [*cf.* Negative Existence, a dark or original view] and *Domarum Mercurii* [*cf.* Positive Existence, a light, derived view]. The Hebrew alphabet indexes both. The sigils are in mirror-image columns of their contrasting aspects. The names of the genii follow using alphabetical acronyms. The collective revelation is greater than the sum of its parts.

Some parts of the first edition in Equinox I (7): 69-74 may not be considered Class A. The double column of Hebrew letters appears between the sigil tables there for the first time. The *Note on the Qabalah of Nine Chambers*, a legacy written by Fr. P. (Aleister Crowley) during his Golden Dawn (Old Æon) period is another.

The original, Latin-Greek title occurs in *Equinox* I (7): 69:

> LIBER ARCANORUM tωn ATV tou TAHVTI QUAS VIDIT
>
> ASAR IN AMMENTI SVB FIGURA CCXXXI
>
> LIBER CARCERORUM tωn QLIPHOTH CVM SUIS GENIIS
>
> ADDVNTUR SIGILLA ET NOMINA EORVM

Translated:

> Book of the Secrets of the Atu of Tahuti
>
> that Asar saw in Amennti. Under Figure 231
>
> Book of the Cells of the Qliphoth with their Spirits
>
> their Sigils and Names having been added.

In the Holy Books of Thelema, Equinox III (9): xxxiii, notes by Crowley include:

Above the body text is the statement, "This book is true up to the grade of Adeptus Exemptus [7°=4▫]"

> This is an account of **the cosmic process** so far as it is indicated by the Tarot Trumps. [Syllabus, Equinox I (10): 45]

> Liber CCXXXI (**XXII Domarum et XXII Carcerorum**) [Index, Equinox I (10): 239 refer to Equinox I (7): 69, the numbers of sigils]

> *Liber CCXXXI vel Arcanorum* is a technical treatise on the Tarot. The sequence of the 22 Trumps is explained as **a formula of initiation**. [Confessions p. 673-74]

> CCXXXI Sum of the numbers [0 + 1 +.... + 20 + 21] printed on the Tarot Trumps. [Syllabus, Equinox I (10): 55].

The title and Class A assignment indicate Tarot is more than a game, more than a method of divination. It presents a reference guide for organizing aspects of the life of an aspirant in the New Æon (and applicable to others as well). It first outlines cosmic development.

The original *Domarum Mercurii* page of the manuscript with handwritten directions and drawings by Crowley survives in the University of London Senate Library Fuller Collection Archive. This manuscript was scanned there in 1988. Other than the 65 pages of The Book of the Law, Liber XXXI, this original manuscript page is the only other recognized Class A page known to exist at present! Crowley made (≈ received?) the original drawings for publication. He penciled directions along its left-hand margin to J. F. C. Fuller. Hebrew letters are index keys to the sigils. A typescript transliteration follows:

> General Design.
> May be a wheel with 22 compartments on the rim.
> The wheel has 8 spokes. At the 4 corners are the Kerubim.
> But this Pillar Scheme is equally good.
> Note the interchange of ה and ו.

> These sigils are dangerously automatic, and should never be exposed or left lying about. ου μη 7°=4▫

> This is perhaps because these are the Atus which Asar beheld in Amennti—they are therefore the governors + inspectors of the disordered fabrications.

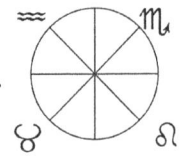

Crowley signed the note as ου μη [7°=4□]. He placed the liber applicable within the realm of manifestation.

The wheel scheme with spokes and compartments is listed before the pillar scheme. However, Crowley published only the pillar scheme during his lifetime. Fuller did an unpublished exploration of the wheel scheme after 1944, using Thoth tarot card images. It is in the University of London Senate Library Manuscript Collection. His arrangement provided some insight into the interpretation presented here. The schemes are complementary. They differ from the traditional Tree of Life and Cube of Space models.

"Note the interchange of ה and ו." This note is enigmatic. The sigils have associated Hebrew letters in pencil on the manuscript. As Class A, they must be respected and cannot be re-arranged, though they are labels out of alphabetic and zodiacal order. They differ in sequence from the text and the names of the genii. The note may be interpreted in at least two ways. The first is: "Be aware. This may seem unusual, but it is Class A. Do not change it." The second is: "Be aware. The sequence needs study. Rearrange them when you prepare the final drawing." At present, there is no way to determine the alternative meant by Crowley.

The rest of the liber is known only through its published version. How well the Equinox I (7) version follows other remaining parts of the original manuscript is moot. All published versions of Liber CCXXXI use the pillar scheme. The fabrications, the sigils collectively, are a distinct presentation. The wheel format has not been much explored. "Disordered" implies irregularities or blinds. It presents possibility for meditation and research.

The final drawing of the sigils, published in Equinox I (7): unnumbered page before page 71 is now in the Rutgers University Fuller Archives. It shows columns of both *Domarum Mercurii* and *Carcerorum Qliphoth* as now published, but without Hebrew letter assignments. The mercuric columns match Crowley's manuscript, including the ה and ו reciprocal exchange. The sigils differ only in detail. The qliphoth sigils are in Hebrew alphabetical order, from left to right, top to bottom. The mercuric sigils go from right to left, top to bottom, except for the sigils already mentioned. A letter shows for most (and presumably originally for all) sigils. They are light and almost undecipherable (? erased when cleansing a finished artwork). Some similar letters seem out of sequence (ט and ס).

A few sigils suggest a Tree of Life model, but there are no assignments of letters or paths to specific connections among the sephiroth.

Tarot Trump Order

On the 3-D Quantum Tree of Life model the glyph path connects Geburah (♨, ♂) to Yesod. It is not visible on 2-d TL models. Its action correlates to the path of Tzaddi from Netzach (צ, ♀) to Yesod. Each has a value of 90. Crowley interchanged the paths of V. Emperor Heh (א) and XVII. The Star Tzaddi (צ). He used the switch of XI. Lust Teth (ט) Leo (♌) and Adjustment VIII Lamed (ל) / Libra (♎) of Marseilles for justification. He illustrated them in The Book of Thoth, page 12. See Figure 5. At each junction, continuation of the path has two alternatives.

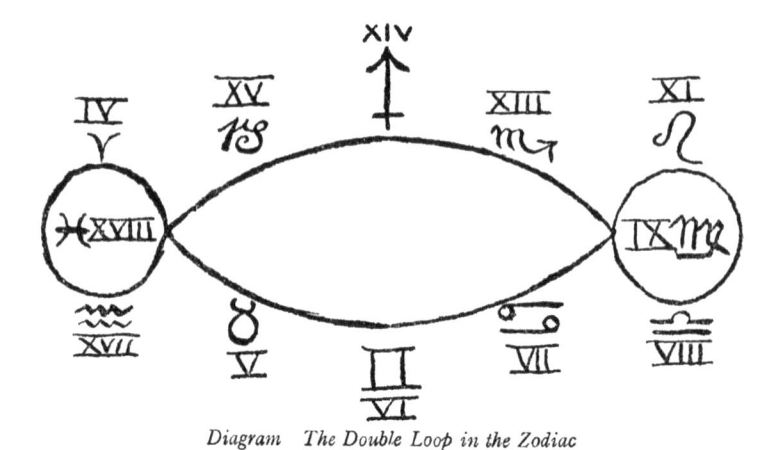

Diagram The Double Loop in the Zodiac

Figure 5. Thoth tarot double path interchange.

Is the prophet Crowley? He was the first and recognized himself to be so. This remains a common assumption today.

Following the line in the diagram shows the sequence of the twelve signs in classic Hebrew alphanumeric and zodiacal / astronomical order. The apparent Teth (ט) / Lamed (ל) switch is explained by phase shift on the Quantum Tree.

Without the earlier Strength (ט, ♌) / Justice (ל, ♎) parallel as a reference, the Emperor (ה, ♈) / Star (צ, ♒) interchange could have involved other paths. The smoother line in the Book of Thoth diagram follows zodiacal order. Switch the lateral loops back. The zodiac and alphabet reappear in traditional order. See Figure 6. Occam's Razor applies.

The platonic virtues correlate to the tarot paths of Prudence / Wisdom (Hermit) (י, ♍), Justice (ל, ♎), Fortitude (Strength ט, ♌) and Temperance (ס, ♐).

The 22 trumps are described in Hebrew alphabetical order by the voice of the Angel (Class A) in the First Æthyr of Liber CDXVIII, *The Vision and the Voice*.

Text	**Tarot Card**	
Thou shalt laugh at the folly of the fool.	0.	The Fool
Thou shalt learn the wisdom of the wise.	I.	Magus
Thou shalt be initiate in holy things.	II.	High Priestess
And thou shalt be learned in the things of love.	III.	Empress
And thou shalt be mighty in the things of war.	IV.	Emperor
And thou shalt be adept in things occult.	V.	Hierophant
And thou shalt interpret the oracles.	VI.	Brothers, Lovers
And thou shalt drive all these before thee in thy car, and though by none of these canst thou reach up to me, yet by each of these must thou attain to me.	VII.	Chariot
And thou must have the strength of the lion,	VIII.	Strength
and the secrecy of the hermit.	IX.	Hermit
And thou must turn the wheel of life.	X.	Wheel of Fortune
And thou must hold the balances of Truth.	XI.	Justice
And thou must pass through the great Waters, a Redeemer.	XII.	Hanged Man
Thou must have the tail of the scorpion,	XIII.	Death
and the poisoned arrows of the Archer,	XIV.	Temperance
and the dreadful horns of the Goat.	XV.	Devil
And so thou shalt break down the fortress that guardeth the Palace of the King my son.	XVI.	Tower
And thou must work by the light of the Star	XVII.	Star
and of the Moon	XVIII.	Moon
and of the Sun,	XIX.	Sun
and by the dreadful light of judgment that is the birth of the Holy Spirit within thee.	XX.	Judgment
When these have destroyed the universe, then mayest thou enter the palace of the Queen my daughter.	XXI.	Universe

The distinction between 'shall' and 'must' parallel the exoteric and esoteric aspects of man.

It is the same sequence for paths, sigils, text, and genii in Liber CCXXXI. The paragraph clearly shows the initiatory process as a sequence. The early paths are shalt guides; the later ones are mostly directive must ones.

The wording of Trumps XX. Judgment (Resurrection, Decision, Choice) and XXI. Universe (options) seems to indicate distinct categories:

1) The birth of the Holy Spirit, [a new dreadful light of judgment] marks a high level of initiation. It contrasts to the dark origin. The Holy Spirit is not only the Holy Guardian Angel, the Inner Self or soul. It is divine enlightenment. The initiate achieves unity with the Holy Spirit. When this is enabled in an initiated Adept, he chooses his concluding relationship to deity and the universe.

2) They that destroy the Universe ($\approx$ who have chosen to leave it) in themselves, enter the palace of the King and unite with Ineffable. This is analogous to the ascent to heaven, heavenly Jerusalem, nirvana or crossing the ultimate Abyss. The microcosmic man unites with the macrocosm.

3) Those that do not destroy the Universe ($\approx$ who have chosen to remain in it) enter the palace of the Queen. They remain in nature (Duality) and return as a Fool or Magus. Elaboration of this occurs in the collect following Death (The End) in the Gnostic Mass.

> The Deacon. Unto them from whose eyes the veil of lifehath fallen may there be granted the accomplishment of their true Wills; whether they will absorption in the Infinite, or to be united with their chosen and preferred, or to be in contemplation, or to be at peace, or to achieve the labour and heroism of incarnation on this planet or another, or in any Star, or aught else, unto them may there be granted the accomplishment of their wills; yea, the accomplishment of their wills. AUMN. AUMN. AUM.
> (Equinox III (1): 263)

Cosmic Process

The cosmic process levels are indicated by the three mother letters.

Aleph is Origin, creation of duality through the expression of Word.

Mem symbolizes the Deluge, cleansing by water.

Shin, the final Abyss, the return of duality to unity.

They parallel Creation, Preservation and Destruction. Unity is imperceptible and leaves no manifest trace.

Formula of Initiation

The sequence for an individual aspiring to initiation also has three levels.

Aleph is Initiate who enters life — Birth activating his Outer Self.

Mem is Baptism or Consecration — Baptism activating his Inner Self.

Shin is spiritual choice — Reincarnation (duality) or Transcendence (unity).

In man, the Aleph (exoteric) and Mem (esoteric) are always present, probably developed to different degree. They reach attainment at Kaph and Resh respectively. They prepare the Adept for the Abyss at Shin in the Consummation at Tau.

In Shin, the initiate Adept opts between duality and unity. He may reincarnate for further development or service as a Magus, Prophet, or Bodhisattva, or may cross the final Abyss into Unity and escape existence, or the wheel of karma.

There is no god but man.

He begins knowing Nothing about Everything.

Through life he learns more and more about less and less.

He ends knowing Everything about Nothing

There is no man but god.

This is the ultimate Abyss, the gulf between duality and unity. It is the event horizon between manifest creation (Nature) and Ineffable. When this Great Work is completed, they are One and they are None. The initiate becomes Ineffable. No evidence remains. The man and God are indistinguishable.

The terminology in *Arcanorum* embodies the nature of the paths. Some terminology used here is not present in The Book of the Law, Liber XXXI vel AL, but occurs in The Vision and the Voice, Liber CDXVIII. Among them is Babalon, accepted here as a name or label for manifest Nuit.

The familiar term Holy Guardian Angel refers guidance for an individual Adept as he attains his spiritual truth. Whether it is an external influence, a distinct entity, or an internal consciousness, or manifest realization is moot.

In Thelema, crossing its Abyss requires action by the inner self. It is a major decision in many ways parallel to the Christian dark night of the soul. Understanding the Abyss is key for followers of Liber AL. In entering Binah on the Tree, it establishes a connection to spiritual Briah. The final Abyss, the Class A abyss model, offers the options of return to Unity with Ineffable, or Reincarnation in Duality. They are distinct.

Chapter Four
Path Messages — Descent from Aleph — Overview

The paths follow the sequence in the Class A Arcanorum and the First Æthyr of Liber 418. They are treated as a symbol of cosmic evolution and individual initiation becoming manifest. The individual cards and letters reflect aspects of the universe and life. The sequence is linear or circular. The three elemental letters describe entry into different phases of initiation. Aleph, Air (א, △), symbolizes creation and word. Mem, Water (מ, ▽) preservation and enlightenment. Shin indicates Fire (ש, △) and final options. The paths form into rows and columns parallel the Tree of Life.

Liber Arcanorum includes the tables of sigils and the columns of genii names. The qliphoth and mercuric aspects indicate the contrasting viewpoints within each path.

Man of Earth Grade — External, Pentagram (א, ☆), Earthly

Fool	Magus	High Priestess	— *Liberty, Nature*
Empress	Emperor	Hierophant	— *Law, Light*
Lovers	Chariot	Fortitude*	— *Love*

Virtues

Fortitude*			
Prudence	Justice	Temperance*	— *Life, Virtues*
(Wisdom)			

Lover Grade — Internal, Spiritual, Hexagram (מ, ✡), Solar

Wheel	Hanged Man	Temperance*	— *Complements*
Death	Devil	Tower	— *Light, Enlightenment*
Star	Moon	Sun	— *Revelation, Initiation*

* expresses the double assignment to Briah and Yetzirah.

Hermit Grade — Stellar, Babalon, Nuit (ש, Heptagram), Universal

Judgment	Universe	— *Will, Abyss, Decision, Resolution*

The Fool (א) is baptized and cleansed. Coincidentally, he is the Hanged Man (מ), a potential emerging Adept. Baptism activates his esoteric self and goes through trial and ordeal. His inner nature (✡) evolves. The process climaxes in the revelation of truth (ר). His enlightened self emerges (ש), opts for Nuit (ת) or reincarnates as a Fool or Magus.

In the traditional approach, the initiate 'climbs' the sephiroth on the Tree of Life. He proceeds upward, a return from Malkuth to Kether.

Air — Man of Earth — Aleph to Kaph

Liber CL, De Lege Libellum, lists the aspects that relate to groups of the tarot paths in sequence from Aleph (א, ✦). These four are Light, Life, Love, and Liberty.

Liberty

The aspirant enters the path of life. He seeks liberty and truth within Nature. This is the alchemical triad. In *Splendour Solis* (1594, BL MS Harley 3469) the student and mentor of Plate 1, set out on a journey in Plate 2. The mentor holds a vial from which emerges the statement:

Eamus Quesitum Quatuor Elementorum Naturas.

We are looking for the answer to the nature of the four elements.

א — **The Fool** — Innocent, Wanderer, Individual   Aspirant

The cosmic cycle begins. The Fool explores Nature. He is the subject, the archetype of the path.

ב — **Magus** — Prophet   Mentor

The Magus is the experienced and enlightened guide for the Fool. He serves as a voice for Ineffable. They explore nature together. As in alchemy, they seek beauty and truth, wisdom, and peace — without and within.

ג — **High Priestess** — Nuit, Isis   Nature, the Universe

This is Nuit. It is how Had as manifest man perceives Nature ($\approx$ Nu). Total comprehension is beyond his mind.

The series of paths explore Nature as expressed through law, love, and will.

Light — Law

The whole of the law ($\approx$ Natural Law) applies to all operations of the universe. Other law describes the application or interpretation by man. The labels relate to natural, temporal, and spiritual realms.

ד — **The Empress** — Nu, Mother Nature   Natural Law

Natural laws are inviolate. They operate consistently even though not known, acknowledged, or even presumed to exist. There is an infinite unknown in man. Man continues to explore and learn.

ה — **The Emperor** — Secular Law   Government

Through the state, laws regulate the outer life of individuals. Man is a social and political species. The rules are fallible guides for manifest man.

This aspect of law defines the direction and responsibilities of communal life. It is the ordering of daily life by government acting in a society and political interactions among men. This law is created within the mind of man and subject to change. The 'king' may be anywhere from beneficent to despotic, from beneficent to dictatorial, accepted and loved, or challenged.

ו — **The Hierophant** — Sacred Law   Religion, Church

The Hierophant is a spiritual leader or priest. His message and action come through religious dogma and ritual. Absolutes can exist as arbitrary constructs within a defined system. Religions differ. Approaches vary. Dogma reflects culture.

This aspect of law expresses the 'will of God, or gods' through an intermediary or messenger to mankind. In many ways these laws are the cultural expression of a community — Christians are a western phenomenon; Hindus have home in India; Jews and Arabs in the Middle East.

Because it comes 'from deity' it often assumes an origin absolute. It becomes dogmatic. It is accepted only by faith. At best it describes one man's understanding of the universe. At worst it becomes dogmatic and absolute, imaginary and irrational.

Love

The whole universe is an act of love, expressed as *Solve et Coagula*, division and unity. Separation and conjunction. Love under will includes attraction, purpose, and respect for others. It involves liberty, independence, and integrity. Each is important for survival and growth. Love expresses itself outwardly and broadly, or inwardly and personally. Its forms include:

ז — **The Brothers or Lovers** — φιλια   Brotherly Love

This is the attraction, outward love and energy expressed toward humanity. It involves respect, tolerance, philanthropy, and charity. Its antonym, hate, is corrosive.

In broad terms this love contains charity, philanthropy, connections within society. These are the human, emotional interactions that bind society. At an individual level it is family and friends, colleagues and classmates. Love is the interaction of contrasts.

The BOTL says, as brothers fight ye. Challenge and contrast are necessary for growth and change, resolution and respect of differences.

ח — **The Chariot** — Αγαπη   Sacred Love

This love or union with god(s) is expressed through religious practice and acts of faith. The path and goals of initiation, *e.g.*, the Grail, are formulated here. A wheel is a frequent symbol for the presence of God — ever changing, ever the same.

Life — Virtues

Do what thou wilt goes beyond the outward awareness of knowledge and love. It guides inner and outer parameters. Virtues are outward expressions of inner ethics. Self-control and discipline control expression. They interpret law within the limits of man. Vices are antonyms. For a Thelemite, unto Nuit provides direction for judgment and action.

Virtues are principles men use to express value when approaching freedom. They involve truth and experience. Liberty grows from the expression of virtue and inner responsibility. Freedom demands self-control, respect for others. In Thelema, virtues derive from the early verses of Liber XXXI. They define individuality and equality. They require tolerance and respect. They each have a path connection on the Middle Triad.

ט — **Fortitude, Strength** — Energy   Desire, Lust

Force is the energy that regulates growth. Fortitude keeps man on track. Strength is expressed as reliability, steadfastness, diligence, endurance, determination, and respect. It is the Azoth, the universal lion-serpent.

Energy can be constrained or excessive. The force works to keep oaths consistent with the goals of life and Will as they are challenged by adversity. It includes the physical aspects of life, from mild to extreme. Crowley relates lust to Babalon. The Book of the Law encourages action toward excess in one's action. But always directed unto Her.

Babalon and the Beast conjoined is a significant expression common in Thelema. A medieval depiction in The Apocalypse in Luther's original German translation of the Bible in 1534 is very similar to the lust card in The Book of Thoth. Babalon rides the multi-headed beast, the whore, abomination. It reflects the description in Revelations.

י — **Hermit** — Knowledge, Prudence   Wisdom, Light

Prudence is the basis for effective action. The Hermit carries a lantern, representing knowledge. He distinguishes light from dark, good from evil. It includes revelation of physical laws of Nature (science) and the metaphysical aspects of initiation (religion). The staff signifies stability. His age shows breadth of experience. Historically the card signified time. Then the Hermit carried a sandglass instead of a lantern.

ל — **Justice** — Balance, Adjustment   Equilibrium

Justice relates back to the manifold application of the universal $0 = 1$ formula — for every action there is an equal and opposite reaction. Justice requires knowledge (external) and wisdom (internal). Their goal is gnosis, universal truth. He who does not know and respect truth cannot be truly just. It derives from fact, knowledge, and experience. It recognizes change and difference.

ס — **Temperance** — Practicality   Restraint, Control

Temperance is the practical application of wisdom, fortitude, and justice. It does not mean being only obsequious or yielding. Rash action can be appropriate. Temperate action may say to quit. Amputation may be necessary to save life. Steel and temperance are tempered by fire and water. Temperance is determination, the application of Will.

כ — **The Wheel of Fortune** — Life   Experience

This path encompasses the ages of man and the life forces that counterbalance one another — Rajas (passion), Sattvas (goodness), and Tamas (destruction, chaos). The totality is realized as karma. The path summarizes the outer life of man.

Water — Adept, Esoteric Self — Mem to Resh

The element of water indicates a complementary aspect to the external life — the inner or esoteric self. It involves ordeal. Every initiation ritual has a shock element and revelation to raise awareness or consciousness. Noah endured the trial of the Deluge during his time in the Ark.

A Thelemic version occurs in the ritual of Liber DCLXXI vel Troa vel Pyramidos. It includes a symbolic crossing of the divide between Yetzirah and Briah. It consecrates the initiate and opens his awareness to the inner self. The process is weighing of souls in Ammenta, is like Noah surviving the Deluge, Jonah surviving the whale, Jesus' baptism and forty days in the desert, and the dark night of the soul for St. John of the Cross and St. Theresa of Avila. For a Thelemite, it begins Ordeal x. Experience on the paths hones the inner awareness and importance of truth.

מ — **The Hanged Man** — Baptism　　　　　　　　　Consecration

The Hanged Man activates the esoteric inner self of The Fool. It is present and puissant in every individual. It exists parallel to the exoteric aspect within every individual life. It represents the entry into the esoteric side of man.

נ — **Death** — Mortality　　　　　　　　　　　　　Challenge

Death ends the external life of an individual. For the initiate it can be the destruction of ego. The inner self of the adept expands in subsequent paths and maintains its identity.

ע — **The Devil** — Temptation　　　　　　　　　　Trial

Here the initiate defines his inner self and refines his life values. He learns to distinguish dark from light, evil from good, ignorance from knowledge. It is a path of question, challenge, and temptation. The initiate progresses from ignorance to gnosis, from understanding to wisdom and self-realization. He refines his ethical values.

פ — **The Tower** — Annihilation, Ordeal　　　　　Enlightenment

This is creative destruction. Other names for this path include the House of God, the Blasted Tower, or the Lightning Struck Tower. Some see it only as destruction or annihilation. The lightning flash is destructive. The lightning flash also represents new knowledge and gnosis. The gross shall pass through fire. The fine shall be tried in intellect. This is purification by fire, the fulfillment of the consecration by water of the Hanged Man.

Enlightenment — Tzaddi to Resh

צ — **The Star** — Emergence　　　　　　　　　　Awakening

The Star is The Hanged Man, the Adept, now inoculated and energized by the Lightning Flash. He recognizes the path toward ecstasy and nirvana.

The darkness of annihilation is broken by the illumination of truth and wisdom from above. Now the Star visualizes his goal.

ק — **The Moon** — Development, Perception　　　Illusion

This is the path of illusion, doubt, and distortion during growth. It is light reflected in darkness, the emerging and partial revelation and understanding. It is emergence during the revelation of truth, as the phases of the moon reflect the light of the Sun. It is the bud before the flower, the unconscious waiting to be revealed.

ר — **The Sun** — Enlightenment, Clarity　　　　　Truth

The initiate finds his Pure Will and perfection. The Sun emerges from eclipse into the full brilliance of truth. The Star fully realizes his true inner self and his relationship with the Universe. He achieves the Great Work. This is the culmination of his esoteric goal.

Fire — Hermit — Shin, Tau

Choice — Reincarnation, Rebirth, Resolution

At this junction, the enlightened Star faces final options. He must choose unity with Ineffable or remain in duality and return in service to mankind. The first is crossing the Abyss. The initiate becomes anonymous and leaves no evidence. He passes beyond the Word and the Fool. If his choice is to remain in duality, he does not cross the Abyss. He reincarnates as another Fool, Hermit or Magus.

ש — **The Æon** — Judgement, Resurrection   Abyss

This decision of the enlightened adept expresses his True Will. The options are to remain in duality or to cross the Abyss to unity.

ת — **The World, Universe** — Will Expressed   Finality

The described options for an enlightened initiate are:

> Duality — reincarnation in Nature below Abyss
>
> Unity — crossing the Abyss and Annihilation

Spirit — crossing the Abyss

> *Liber XXXI vel AL*, I (46-7): Nothing is a secret key of this law. Sixty-one the Jews call it; I call it eight, eighty, four hundred & eighteen. But they have the half; unite by thine art so that all disappear.

Arcana Principles

Tarot trumps sort into qabalistic groups — elemental, double (planetary) and single (zodiacal). The traditional designs of the tarot cards tend not to depict contrast. They address the initiatory view more strongly than the cosmic one.

In Liber CCXXXI the letters correlate sigils, text, and genii. They are guides for meditation. The contrast helps express the truth present in each path. The response is individual.

The sigils indicate qliphothic and mercuric contrast and the cosmic truths of the path. The genii give a sense of the divine nature within the contrast. They personify guardian spirits and individual gods. Augustine attributed the rational nature and ability of men to their genius, hence the more modern usage for the term. The Arabs demonized the djinn or genies as good or evil supernatural creatures.

The design for each card here is dual. It can be viewed upright or inverse. The views are different, unlike the court cards of a deck of playing cards. The new drawings interpret them from many religious, mythological, and occult traditions. Their contrasting aspects are guides for wider exploration and meditation. They reflect universality of the underlying message. Both mercuric and qliphothic aspects are present and contrasting. Each card expresses a common underlying message.

The sequence of paths for both cosmic evolution and initiation proceeds from Aleph to Tau. If applied to the Tree of Life, the paths proceed downward from Aleph at Kether to Tau at Malkuth. This might be the same as the circular arrangement sequence drawn with Malkuth connecting to Kether. The initiatory path practiced by Thelemites proceeds from Malkuth toward Kether on the Tree of Life.

The circular arrangement was suggested by Crowley. Fuller used an assemblage of individual tarot trump as a base. He used the three dimensions as the surface of a donut-shaped torus with the 78 Tarot cards.

The New Æon is a Twentieth Century phenomenon. Mathematics and sciences of physics, astronomy, chemistry, and biology have greatly expanded the understanding of the universe by man. New knowledge provides new answers and creates awareness of further dimensions and ignorance. It is approached asymptotically. There is much to do.

Individual interpretation has limits. It evaluates fact. It may propose new hypotheses. The box is not fixed in size or shape. The borders of ignorance are constantly being challenged and eroded. Each attack brings us closer to Truth (light), reducing ignorance and expanding knowledge. The absolute is impossible to attain. The unknown will always exist.

To test the limit is to challenge. Acceptance and agreement may follow — or not. The dangers are to accept new ideas that are not true or to deny those that are true. Such errors are inherent in every decision. The system is self-corrective. Apply this principle to every exploration and every prophet.

$$0 = 1 \text{ is the formula of Unity}$$
The ineffable part of the journey — Anonymity.

$$0 = 1 = 2 \text{ is the formula of Duality}$$
Nature (the Universe) is revealed through difference — Contrast.

$$0 = 1 = 2 = \infty \text{ is the inclusive formula for All.}$$
Every number is infinite: There is no difference — Universality.

Chapter Five
Arcana 231 — Tarot Path Accounts

The 22 individual path accounts are in Hebrew alphabetic order. The commentary for each path begins with a page of the Class A material extracted from *Liber CCXXXI vel Arcanorum*.

The text for each path reviews some traditional aspects of the path and confounding symbols.

Message and contrast show how the text and sigils have been interpreted as guides for meditation. The message includes both cosmic evolution and initiation. It provides context for aspects suggested by Crowley.

Hebrew letter comparisons elaborate on the table between the columns of sigils. They are a system of cross-references among the letters and sigils.

The analysis of Genii names uses Hebrew and Greek roots for the components. Each syllable has its connotations. They combine to express meaning.

The paths correlate (in reverse order ש, מ, א) to the Three Grades in Liber XXXI, I: page 10 - 11 (verse 40), the Hermit, the Lover, and the Man of Earth.

This collection is presented for personal meditation and interpretation. The text is one man's reading of the Arcana figures. Both mercuric and qliphothic aspects are included. The two aspects are different or contrasting views of the meaning of the path. The two aspects contrast, but are neutral, not ethically good and bad, which may be implied in personal interpretation.

The accounts include drawings by Barry William Hale. His art visualizes the message of each path and interprets its contrasting elements. Each drawing has symbolic magical interpretations. The breadth of the many religious, magical, or mythical examples shows a world view. The following discussion by the author provides background, context, suggestions, and orientation for interpreting the drawings.

א

The Fool — Aspirant, Innocent

Air (△) — Ineffable and Word

0.   A, the heart of IAO,
dwelleth in ecstasy in the secret place of the thunders.
Between Asar and Asi he abideth in joy.

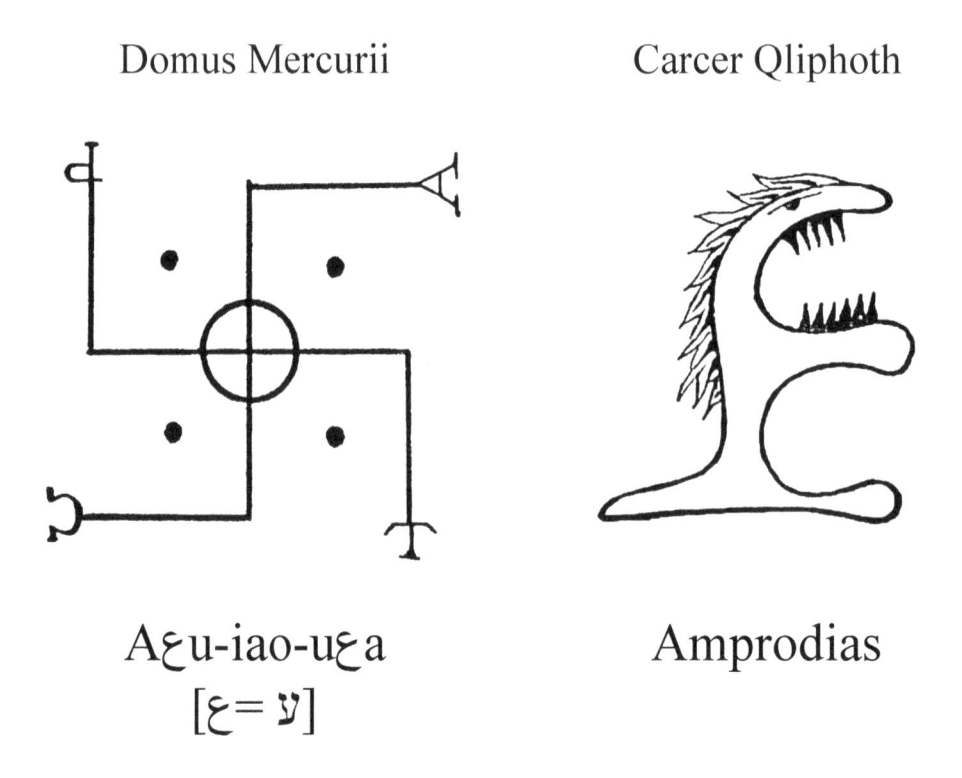

Domus Mercurii   Carcer Qliphoth

Aεu-iao-uεa   Amprodias
[ε = ע]

Aleph (א) compares to Tzaddi (צ)

Aleph (א) is the first elemental Hebrew letter. It relates to Air (△) and Tarot 0. The Fool. It has a numerical value one (1).

The elemental letters Aleph (א), Mem (מ) and Shin (ש) indicate three aspects of life. They correlate to Air, Water and Fire. The alphabetical paths before Mem (מ) describe exoteric (external) aspects of life, law, love, and liberty for The Fool, Men of Earth, and Magicians. The Fool is the innocent beginner, the wanderer, the explorer seeking light and truth, wisdom, and peace — the Aspirant.

The path emphasizes origins and fertility. It emanates from cosmic darkness and absence. It is the source of light. Hence, the message of the two columns of sigils — contrast — is the way to discover and understand. All light comes from dark. All knowledge comes from ignorance.

In the text, A, the heart of IAO is the Serpent (of the Garden of Eden) Apophis. 'A' is the transform between the complements in the IAO formula. The central heart is active, a verb between nouns. Aleph relates to the abode of God beyond comprehension. Silence is perfection, the unknown Nothing. Unity precedes and transcends consciousness.

Thunder, created by lightning, is the Voice in the Silence, the Light, and the Word, of the beginning. *Liber DCLXXI vel Pyramidos*, a ritual of self-initiation, says: But I have heard one cry ring through eternity; Arise and follow me!

What does it require to know anything? Contrast! Contrast derives from Ineffable and Word, dark and light, Asar and Asi, left and right. knowledge and awareness cannot occur without it. Ineffable is beyond definition but is the source of the Word. Ineffable is contrasting Asar and Asi. They are analogous to manifest Nu and Had in Thelemic symbolism. Their combination, union, reinstates ecstasy.

Nuit personifies Nature, the macrocosmic universe. Had personifies man, manifest within it. The unveiling of the company of heaven reveals the nature of Nature, the Universe in its broadest dimensions and ramification.

The Visconti Fool shows a simple man with a staff over his right shoulder. The Marseilles Tarot has *Le Mat*, a man walking. He holds a sack on a stick with his right hand, and a walking stick in his left. A lion nips at his left leg. This is the general pattern followed in subsequent decks. Wirth has *Le Fou* with a similar design. A lion is nipping at his leg. It is placed between Shin and Tau in sequence. In some, the Fool is not numbered. The Rider/Waite card numbers The Fool as zero. He walks a precipice. A dog is at his left leg, warning about danger and keeping him on the path.

The Thoth card shows a green Fool with a lion at his left leg. The card is filled with symbols of Spring, origin, growth, and fruition. The Lion steadies his path. The dove and the whirling air signal the message of the New Æon.

Aleph in Cosmos

The qliphothic sigil is an open-mouthed head in the form of a reversed Beth. It indicates breath or Word. The Word of Ineffable is the act of Creation. The eye represents awareness. The fiery mane indicates primal energy, and energy is matter. The five upper and six lower teeth suggest Nu (= 56), a manifest expression of the universe in Thelema. The Word is light, chaos, represented by the mercuric swastika or the qabalistic whirlings, the gilgalim. Beth, meaning house, is also the mouth that creates the Word.

Aleph starts with a cosmic view. Nothing expresses no definition or form. It is all-encompassing absence.

It begins before time and space. Nothing was aware. Nothing was differentiated. It was beyond and before space, time, and mass, the dimensions of the Universe. Nothing is a key of the Law.

I am what, I am, or I will be what I will be. אהיה אשר אהיה

This rephrasing is the voice of Ineffable crying in the wilderness (the void). Is the voice a sound? When a tree falls alone, does it make a sound if there is no receptor? Does it matter? An event has occurred!

Hoor-Paar-Kraat is the background authority behind Liber XXXI vel AL, the initial revelation in the New Æon. Aiwass transmitted The Book of the Law under his authority. Ra-Hoor-Khuit (Ineffable) is behind the manifest Lord of the Æon, the ruler, Ra-Hoor-Khu(t). They correspond to the Silence and the Word.

The mercuric sigil is a swastika with TARO (*TARO* in Greek) at its four ends. It is Chaos, entropy toward which all turns back. As ROTA it indicates a wheel or cycle.

The symbolic swastika with its four dots goes back to ancient India and Tibet, or earlier. The central crossing represents origin. The arms represent creation, sun, good fortune, or Brahman in his universal manifestation. The circle is the sun, center of an evolving universe. The four dots indicate alchemical elements. The whole indicates early evolving development, gilgalim. When Liber Arcanorum was received, this symbol was historic and had very positive connotations.

Cosmic evolution proceeds toward manifestation, from energy to space, time, and mass. They are complementary aspects of the same thing. In every beginning, there is an end. In every end, there is a beginning. Consider the formula *Solve et Coagula*, the universal rule of action, and the Tai Chi Yang / Yin symbol.

Aleph in Initiation

The elemental letters Aleph (א), Mem (מ) and Shin (ש) indicate the three major aspects of the initiate's path — exoteric, esoteric, and spiritual. The intermediate paths add depth and details. They are approaches to discovery and understanding.

Birth and conception relate to origin, innocence, and fertility. A new individual enters the path as a man of earth to become a Magician. The Fool begins at 1°=10° — blind, limited and innocent. He knows nothing. He seeks wisdom and peace.

Conceived in the darkness of midnight, man is born into the light of morning. The Sun rises. The egg is inherent potential for becoming an independent mature organism.

The Green Man personifies fertility and growth, optimism, and inspiration. In the annual cycle he represents Spring and the awakening of life. Spring brings promise. The Sun crosses the equator in its progression northward. It enters Aries (♈), at the Equinox.

For IAO-OAI see the Class A ritual formula in *Liber LXVI vel Stellae Rubeae* and the path of Beth. The letters I and O show contrast. The A is the Serpent, Da'ath — knowledge and truth. See Liber CDXVIII, Fifth Æthyr.

The Fool explores, wanders, and carries his sack full of follies, illusions, and ideals. This burden is his karma. He is unaware of dangers. The animal nipping at his heels threatens stability as he treads a precipice, but also keeps him on the path (directed, away from sin). Life is compromise between promise and limitation. Experience tempers the intoxication of youth.

Table of Letter Comparisons

Aleph (א) compares to Tzaddi (צ)

The paths of Aleph and Tzaddi each relate to a stage of initiation. The Fool (א) begins his tour of exoteric life with birth. The latter swastika indicates the fluidic fire. As a Star (צ), he emerges as an esoterically developed Adept.

On the mercuric side, both sigils contain swastikas. On the qliphothic side a comparison is not obvious. The tall head may represent the ecstasy of the Word and the fertile seed at the top. Mental focus is necessary for Will.

Genii

Qliphoth — Amprodias

The Voice in the Silence

This genius of origins announces contrast or separation between Ineffable and universe. It breaks the perfection of Silence. The initial trigram of Liber XXVII vel Trigrammaton point this out.

Mercurii — Aξu-iao-uξa

Creator is Creation. Naught is All.

Aξu- equals AOU, the paths of The Fool, The Devil and the Hierophant. It has the same pattern as the IAO formula with sexual connotations. Here, the Devil is the dark god. He tempts The Fool as he responds to the light and the dark, good, and evil.

The -iao- is the universal god form with its components.

The uξa is the mirror image of aξu. The name then translates to IAO = OAI, or △▽▲ IAO ▲▽△. This is the Air – Water – Fire of the elemental letters, and the formula (-1) = (+1) of the universe and initiation as IAO. It is expressed in the Class A Liber DCVI vel Stellae Rubeae, the Ritual of the Ruby Star.

Arcana 231

The message of Aleph is origin, creation, and fertility. The rebus at the center suggests the initial chaos or subconscious origins. The surrounding wreath of flowers suggests fertility. A goat and a leopard emerge from this early chaotic expression of organization. The goat symbolizes fertility. It relates to Dionysus / Bacchus and the satyr Pan. The leopard is connected to the lion-serpent that symbolizes the Azoth, the vital force of life.

The qliphothic aspect shows Pan, the wild man holding a gnarled staff. He is a horned and hairy Greek god of fertility. As the Green Man, he relates to the renewal of Spring. On his right shoulder is the head of a goat, symbol of fertility. He is holding a panpipe. It indicates that the message of the tarot is symbolic, through the language of the birds, not in words. The horns reflect a basic pattern of organization.

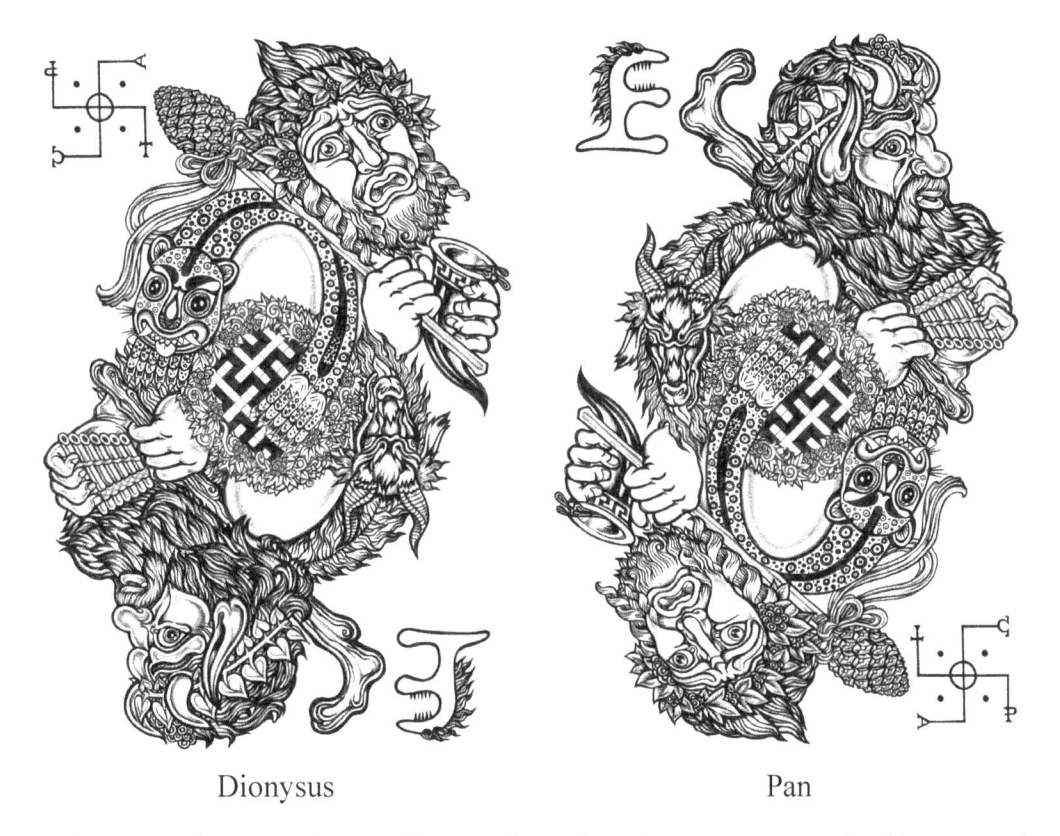

Dionysus   Pan

The mercuric aspect shows Dionysus / Bacchus. He wears a wreath of leaves again representing fertility. The thyrsus in his right hand represents a fertile phallus. Its pinecone tip represents the seed. It signals the mystical nature of the Way. He carries a kantharos, a wine-cup, in his left hand. Together they represent male and female, parallel to wand and cup, or the royal scepter and orb of the Greater Mysteries. Near his shoulder is the leopard, traditional symbol of Dionysus, symbol of vitality. It relates to the lion-serpent, Baphomet. The staff and pinecone symbolize initiation.

ב

The Magus — Prophet

Mercury (☿) — Messenger and Mentor

1. The lightnings increased
and the Lord Tahuti stood forth.
The Voice came from the Silence.
Then the One ran and returned.

Domus Mercurii   Carcer Qliphoth

Beξθaoooabitom   Baratchial

Beth (ב) compares to Gimel (ג)

The second path is Beth (ב), 1. The Magus. It has a numerical value of two (2). It relates to the planet Mercury (☿). The Magus is the prophet connecting the Word of Ineffable to the New Æon. He is a complete initiate.

Beth is the initial letter of Genesis 1: 1. בראשות. In the beginning. The path recognizes Nature as separate and emanated from Ineffable, inherent within it. The Word expresses universal nature and wisdom.

Aleph is breath, the Word. Breath begins the universe and life. Beth is the mouth expressing the Word of Aleph. Beth is how Ineffable communicates. From an initiatory view, a Magus or Prophet carries it.

In *Splendour Solis* (1582), the first illustration shows a teacher with student at the beginning of a joint initiatory journey. They seek Nature. This alchemical triad is a basic outline of the initiatory process.

The Magus is the messenger or mentor of the mysteries. He uses his own initiation and experience with the elements (Nature) as a guide for the next generation. In the Book of Lies commentary to Κεφαλη B, The Cry of the Hawk, Horus, the ruler of the New Æon, shows this mercurial nature of the Magus of the Tarot.

The traditional Juggler or Conjuror has a table in front of him. He maneuvers the elements on it. In doing so, he presents his message. He promulgates falsehood because Ineffable truth cannot be communicated fully or directly. The path is a blessing (ברכה) for the Man of Earth and the Magician.

Lightnings symbolize the Words and Knowledge transmitted to the Universe. As they occur, the cosmos evolves. The lightnings produce thunder, the sound of the Word. Knowledge of the Word is key to understanding the Universe. The rays of the sun carry light and energy to life on earth. By analogy in biological context, the phallus transmits the Word, the seed.

The first two lines name Lord Tahuti as the Magus and guide for The Fool. Tahuti is the Egyptian personification of communication and writing. He is analogous to Greek Hermes or Roman Mercury. In his union with the macrocosm, the Magus has given his last drop of blood to Nuit.

The Visconti Tarot shows *Il Bagatto* (The Juggler) sitting behind a table with symbols of three elements on it. He holds a long wand in his left hand, and appears to be throwing sand (chance, chaos) from his right one. The Marseilles card has *Le Bateleur* similar but standing. It is numbered I. The Wirth card, *I. le Bateleur*, stands behind a table with a sword, cup, and disc. It is labeled I. א. on The Rider / Waite card, I. The Magician is standing with a wand in his right hand and four elements on the table. The lemniscus (∞) above his head indicates relationship to the Infinite.

The Thoth card, I. Magus, has a central man in front of a phoenix wand with the symbolized elements around him. It emphasizes his mercuric aspects as messenger of the gods. The Book of Thoth describes his duality, representing truth and falsehood, wisdom and folly.

On the Stele of Revealing, the Magus is the priest before god at the altar. The serpents (wisdom, word) are opposites — active / passive, lion / eagle, macrocosm / microcosm.

Beth begins creation. Chaos, an organizing phase, followed. The Torah starts with ב, בראשית, meaning 'at the beginning'. It also begins blessing, ברכה. Genesis I: 3. And God said: Let there be light. יהי אור. At Creation, light came from dark, bringing contrast.

Both sigils for Beth recognize contrast. Beth is intersection between cosmos and intelligence. It is ultimate blessing, revealer of wisdom.

The qliphothic sigil shows symbolizes the course of the boat of Ra through Amennti. The lateral bent swords are the pillars of the eastern and western horizon, dividing night from day. The moon is overhead. The central Sun, Ra in his boat, shines toward the moon. Tahuti is the wavy line at the prow. Ra-Hoor is the wavy line at the helm. The sun arises from the dark in the east at sunrise. It descends into the dark in the west at sunset. This is the daily cycle. It is the repeated cycle from firmament (△) to sea (▽) to Amennti (△). The practice of Liber CC vel Resh recognizes the light / dark cycle in daily ritual.

Beth in Initiation

The day / night cycle parallels the process of initiation.

The mercuric sigil for Beth is a composite IAO. The inverted T or I is the lingam. The vesica, O, is the yoni or vulva. The two are sexual contrasts expressing the *Solve* phase. The middle staff symbolizes the crowned axis of the magician or Ra-Hoor-Khuit, the union of opposites. He is *Coagula*, expressed in the first gesture in Liber V vel Reguli. *Solve et Coagula* is the basic and universal formula acting throughout nature. It is the pattern for change.

Class A Liber B vel Magi sub Figura I elaborates the role and responsibility of the Magus by Masters (*Magistri*) of the Temple (Syllabus in Equinox I (10): 43)). Regarding this liber, Crowley says in Confessions, p. 673 it describes the conditions of this grade.

The Magus is a reincarnation of the perfected Initiate or Hermit. The Magus wills to be a Magister or mentor (ב) for Speech in Silence (ב). He fulfills the role of prophet (ב) of the Word of the Ineffable (א). Liber B expresses the contrast between Truth and Falsehood and the place of Love.

Table of Letter Comparisons

Beth (ב) compares to Gimel (ג).

Beth (ב) communicates Nature to man. Beth means house. The path of Beth explores the contrast between dark and light. The path of Gimel elaborates the alchemical elements of Nature in multi-dimensional state.

Tau (ת) compares to Beth (ב). This pairing supports the interpretation that the enlightened Fool or perfected Initiate chooses to return as a Magus. The mercuric sigils relate to IAO.

Genii

Qliphoth — Baratchial

Angel connecting Creation to Man

This genius connects deity to the universe. Aiwass, the minister of Hoor-Paar-Kraat, transmitted the Word by dictating *Liber XXXI AL vel Legis*, The Book of the Law, to Crowley in April 1904.

Bara	בר	Active production, emanation, Movement to manifest the creative force in existence
tch	תה	An intermediate link
ial	יאל	An enclitic meaning angel, genius, or spirit (also -iel)

Mercurii — Beθξaoooabitom

Beth	בט	House
ooo	עעע	210, the number of NOX, Nothing, the dark origin of the Universe
bitom	בתמ	Relates fire and energy. the light. It is seen in the Enochian Tablet of Union

Beth is the Magus who transmits the Word from Ineffable. He brings fire from heaven, as symbolized by Prometheus. He connects the word of the Æon from Ineffable to man. When the mind of man is silenced, in meditation, it synchronizes to Ineffable. When he hears the Word, illumination may occur.

Arcana 231

Magician
Ge Xuan

Exorcist
Wan Fu Zu Shi

The Magus holds a distinctive position among the paths. He is a spiritual Hermit who has completed his connection with the Universe at the path of Shin and reincarnates. He is an enlightened individual, not a god, who has chosen to bring the experience of enlightenment to man. A few examples are mentioned in the collects of Liber XV, the Gnostic Mass. Crowley selected them for inclusion. They range from founders of a religion and local, mythic, and historic persons. The Magi of major religions are Laotze, Siddartha, Krishna, Moses, and Mohammed. Abraham, Jesus, and Taoist masters could be included. Among the saints, mythical or otherwise, is a long list of other magi.

The illustration shows two Taoist masters as Magician and Exorcist. See Liber XXXI II:7.

The Magus, Ge Xuan, has many different roles — magician, teacher, mentor, and prophet. His burden is to assist the initiate on his journey. The traditional card shows the magician working his will through the four elements (manifestation). The sign of infinity shows the goal as Ineffable.

The qliphothic figure is Wan Fa Zu Shi (万法祖师), patriarch of Taoist magical skills. He has one eye smaller than the other. His left eye sees the heavenly realm. His right eye sees the earthly realm. He sees the contrasts and changes in life.

Wan Fa Zu Shi ultimately glided to heaven on Qi Lin (麒麟) from Kong Tong Mountain (崆峒山). Qi Lin is a Chinese unicorn with the body of a deer, the hooves of a horse, and a long horn. Kong Tong Mountain is a sacred mountain in Taoism. The story parallels the ascent of Ezekiel to heaven in a chariot. It implies when his role as a Magus is completed, then the master may cross the Abyss into Unity.

The central figure is a pearl, like the jewel in the lotus.

In the Classic of Purity, Ge Xuan (葛玄), the mercuric, includes the thought that the inner spirit of people love purity, but the mind is often rebellious. The characters on his lapel are a Chinese equivalent of "Do what thou wilt shall be the whole of the Law". He was the founder of the Ling Bao School. He introduced the concept of æonic cycles (the axle with wheel and the cube). His headdress identifies his Taoist position, a representation of the jewel (pearl) in the lotus (flower). He is holding the brush and the inkpot as an analogy to Tahuti. The scroll of paper is nearby. The snake at his upper left is a symbol for the word and knowledge. The Five Taoist Elements: Fire, Earth, Metal, Water and Wood relate to the traditional four elements of alchemy. Aleister Crowley claimed Ge Xuan as a great previous incarnation. Under the pseudonym Ko Yuen, Crowley translated his work Tao Teh King (via Legge).

Out of the darkness comes light, the Word. The message begins with the path of Aleph. Dark / light is the symbolic contrast. It is contrast between ignorance and knowledge.

ג

The High Priestess — Nuit, Nature

Moon (☽) — Chaos in Organization

2. Now hath Nuit veiled herself,
that she may open the gate of her sister.

Domus Mercurii	Carcer Qliphoth
Gitωnosapφωllois	Gargophias

Gimel (ג) compares to Beth (ב)

The third path is II. The High Priestess, Nuit, Nature. It has a numerical value of three (3). The Hebrew letter Gimel (ג) means camel and relates to the Moon. This is the expression of Ineffable, Nature above the veil of Isis. It is the Shekinah of Hebrew qabalah. The Shekinah in exile is her counterpart below the veil.

This path begins cosmic and initiatory processes represented in the Tarot. Gimel represents all-encompassing Nature. The sky-goddess, Nuit, is the non-manifest expression. The Sun is just one star within the universe. Recognizing this, Liber CCXXXI acknowledges a stellar perspective. Knowledge exposes truth. From outside, her veil separates duality from unity. Man perceives the secrets of Nuit / Isis as hidden or dark. The universe is dark. Striking the veil reveals truth and contributes to understanding. Man learns from the unknown. He never reaches absolute unity. The veil separates the paths of Gimel from Daleth.

The first four verses of Liber XXXI, Chapter II are the introduction of the nature of Nature to man.

Man can never expect to comprehend the All, Ineffable. He can recognize new knowledge and increase his understanding. Observations and experiences beyond explanation are called miracles. They indicate unknown areas for further revelation. Through initiation, the aspirant learns from others the mysteries of life and death.

The sister of Isis is Nephthys, related to the qliphoth. As Isis represents light, so Nephthys represents dark. Nephthys symbolizes death, decay, and immobility. In ancient Egypt, Nephthys is the sister of Isis. She is the wife of Set and the mother of Anubis, associated with mummies and funeral rites. Together they protect the deceased in his afterlife journey. Nephthys is associated with the journey of Ra as he enters the Duat at dusk. The action of Isis is parallel at dawn. Isis symbolizes birth, development, and action.

The Visconti Tarot shows the enthroned Popess with a triple crown and holding a blue book symbolizing the universe (truth) in her left hand. Her right hand holds a scepter with cross on top. The Marseilles tarot card shows the seated *La Papesse* holding only a book. The Wirth *la Papesse* holds a book with Yang / Yin in her right hand and keys in her left. It is numbered II and ג. The Rider / Waite card shows the High Priestess with a moon crown, holding a TORA. She sits between the columns of Boaz and Jachin.

The Thoth card shows The Priestess as a stellar figure. Above, a bow and arrow and a numinous veil signify an abyss or separation. Below are symbols of manifestation. The camel, flowers and fruit, and rocks represent the kingdoms of earth — animal, vegetable, and mineral.

Gimel in Cosmos

The qliphothic sigil illustrates emanation of Ineffable. It shows the four alchemical elements. Alchemists sought their knowledge through the symmetry, beauty, and structure of Nature. The Universe, Mother Nature, appears as a face. The bilateral symmetry of the sigil indicates duality — contrast devolves from Ineffable unity. The three original elements are air (△) the sword; water (▽) the bottom bowl, and fire (△) the lateral wands. The oval is the primordial egg with its fertile seed. It represents the fourth element earth (▽). The complex represents the manifest universe. The eyes may indicate the presence of Ineffable, the element of spirit (ש) in a five-element interpretation.

Gimel in Initiation

Initiation in the aspirant is a process parallel to evolution in Nature. The initiate aspires to improve his understanding of universal Nature.

The Mercuric sigil has two flags in mirror image position, but with contrasting direction of the fill-in lines. They indicate the complementary aspects of Isis and Nephthys. The lower ends suggest the phallus and vulva, sexual polarity, or symbolic universal law. Between them, the empty space suggests a woman or the birth canal.

Here is the expression of the universe in nascent manifest form. This level has Nuit and Hadit as non-manifest gods. The sigil shows the dual nature of Nature, the basis for its operation.

Table of Letter Comparisons

Gimel (ג) compares to Beth (ב)

This is a reciprocal path of Beth. It indicates their close relationship. Nuit is the non-manifest personification of Nature. Nuit cannot be experienced directly, but only through manifest Nature. Direct experience is illusory, hence assignment to the Moon.

Genii

Qliphoth — Gargophias

Spirit of Action in Nature

Gar	גר	To dwell, movement bringing being upon itself
goph	גיפ	Body or person
ias	יאס	A form of spirit, possibly a Holy Guardian Angel

Mercurii — Gitωnosapφωllois

Spirit of the early force of manifestation

Gitωn	Gitωn	The giants or Nephalim of Genesis 6: 4, the Titans
os	ος	A relative pronoun
ap	απ	Provides emphasis
φωlloις		A play on φαλλος, phallus and φολεος, φωλλοι The corresponding verb φωλευω, means to lurk, or lie torpid in a den, as in hibernating bears.

Arcana 231

Artemis / Diana   Hecate

This is the path of the exalted feminine, Nu. It is Mother Nature in broadest aspect. The figures show commonality and contrast through Diana and Hecate. Hecate is the feminine High Priestess keeper at the veil guarding the mysteries. She relates to the dark side of the Moon, especially those days adjacent to the New Moon, and the dark within us. In that sense, she is a key to opening the dark side, the veil of Nuit (Isis), and the mysteries.

Qliphothic

Hecate is Mother Nature in early personification. She is a star goddess, an expression of Nuit. As goddess of the Moon, she symbolizes illusion, darkness, and remoteness. She relates to entrances, origin, and childbirth. Her triple form parallels phases of the Moon. She is Selene – the heavenly moon, Artemis the earthly huntress, and Persephone, queen of the underworld.

Signified here by her three heads and three sets of hands, she ruled over the firmament, the sea and the earth. The three heads reflect the more modern interpretation as maiden, mother and crone, and the cycles of Nature.

Hekate is the only goddess who used two torches as she guided individuals through the mysteries. In her right hands also are a dagger (athame) for initiation and a mallet. In her left hands are a snake (for revelation) and a rope (umbilical cord for childbirth).

Mercuric

Diana, the huntress, is associated with remote places, high mountains, and sacred woods. She is a triple goddess comprising Luna in Heaven, Diana on Earth, and Proserpina in the Underworld. The parallels to Hekate and Artemis are clear.

Diana / Artemis is recognized by the stag. She also carries a bow, quiver and arrows as a huntress. The crescent moon on her forehead attributes to the path of Gimel. Her hunting dogs are included. The stag refers to the story of the hunter Actaeon, who discovered her naked while bathing in the forest and tried to rape her. As the result, she turned him into a stag. A stag and a dog are on the medallions at her shoulders.

The central horizontal bow represents the veil of Nuit (or Isis), separating Ineffable from emanated Universe. The veil of Isis separates the two aspects of the path image. The central image of the Sun in the arms of the Moon is an analogy to sexual union and magic, and the operational formula of Nature. The formula *Solve et Coagula* explains the universe through its interplay.

ד

The Empress — Nu, Mother
Venus (♀) — Natural Law

3. The Virgin of God is enthroned upon an oyster-shell;
    she is like a pearl,
    and seeketh Seventy to her Four.
    In her heart is Hadit the invisible glory.

Domus Mercurii   Carcer Qliphoth

Dηnaʒartarωθ   Dagdagiel
[ʒ = st]
[Dynastartaroth]

Daleth (ד) compares to Ayin (ע)

The fourth path is Daleth (ד), III. The Empress. Its numerical value is four (4). Daleth means door or gate. The expansion of the number four is the basis of the universe in space/time. This is the first path on the effable side of the veil of Nuit / Isis. The path relates to the planet Venus (♀), the Morning Star.

The Empress rules innate understanding and tradition. As interpretation, it is subject to error but is the gateway to increased understanding of the rules of the universe. Gimel is to Daleth as Nature is to Natural law. The first is a noun, the latter acts as a verb.

This path expresses natural law in operation. It functions independently of individuals. Manifest fact and understanding are necessarily incompletely known. The scientific method serves to expand and verify man's understanding and knowledge of Nature. Broadly speaking, tradition is the timely limited application of natural law.

Four is the number of elemental physical forces. Four is the number of dimensions in space/time. Four is the number of 'states' of matter. Four is the number of nucleotides in the DNA biological code.

Virgin traditionally means not having borne a child. The Virgin of God is identified in the third path as Nu, the manifest complement to Nuit.

The aphorism says the hand that rocks the cradle rules the world — the mother.

This is Nu within the realm of perception and comprehension. Hadit is her non-manifest consort. In qabalistic terms, the initial Heh (ה) of IHVH (יהוה) is raised to the throne of the Mother (final Heh).

The oyster-shell is an altar. The seashell is a classic symbol for the vulva. Bivalve mollusks, clamshells, symbolize fertility and birth. Some produce pearls, pure and innocent products of an organism living within the shell. Both oysters and scallops are associated with the birth of Venus. She is perceived Nature in broadest material sense. She is mother. Venus is love. Love is the law, love under Will.

The pearl symbolizes feminine attributes — sea and water (Mare, Mary, Maria); love (Venus, Aphrodite); and mystery, beauty, and purity (Moon). The pearl in the oyster is its mystic center. It is the same for anyone who wears one. It is natural, organic in origin, pure, perfect and spherical, and white. It symbolizes the inner self.

The number 70 is the product of 7 and 10, spiritual perfection and completeness. Here it implies perfect order in Tetragrammaton as applied to qabalah and Tarot. Seventy is also סוד, the secret seed behind the gate or veil, Daleth, ד (4). It describes perfection of Microcosm and Macrocosm.

In the Fourth Æthyr of Liber CDXVIII the Angel says that the wisdom of the Magus shows different views of the material universe by the major historic religions. Dark and evil are perceived differently. Their reactions range from ecstatic to intellectual, violent to peaceful.

The present æon professes its view in the ritual of the Gnostic Mass. The Virgin Intacta enters (cf. the Princess of Tarot, the final Heh of Tetragrammaton). She invokes the power of iron (fire, spirit, solar energy) to consecrate by water and fire the man who emerges from the tomb. Then, as Priest he enthrones the Virgin on the summit of the earth (altar, the oyster-shell) He consecrates her as Priestess by water and fire and closes the veil.

Behind the veil, the Priestess is exalted to represent Nuit (the initial Heh, the queen of Tarot). She recites the exhortation of Nuit from Liber XXXI, Ch. 1, pp. 19-21 (Liber CCXX, Ch. 1: v. 61). The Priest ascends the steps. He opens the veil to meet Nu. He consecrates the Priestess cons and then consecrates the elements. He performs the Mystic Marriage as Babalon her consort. Then, the congregation experiences the universal mystery of Nature as Nu / Had by consuming the symbolic cake of light and wine.

Most traditional cards show The Empress on a throne. The Visconti tarot card shows *L'Imperatrice* seated and holding her shield. The Marseilles card, *III L'Imperatrice* has her crowned and holding shield and scepter. The Wirth tarot card is similar, but the throne has wings. It is labeled III and Gimel (ג). The Rider / Waite Empress is seated and wears a crown of stars. She holds a scepter in her right hand. The heart-shaped shield has the sign of Venus (♀).

The Thoth Empress is more expressive and mystical. She sits under an arch. She holds a lotus. The shields show the pelican and the White Eagle. A few moons are evident.

Daleth in Cosmos

The path of Daleth has Nu as Venus. She represents the highest form of the feminine approachable and comprehensible to man. Venus is the brightest of the planets. She personifies love. This path presents love in the broad sense as *Solve et Coagula*. It harmonizes life and its environment. It is maternal and familial love that engenders the behavior of man to his fellow man and his environment.

It refers to the underlying operational formula of Nature. The laws of nature are never broken.

The qliphothic sigil shows Daleth, as gallows or gate standing on a shell-like base. A suspended triangle represents The Fool with his feathered cap. He is tethered. He is blind at the beginning of his journey. Below are the letters AVD, life force. They have a numerical value of 11. Nu has a value of 56, and by Temurah, equivalent to qabalistic 11. Collectively they represent Nu and The Fool on his path. It expresses his approach to the perceptible universe below the veil of Isis.

Daleth in Initiation

Crowley's comment to Κεφαλη MB (42) in the Book of Lies describes a camel (Gimel, ג) as analogous to the traveler, uniting Macrocosm to Microcosm in his initiation.

AVD (אוד) is a powerful force as a guiding initiation. It is the key to spiritual life through love.

In heart metaphysically, The Empress has the secret of Hadit. The Empress is to the Emperor as Nuit (Isis) is to Hadit. She is the gate to higher consciousness and mystical attainment. Plato considered Venus to be an earthly goddess that aroused physical love, and a heavenly goddess that inspired intellectual love. Daleth is the path of the formative mother.

In the mercuric sigil, the lateral arcs represent the gate, the virgin Venus at the veil of Nuit, between Macrocosm and Microcosm. The T is a phallus. The D is a vulva or gate (ד). The flowering central thistle-head indicates seed and fertility. The tetractys indicates subsequent progression. The whole indicates a veil rent, permitting access to the non-manifest. Light appears. Knowledge increases. The Universe takes form and occupies space. Contrast is established. The sigil projects a similar image of an abyss crossing in chapter 42 of the Book of Lies.

Table of Letter Comparisons

Daleth (ד) compares to Ayin (ע)

The paths of Gimel and Daleth express Nature and its operation, with the Veil of Isis separating them. It is like Tai Chi Yin and Yang. The paths are reciprocal. They reflect the Emerald tablet aphorism, As above, so below.

They relate to the four devils [4 (ד) x 70 (ע)], views of Satan. The names of the genii mean that Nothingness becomes manifest. Logically, this occurs at the veil of Isis. But see the path of Ayin for elaboration.

The two paths are at the beginning of different levels of mystical attainment. Daleth is the first challenge to initiation for The Fool. Ayin is the gate or temptation the Fool experiences as his Inner Self evolves.

The koppa (ϙ) in the middle of the mercuric sigil has the value of 90, as does Tzaddi, the opening path to higher initiation. It indicates movement and discrimination during initiation. It is the sperm fertilizing the egg (the square) and so produces the thistle fruit and seeds. The seeds represent new revelations.

Genii

Qliphoth — Dagdagiel

Angel of Fertility

Dag	דג	Hebrew root דג meaning fruitful. It also means fish. It is duplicated for emphasis.
iel	יאל	Ending denoting an angel.

Mercurii — Dηnaʒartarωθ

The transliteration is Dynastartaroth.

The Force of Love in Tarot

Dyn	Δην	A prefix meaning force or power, *cf.* dynamic.
Astarta	aʒartar	A spelling of Astarte, the Babylonian fertility goddess equivalent to Venus.
Taroth	ταρωθ	A form of TARO found in the mercuric sigil for Aleph.

Arcana 231

Nu, Queen of Heaven | Babalon

The central eight-pointed star with radiating flames indicates initiation. The two views show different perceptions. It shows Nu at the veil. Babalon expresses a manifest sexual level. Within the path are differences in love expressed by Nuit, Nu, and Babalon.

The qliphothic aspect shows Babalon with fire and light in her eyes and masses of flaming hair about her, as described in Liber XXXI, II: 24. She has a strawberry crown, a symbol of Venus because of its heart shape and color. Her central brooch shows the seven-pointed star of Babalon. In her right hand is her cup of fornication. In her left hand is the beast with seven crowns and the heads of a man, eagle, dog, unicorn, lion, boar, and goat. Compare the description of Babalon from Apocalypse, Chapter 14.

Nu is figured on the mercuric side. She wears a radiant crown of twelve stars, showing a stellar nature. The wing to the right implies transcendence. It indicates the mystery of the pelican. She holds the paw of the lion, one of the seven-headed beasts, occurring later in the path of Teth. The beast is tamed and outside the veil. On her back is a wing to the right and a fiery scepter at the left.

ה

The Emperor — Ra-Hoor-Khuit

Aries (♈) — Secular Law and Government

4.   Now riseth Ra-Hoor-Khuit,
and dominion is established
in the Star of the Flame.

Domus Mercurii   Carcer Qliphoth

Hoo-oorω-iƺ   Hemethterith

Heh (ה) compares to Cheth (ח)

The fifth path is Heh (ה), IV. The Emperor. It has a numerical value of five (5). This is the first path specifically referring to the New Æon. The text recognizes the dominion of Ra-Hoor-Khuit as the ruler or Lord of the New Æon. The path relates to Aries (♈) and Mars. The Sun is exalted. Mars represents the most material aspect of energy, fire (△).

The Emperor represents the manifest Ra-Hoor-Khu(t). He governs secular law and governance. Red is his color. In Liber DCCCVIII vel Ararita I: 4, he is jocund, ruddy, and full of majesty. When unbalanced, he becomes despotic instead of beneficent.

Liber XXXI, Chapter I, expresses the viewpoint of Nuit. Chapter II has the viewpoint of Hadit. Chapter III starts with the viewpoint of Ra-Hoor-Khut. As half of Heru-Ra-Ha (= 418), Ra-hoor-Khut is 209. This sets his role as chief seer or prophet (אבראה = 222). Ahaahadabra and reward (אגרה) are each 222, the sum of 209 plus 13 (Unity, אחד). Qabalistically, it labels the prime role of Ra-Hoor-Khut. The commentary to the First Æthyr in The Vision and the Voice announced: The final manifestation is the Crowned Child, Horus (≈ Ra-hoor-Khuit), the Lord of the New Æon.

The Star of the Flame is the dominion ruled by Ra-Hoor-Khut in the New Æon.

The seated Emperor is holding a scepter in his right hand. The Visconti Tarot has *L'Imparatore* sitting on a gold throne. He wears red shoes. On the Marseilles card *IIII, L'Empereur* is sitting sideways with a shield below him. The Wirth *l 'Empereur* is similar. The card for The Emperor is number IV in the Rider / Waite deck. (The Fool is moved to near the end of the sequence) He sits on a throne marked with the heads of rams. The scepter and orb are symbols of authority. The Emperor can express himself as a wild ram or a gentle lamb.

Crowley's Thoth card for The Emperor is red. The crowned Emperor sits on a ram's head throne. The card has a lamb, a ram (♈) and a shield with a double-headed eagle. He sits in the position of sulfur (🜍), a fiery element.

Heh in Cosmos

The qliphothic sigil pictures the face of a man, the Emperor wearing a chain of office. The text associates it with Ra-Hoor-Khuit and the letter Heh [ה = 5]. On the Tree of Life model, Crowley puts The Emperor on path 17, instead. He attributed it to Tzaddi and Aquarius. This contrasts to its position in *Arcanorum CCXXXI* and other Class A libers.

The mercuric sigil is an upright star with the five elements interspersed between the arms. Clockwise from the upper left are Salt (🜔), Mercury (☿), Aqua, water (▽), Sulfur (🜍) and Ignis, fire (△). Together they create upright and inverted pentagrams. They define dominion in the New Æon.

Heh in Initiation

The Emperor rules the law and government in secular life. He may be tyrannical, dictatorial, or beneficial. He rules through fiat and statute. Wisdom, discretion and prudence regulate his actions. Any or all may be fallible, good, or bad. Render unto Caesar….

Salt, Mercury, and Sulfur symbolize material elements. Water and fire are consecrating elements. The two pentagrams reflect the mercuric and qliphothic, light and dark sides of life in the Microcosm. They delimit the dominion of the king and are guides for The Fool.

Table of Letter Comparisons

Heh (ה) compares to Cheth (ח)

These two paths are complementary, related to secular and sacred law.

The letters ה (Heh) and ח (Cheth) are similar in form. The difference is the gap in the upper left corner of ה (Heh). Each may appear as a substitution or blind for the other. Compare, for example, the middle syllable of Abra-had-abra, Abra-cad-abra and Aha-ahad-abra. They have different qabalistic values, correlations, and meanings.

The qliphothic sigils and text show no overt correlation.

The mercuric sigils both have five-pointed upright and inverted pentagrams related to the alchemical elements of the macrocosm.

The positions of the mercuric sigils for Heh and Vau would fit the alphabetical sequence better if they were interchanged. The letters and names of the genii follow the normal sequence. A discussion of this enigma occurs in the introductory chapter.

Genii

Qliphoth — Hemethterith

Spirit of a red ruling warrior (Horus)

Heme	εματο	Prefix related to blood, red or iron.
teri	θερι(ον)	Greek Θεριον, therion, a small wild animal.
ith	ιθ	Indicating spirit or genius.

Mercurii — Hoo-oorω-iζ

Genius of Horus, Hoor-paar-kraat

Hoor	ooρ	Hoor-Paar-Kraat, Horus.
oorω	ooρω	Ra-Hoor-Khu, Horus
iζ	-ιστ	Genius designation (compare -iel)

Arcana 231

Odin   Tyr

The path describes the character of a secular ruler. The contrast is between a Tyr(annical) ruler and a beneficent one. While they may seem contradictory to one another in style, each has benevolent and destructive aspects. At any time, one may seem more appropriate than the other.

The chief ruler of Olympus was Zeus, a sky god, who with Poseidon and Hades won the battle of the titans against Chronos their father and replaced him. Chronos was universal in his rule. Zeus, as highest among the Olympians, shared the different dominions with his brothers. The Roman equivalent of Zeus was Jupiter. In the Norse tradition, Tyr is analogous to a Titan, and Odin to an Olympian.

Here, the symbol of rule is the thunderbolt, indicating power and sharp decision. A tyrant is one who usurps power and rules by absolute authority. The orb and scepter are the symbols of sovereignty and imply steadier and more beneficial rule, and tradition.

The Norse Tyr and Odin reflect the parallel story of power and rule. Tyr is a sky god, the highest Germanic and Norse god associated with law and legislation. His symbol is a thunderbolt.

The myth is a story about control and power. Prophecy foretold great danger from the wolf Fenrir because of its rapid growth. It became dangerous and out of control. Tyr put his hand into the mouth of Fenrir so the wolf could be chained. The chains were able to control it. The cost was Fenrir biting off the right hand of Tyr. Symbolically, he lost his hand upholding courage, honor, and justice against the wolf. In doing so, he lost the ability to use a sword and be effective in war. He became a god of peace. His rule expressed universal consistency and regulation.

Odin was the Norse god corresponding to Jupiter, king of the gods and god of war. Odin had one blind eye, a long-beard and wore a broad-brimmed hat. He sacrificed his eye to gain wisdom. He was associated with magic, runes, and poetry. Wolves and ravens accompanied him. They brought him knowledge from the Middle Earth abode of man.

The myth is about government rule changing with time and circumstance. Each style has benefits and disadvantages and is appropriate at different times. A ruler at any time may act wisely or not. His effectiveness and success depend upon how judgment and temperance influence his actions.

ו

The Hierophant — Prophet

Taurus (♉) — Sacred Law, Religious dogma

5.   Also is the Star of the Flame exalted, bringing benediction to the universe.

Domus Mercurii   Carcer Qliphoth

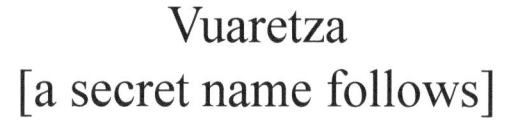

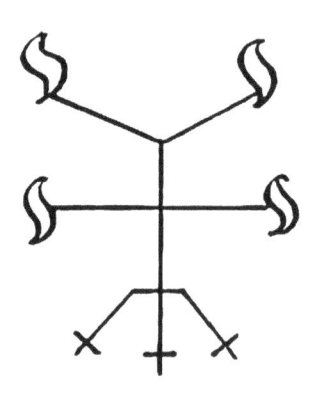

Vuaretza   **Uriens**
[a secret name follows]

Vau (ו) compares to Kaph (כ)

The sixth path is V. The Hierophant. Its Hebrew letter is Vau (ו), meaning nail. It has a numerical value of six (6) and relates to zodiacal Taurus (♉). This path connects the top triad of Briah to the top triad of Yetzirah on the Pillar of Mercy.

The Hierophant is a manifest messenger of the gods. He deals with the sacred aspects of the universe. He expounds sacred law and rule. He acts as psychopomp in initiation rituals.

The Star of the Flame is the individual enlightened mentor or prophet, the Hierophant. He leads through advice and sacred revelation. Liber XXXI promises new prophets for the New Æon. The clergy function in this path at a more individual level. They instruct the initiate in sacred law. They connect Macrocosm to Microcosm.

The cosmic aspect is usually presented as evolution. The process of initiation usually is presented as return. The models found on the Liber CCXXXI manuscript are linear. They begin with Ineffable.

The Visconti card, reflecting the Christian environment of its time, calls this tarot path *Il Papa* (The Pope). He wears the Triple Crown and has a triple-crossed staff. He holds one hand in benediction. The Marseilles card *V. le Pape* is similar. Rider / Waite changes the card name to V. The Hierophant, but the action is similar. It adds the papal keys at his feet.

The Thoth card, V. The Hierophant shows a central figure seated on a bull. The union of macrocosmic hexagram and microcosmic pentagram represents his message. Within the pentagram is the child of the New Æon, RHK. The woman girt with a sword is below him. The distinctive wand of the Hierophant represents the æons of Isis, Osiris, and Horus.

Vau in Cosmos

The Star of the Flame of the path is the messenger of sacred knowledge and revelation. He is the prophet or hierophant. The mercuric sigil has the upright VVVVV for the motto of Crowley.

The qliphothic sigil shows a branched structure with Yods (י, light, knowledge) at the apices. They appear on the upper triads of a Tree of Life model. The bottom shows a three-branched arrangement with a cross at each end. These may be interpreted as bases of pillars of the Tree of Life. The central axis locates the Hierophant who connects the two regions. The sigil is analogous to a hierophantic staff.

Vau in Initiation

The mercuric table of sigils interchanges the positions of ה and ו reciprocally. Crowley makes specific note of this on the manuscript. The sigils have penciled ה and ו present. The sigils match the respective text and genii. A logical interpretation suggests this was a subsequent note to Fuller to pay attention. See the Introduction.

The outer Circle of Fire indicates energy. This perimeter represents Ra-Hoor-Khut, as the ruler of the æon. The center is an Udjat, the Eye of Ra. It recognizes the Sun, Ra, as his basis. Between the two are indications of a high prophet or the Magus of the Æon.

An inverted pentagram shows grades of Initiation.

Description	Elemental	Level	Title
0 = ∞	Origin, Birth	≈ א Aleph	Man of Earth
8 = 3	Cleansing	≈ מ Mem	Adept, Initiate, M.T.
10 = 1	Resolution	≈ ש Shin	Prophet

Table of Letter Comparisons

Vau (ו) compares to Kaph (כ)

The qliphothic sigils are both based in the microcosm. Three bottom crosses indicate manifest nature in a fixed state.

The mercuric sigils are both circles. Vau relates to the messenger of the æon. Kaph summarizes the cycle of life or the ages of man. The result of action in life is karma.

Genii

Qliphoth — Uriens

Spirit of Uranus, God of heavens

Mercurii — Vuaretza — [a secret name follows]

Genius connecting heaven and earth.

Vu	ו	Represents Vau (ו), connector, nail, or phallus
aretza	ארץ	Earth, world. [a secret name follows]

Arcana 231

Theseus   Minotaur

The story of Theseus and the Minotaur relates to classic Athens and pre-Greek Minoan civilization. The labyrinth is the maze connecting inner to outer. Both the outer labyrinth of Minos, and the inner labyrinth of the aspirant require focus to master. The path connects the outer entrance and the inner goal, microcosm and macrocosm, the pentagram and the hexagram.

The Minotaur was half-man, half-bull. In Egypt, the bull represented Ka, life force and power. The Minotaur was a symbol of Cretan power. His mother was the daughter of King Minos of Crete. The Minotaur lived captive in a labyrinth thought to be part of the palace. He ate human flesh. As the result of winning a war with Athens, Minos demanded periodic tribute of Athenian boys and girls to be devoured by the Minotaur. Theseus killed the Minotaur and released the need for further tribute.

There are many analogies to the labors of Hercules. Theseus overpowered the Minotaur and killed it with his sword (knowledge). For his victories, he became a great unifier of Attica and Greek civilization. Theseus was a hero to Athenians who battled against the old religion and social order.

The labyrinths are the key to the story. Tracing the labyrinth is the path to God (at the center) from the entrance (birth), or a model for a medieval ritual pilgrimage.

Daedalus designed the one at Minos to keep the Minotaur under control. It was a challenge to find his location in the middle and escape. The Minotaur roams the labyrinth. The brain of an initiate (cf. labyrinth) is where he confronts the spiritual side. The resolution of that encounter determines his success as an initiate.

The background shows a branching labyrinth that requires many choices to traverse. It requires judgment and knowledge to succeed. Theseus conquered the maze by leaving the trail of thread suggested and provided by Ariadne, who fell in love with him.

The thread is the key to the mysteries because it marks the course between the outer and inner through the labyrinth. The thread represents preparation, direction, and connection. It unites the outer to the inner self during the Fool's journey. Knowledge and inspiration opened his route to success. The central labyrinth shows the continuous and extended solution representing fortitude necessary to accomplish goals. The branched maze represents the complexity and decisions of life.

ז

The Lovers, The Brothers

Gemini (♊) — Brotherly Love — φιλια

6. Here then beneath the winged Eros is youth,
    delighting in the one and the other.
    He is Asar between Asi and Nepthi;
    he cometh forth from the veil.

Domus Mercurii	Carcer Qliphoth
Zooωasar	Zamradiel

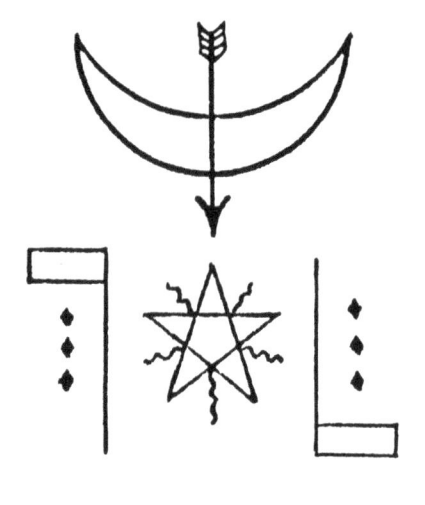

Zain (ז) compares to Daleth (ד)

The seventh path is VI. The Lovers or Brothers. Its Hebrew letter is Zain (ז), meaning sword. It has a numerical value of seven (7) and correlates to zodiacal Gemini (♊). This is the first of three paths related to love.

The message in Nature is attraction, gravity, and magnetism — and repulsion. Magnets attract when the polarity is opposite. They repel when similar. They can even alternate. They depend on circumstances. Similar ambiguity exists between the brothers as independent or coming together. Lovers have similar interactions. Brothers have a common origin; lovers do not. The path represents attraction (Mercuric) / repulsion (Qliphothic) in their broadest and original state.

Eros is energy, the force of attraction expressed through love. In the text, Asar (Osiris) is placed between Asi (Isis) and Nephthi (Nephthys). The two represent contrast, dark and light. Asar is Had, manifest below the veil of Isis.

Some love is superficial or transitory. Some is philanthropic and humanitarian. Some is deep and long lasting. Effective love is reciprocal. When unrequited, frustration and anger occur. Love then seems to disappear.

The key is brotherly love, φιλια. It implies respect for one another. It may express itself through compromise or charity. Do unto others, as you would have them do unto you.

Love expresses itself from individuals to the full expanse of society, and Nature. Young love includes attraction, infatuation, closeness, and warmth. It expresses itself through emotion, friendship, and respect. It is independent of class, gender, age, politics, religion, and economics.

Love can become competition, jealousy, and antagonism. Enmity and war may result. The New Æon views love as universal law. It respects every man and every woman as a Star.

The sigils illustrate the text. They show Eros in unbalanced and balanced state.

The qliphothic sigil has an upper, unbalanced moon, or scimitar. A line extends upward from an L, the letter of balance. At its sides are G(amete) symbols indicating the relationships of sexuality. The upper part of the sigil indicates imbalance or opposites, the lower part shows balance of opposites.

The mercuric sigil expresses balance and diversity in love. In the upper half, Eros the god of love is the vital force. The arrow pierces the moon, illusion. The lower half has the Asar and Asi (≈ neters, the upright and inverted flags) as opposites. The central image shows two pentagrams (sun and dark sun) conjoined. The pentagrams signify the contrasting qliphothic and mercuric aspects of the universe, the dark and light aspects of nature. The whole sigil represents love in union and division, underlying forces of universal action.

On tarot cards, Eros or Cupid points down, instilling the force of love with its arrows. The Visconti card is called *L'Amore* (Love). It shows a blindfolded Eros with lances above, and a pair of lovers below. The Marseilles *VI. Lamoureaux* card has Eros above pointing his arrow. Three figures are below — a central man and lateral woman. Wirth's *VI. l'Amoureux*, is similar. The figures are more distinct. The Rider / Waite VI. Lovers has a winged figure giving a blessing above, and a male and female below. Serpent and tree symbols suggest them to be Adam and Eve in the Garden of Eden as the early prototype of a loving relationship.

The Thoth card, VI. The Lovers is a major change from previous decks. Crowley notes the dual nature of the symbolism. Isis and Nepthys contrast at the top. The alchemical Red Lion and the White Eagle, the black and white children show union at the bottom. He attributed it to the original creation story. Contrast is inherent — analysis and synthesis are counterpoised. He considered the path of Temperance complementary.

Zain in Cosmos

The forces of Nature — including entropy, gravity, and magnetism — regulate the operation of the Universe. For every action there is an equal and opposite reaction — *Solve et Coagula*, involving division and fusion alternately. Man expresses this in the microcosm of nature.

Zain in Initiation

Fraternal or brotherly love is broad. It is the basis for benefaction and humanitarian contributions, and respect for man. When the beneficent aspect is reduced, self-survival may replace it. Xenophobia, hatred, and retribution elevate hostility to war. On a lesser scale, feuds develop when just relations are disregarded.

Initiation has many routes to success. True ones result in balanced individuals. They become wiser, dedicated, and focused on will. The ideal of love is symbolized through Nuit in universal aspect. The moon is the illusion that must be penetrated for balance to occur. See Liber Librae.

Table of Letter Comparisons

Zain (ז) compares to Daleth (ד)

This path connects love to the AVD force and Nature. See the reciprocal in the path of Samech also. The comparison shows love to be the gateway to initiation.

Genii

Qliphoth — Zamradiel

Love is key to action.

Zam	זמ	A system, operation or plan
rad	רד	A sphere or wheel, cycle
iel	יאל	The ending denoting an angel

Mercurii — Zooωasar

Horus/Asar

Zoo	ζωον	Animal, life
ω	ω	Expression of address
Asar	Aσαρ	Horus

Arcana 231

Abel   Cain

The illustration shows Abel and Cain. The central squares show the fires of sacrifice. Abel carries the lamb around his neck. The darker Cain has plant products below his left hand. His right hand swings the bone with which he slew Abel.

Cain and Abel are the first biblical brothers, the first sons of Adam. Cain, the firstborn, was dedicated to the Lord, a farmer. Abel was a shepherd. Their offerings to God were offered differently — proudly or humbly. The pride of Cain moved him to slay Abel. Cain's punishment and remorse followed. Finally, he received a mark of protection from God.

According to a commentary in the Zohar, *Bereshit 180*, Cain and Abel entered the world only to demonstrate the superiority and exaltation of יהוה over אלהים and the secret sin in Adam and Eve's fall. The sin of pride analogy relates to idolatry — pride goeth before a fall. The name יהוה correlates to the Tree of Life that Adamould eat. The name אלהים is equivocal and has many applications. It could refer to different gods, angels, etc. This name related to the Tree of Knowledge of good and evil. Adam was forbidden to eat from it.

The disobedience of Adam and Eve relates to eating an apple from the Tree of Knowledge — of good and evil. That original sin separated them from the Lord. The Zohar describes it as separation of fruit (אלהים) from the tree (יהוה). The hidden aspect is pride or hubris, that created a deadly relationship to God. The attempt at cover-up is a different sin. Adam and Eve were expelled from the Garden for their denial. After their admission of guilt, repentance, and forgiveness, they did not die, but had shorter lives.

In Genesis, Chapter 4, Cain proudly offered the fruit of the ground to the Lord. Abel humbly offered the firstlings of his flock. Their attitudes made Abel's offering acceptable. Cain was angered by the response of the Lord. Soon after, he killed Abel, presumably resulting from competition or jealousy. The Lord faced Cain with the crime, which he first denied, and cursed him for his pride. Cain suffered and was under threat of death. When he repented and acknowledged his sin, the Lord forgave him. He put a mark on Cain to protect him from further dangerous threats. The mark of Cain has become a mark of initiation. See the role of the path of The Devil below.

We see the salutary complex and negative sides of love. The Lord is jealous, loving, harsh and chastising — but forgiving.

The two stories show that love involves respect, truth, and honesty. Failure, as separation, is not fatal of itself. Admission can replace denial. Forgiveness is a response from love. The cover-up is more serious than the original sin.

Brotherly love requires interpersonal relationships. Despite differences, past experiences and emotion, it is important to comport oneself well. *Pax templi* relies on a virtuous response to differences among members of any group. It is the support expected as a group joins in mutual respect and pursues joint objectives. Sometimes, brotherly love means sharing with others, charity, and compassion.

ח

The Chariot — Sacred love

Cancer (♋) — Will and Want — Αγαπη

7.   He rideth upon the chariot of eternity;
the white and the black are harnessed to his car.
Therefore he reflecteth the Fool,
and the sevenfold veil is reveiled.

Domus Mercurii　　　　　　　Carcer Qliphoth

Chiva-abrahadabra-cadaxviii　　　　Characith

Cheth (ח) compares to Heh (ה)

The eighth path is VII. The Chariot. Its Hebrew letter designation is Cheth (ח), meaning fence. It has a numerical value of seven (7) and relates to zodiacal Cancer (♋). With the Hierophant, the two paths connect the upper triad of Briah to the upper triad of Yetzirah.

The path focuses on spiritual love and goals. Its message is aspiration and the goal of initiation. It shows truth through sacred knowledge and revelation. The Charioteer, He, is the Fool on his journey. A similar story tells how Elijah, a successful initiate, achieved union with God. In 2 Kings 2: 11, God sent the chariot from heaven to Elijah. It brought him to heaven.

From a cosmic aspect, the Chariot is the symbol of Ineffable toward the Universe. Seven-fold are the barriers between God and man. Seven-fold describes the image as the seven heavens, the veils of Babalon, the seven creative archons of the Gnostics, or the seven planetary forces. Therefore, they seem dark or evil. They are emanations of the Creator. In mind, they function as angels or demons. Each is a barrier to cross.

The qliphothic sigil shows two figures, one above the other. The mummy-like lower one is the Fool or Magician, lying prone. The upper figure is a stylized lion-serpent, the life force. It also is a camel-headed serpent representing knowledge. Knowledge and use of the astral expands understanding and awareness of the scope of life. They represent the conscience and unconscious sides of man, the material and astral aspects.

The Black Sun is the mercuric sigil symbolizes the nigredo of alchemy and hermetics. It is the Sun in the underworld. Its fire causes putrefaction of the body. The consuming fire removes the dross and purifies the gold. This is an early stage of initiation. See *Splendour Solis*.

The Black Sun also personifies Nuit. She is the dark and brilliant source of light and truth that becomes manifest through Nu. Union with her is culmination of the Fool's search for the Grail, an expression for the Great Work.

The Visconti Tarot card, *Il Carro,* shows the side view of a triumphal queen riding in a chariot. Her helmet is crowned by the crab (Cancer, ♋). In front of the chariot are four-winged cherubic animals — bull, eagle, man, lion — sphinxlike with countercharged parts.

Cheth in Cosmos

The mercuric sigil shows the Dark Sun behind the Sun. The symbol is an upright pentagram with acute points and an inverted one with sinuous points. The two represent the goddess (earth, downward, matter over spirit) and the god (sky, upright, spirit over matter), good and evil, known and unknown. It represents the universe in its qliphothic and mercuric aspects. The totally black image suggests the Magician still needs to distinguish the contrast. The dark Sun emits illumination.

Cheth in Initiation

From an initiatory view, the Charioteer is seeking the Grail. He is the initiate in action. His innocence is prerequisite for success. Once he starts on the path, he is bound to continue until completion. He has free rein (no limits, no hands) to explore. He falls short if his will is compromised. That is Thelemic sin. The chariot is the conduit between the initiate and the gods. The chariot is his mind and the vehicle of his action. The black and white represent its conscious and unconscious aspects. The black and white tiles of a temple floor also reflect this.

Table of Letter Comparisons

Cheth (ח) compares to Heh (ה)

The two letters are similar in shape. Each may serve as a blind for the other. Heh is distinguished by the break, the window, in the upper left corner.

The mercuric sigils of Cheth (ח) and Heh (ה) are like noon and midnight. The bright Heh (5) relates to Ra-Hoor-Khu, the ruler of the æon. The dark Cheth (8) is brilliance at midnight. Hoor-Paar-Kraat is the silent source of knowledge and the Book of the Law.

Genii

Qliphoth — Characith

Spirit of Hoor-paar-kraat

Char	חר	Elementary existence
chith	חת	Veil of darkness

Mercurii — Chiva-abrahadabra-cadaxviii

Magic force of Ra-Hoor-Khu in the Æon

Chiva	חיוה	The Beast. Cf. חוה, Eve
Abrahadabra		Formula of the Æon and of Great Work, 418.
Cadaxviii		AA + CDXVIII = A∴ A∴ + 418

This major formula of the æon is sometimes considered a word of the æon. Note the difference between Abracadabra with a Cheth, ח and its two spellings with a Heh, ה Abrahadabra and Ahaahadabra, in Liber XXXI, III: verses 1, 47 and 75. Qabalistically, they have different values and meanings. Change not as much as the style of a letter (Liber XXXI, 1: 54)!

Arcana 231

Grail Seeker					Satan

Satan, the Devil, characterizes the adversary. He represents the dark side. He has bat-like wings and a beard of fiery flames. The double-hooked rod is his symbol. It expresses duality and opposition. Diaboly, διαβολη, is his false accusation, slander, or calumny. These are his means and methods of operation. The downward pointing star with the wavy arms represents him in the sigil.

The other view shows the Charioteer, rather than the traditional Charioteer in his Chariot. He is the knight in shining armor with a cause, the innocent Grail seeker. His goal is to understand the universe and truth. He wields the sword with Θελημα, Will, emblazoned on its blade. It signifies the 93 Current of the present æon. The upright star with straight points represents him. The qliphothic Satan and the mercuric Charioteer may contrast Want and Will respectively. What is the reward behind the veil? It is accomplishing the Great Work, Abrahadabra, within the initiate.

ט

Fortitude, Strength

Leo (♌) — Life Force, Ἐρος

8.   Also came forth the mother Earth with her lion, even Sekhet, the lady of Asi.

Domus Mercurii   Carcer Qliphoth

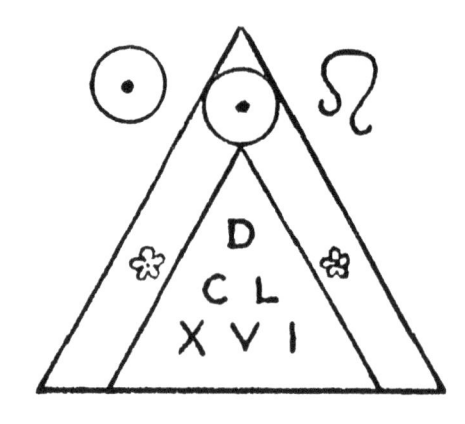

Θalεζer-ā-dekerval   Temphioth

Teth (ט) compares to Shin (ש)

The ninth path is Teth (ט), VIII. Fortitude. It is one of the classic virtues, along with Prudence (Wisdom), Justice and Temperance. It has a numerical value of nine (9). Teth is a serpent. It attributes to Leo (♌) in the zodiac. It is ruled by the Sun. The lion is a traditional symbol for strength and inner feeling.

The path characterizes life force, energy, or azoth. The lion-serpent is one traditional symbol. Life force is either constrained or excessive in different editions of the tarot cards. Traditional cards show a woman holding open the mouth of the lion (restraint). In the early alternatives she is standing by a broken column (excess force).

As virtue, fortitude contains elements of strength, force, and vigor, also include purpose, reliability, steadfastness, courage, and self-discipline It includes courage, determination, and responsibility. It affects morality and ethics. It responds to fear and adversity, trends toward good, and avoids evil. It is stamina driving an individual toward perfection. It is the love of Nuit, unbridled and unlimited, surrendering to the last drop of blood, and the last speck of dust. Force, freedom, and lust are balanced by self-constraint and responsibility.

Mother Earth with her lion expresses solar power. It is life force from the sun. Sekhet, the lion-headed goddess, bears a solar disc and uraeus on her head. The eye of Horus is also her symbol. She is a great power, a female warrior goddess, and a protector of royal power. She is the daughter of Ra and the wife of Ptah. She is associated with Justice (Maat ≈ Isis, Nature, Lady of Asi). She is the whore of Babalon.

The Grigonnier Tarot shows a woman standing by a broken pillar. The Visconti card, *XI La Forza* (Fortitude or Force), shows a standing man with a cudgel beating a lion. It illustrates force (the lion) controlled rather violently. The Marseilles card, *XI la Force*, shows a woman restraining the mouth of a lion. The application of force is judicious. The Wirth card, *XI la Force*, is assigned to Kaph (כ). The Rider / Waite card, VIII Strength, has the woman restraining a standing lion. She has a lemniscus (∞) above her head. These cards show how the presentation varies in time. It also indicates different aspects and sequences of the path.

The Thoth card, XI. Lust shows Babalon riding The Beast. The basic design occurs in the biblical book Revelations, chapter 14. She raises the grail in her right hand, indicating the spiritual goal. In her left hand, she holds the reins of constraint. The beast has seven heads representing her different characteristics — Angel, Saint, Poet, Adulterous Woman, Person of Valor, Satyr and Lion-serpent. She expresses joy and ecstasy. The card expresses a physical formula for attaining initiation, also symbolized is the interaction of Sun and Moon.

In the New Æon, the Thoth message directly emphasizes physical love, sexual exploration, and Eros, as Babalon and the Beast. It is the path of sex magic. Here is Babalon and the Scarlet Woman — different expressions of love unto Nuit. It puts all manifest expression of love under the ægis of Nuit. At the individual level, it embodies respect of one Star for another. It is not a license for licentiousness.

The act of union, *Coagula*, brings together male and female, sexually and magically. The power of Nuit ultimately conquers and rules. The sperm carries the message to the womb, the center of power. The aspirant practices 'Do what thou wilt shall be the whole of the Law'. As he continues further, he understands the depth and truth in this statement. He cannot defy Nu. Natural law is always consistent. His Will incorporates it.

The key to success is understanding Will. The Thelemic response clearly states that love is the law, love under Will. It goes beyond desire or want. All acts of love follow that law. To advance in the Great Work requires the inclusion of pure Will. Sin is anything that detracts from this. Consider the stories of the knights of the Round Table in their quest.

Teth in Cosmos

The qliphothic sigil shows the lion-serpent, Baphomet. Liber CCXXXI reveals the combined solar / phallic nature of the path. Its overt sexual application was shadowed by underlying views at the time of revelation. In the Thoth Tarot, Crowley emphasizes the positive strength and sexual prowess of the lion. Babalon and the Scarlet Woman are manifest expressions of Nuit (or Isis) who represents fundamental feminine power.

Teth in Initiation

The DCLXVI, 666, of the mercuric sigil is the number of the Beast. The Beast is under the wings [influence, protection] of Babalon. The ruling planet, the Sun (☉), is at the apex. It rules the lion, Leo (♌). A red or a white rose is on each wing. The white rose is the blood of Venus. The red rose is the seed of Mars. Conversely, they are the white and red tinctures of alchemists.

Babalon and the Beast conjoined produce the elixir for the next generation, the magical Child. For the aspirant, this is manifestation of sex magic. The experience at the point of orgasm (union), the concentration of Will, provides access to revelation and growth in initiation.

In the Gnostic Mass, before partaking the consecrated elements, the priest repeats three times: O Lion and O Serpent that destroy the destroyer be mighty among us. This is one mystery in the Mass. It invokes Baphomet, the solar / phallic force that conquers death. Consummation symbolizes accomplishment of the Great Work.

Crowley focuses on the sexual nature of the traditional path by calling it Lust. The mercuric sigil recognizes this. It also follows by describing individual force and its restriction or control. The last sentence distinguishes will from want or desire. Here is the difference between lust unto Nu and lust unto result.

Table of Letter Comparisons

Teth (ט) compares to Shin (ש)

The qliphothic sigil of Teth shows Baphomet, the solar / phallic creative force as the lion-serpent. The pyramid tomb in Shin holds the results and choice of a successful initiate, who has completed his Great Work. He will decide the final step in his journey.

The mercuric sigil for Teth is the two-dimensional analog of the solid pyramid in Shin. The Beast is surrounded in Teth. The Pharaoh in the king's chamber is surrounded by the mass of the pyramid. Both are initiation temples and experiences. Both associate force and fire with energy.

Genii

Qliphoth — Temphioth

A Beast

Tem	טמ	Spirit of contamination, either impure or profane.
phioth	פעיט	Dilation, open to penetration, space. Metaphorically, it implies a Fool or simpleton, the action of persuasion and deceit. Lust.

Mercurii — Θalεζer-ā-dekerval

Alester de Kerval

Θ	Θerion	The Beast
alεζer	aloster	Alester
ā		a
dekerval		Dekerval

In Roman characters, this becomes The Beast (Therion) Alester (sic) de Kerval. Theta is the path of the Beast. The remainder of the genius's name is Alester (sic) and Crowley's implied connection to the Breton family de Quérouaille or de Kerval.

Arcana 231

Sekhet   Babalon, Forteza/Fortitude

The broken pillar version is the earlier. The restrained lion is the more frequent. Each version shows the two holding and sharing the wand, the symbol of energy.

The headdress of Sekhet takes the form of a lioness, a symbol of feminine force and sexual prowess. She has determined demeanor. She controls the Beast. Sekhet is a complement of Babalon. Her left hand holds an ankh, the symbol of life force. Her right hand shares the wand of power. The column broken by Babalon represents excess force.

Babalon holds magical power. In this path she is the Scarlet Woman, Sekhet and Isis (Asi) of other levels. The drawing represents the vital force of life applied peacefully. The Serpent flame is the initiatory drive of energy, the azoth. The message of the path expresses the power of the female.

י

The Hermit — Wisdom, Light

Virgo (♍) — Prudence

9.   Also the Priest veiled himself,
lest his glory be profaned,
lest his word be lost in the multitude.

Domus Mercurii   Carcer Qliphoth

Iehuvahaʒanɛθatan   Yamatu

Yod (י) compares to Mem (מ)

The tenth path is Yod (י), IX The Hermit. It has a numerical value of ten (10) and attributes to Virgo (♍) in the zodiac. Yod (י ≈ seed) is the basis for the other letters of the Hebrew alphabet.

This path explores communication and wisdom. Wisdom replaces the earlier virtue aspect Prudence. The Hermit is the communicator between deity and man. Mercury rules the path. The message, truth, is more important than the messenger. Wisdom is the precursor to all just action.

Plato proposes that wisdom involves giving good counsel and advice to others. This application of wisdom is Prudence. It is necessary to preserve stability and harmony, but still allow for change. Prudence generally avoids extreme thoughts. Yet, breakthroughs to wisdom also come from seemingly radical expressions. Prudence considers the short- and long-term consequences of wisdom.

Good and evil are judgmental evaluations of men. Understanding good depends on understanding reality. Reason (knowledge, *ratio*) explores truth, which is independent of man. The result of a decision determines its merit. It requires memory, foresight, open mindedness, and objectivity. He who rejects truth cannot be prudent. Reality influences conscious action.

Freedom requires knowledge. It does not come from slavishly following traditions or previous understanding, though they provide valid bases. The difficulty is separating truth from illusion. Faith and fact in any model or system need challenge regularly, and the difference accepted.

In the tarot the Hermit first carried a sandglass. It represented time and experience. Later, the Hermit becomes the voice and messenger of truth. He has light in his lantern. Its highest and most refined form is gnosis. Knowledge and truth are his weapons. They can be so bright and dazzling they blind perception. Expressed or silent, truth can be sensed. The *cognoscenti* recognize its undistorted nature.

The goals of each initiate begin with light and truth, wisdom, and peace. The separation of the pairs is clear. Truth is Nature — emanation of Ineffable, independent of the mind of man. Light transmits the message of truth. The Initiate receives light as revelation (religion) or as answers to questions (science). Both increase understanding. Prudence requires knowledge for decision and problem solving. Prudence discerns. It distinguishes wisdom from folly. It directs action and thought.

Included within prudence are foresight, objectivity, and clarity of decision. Imprudence is often impulsive, thoughtless, indecisive, and negligent. Prudence cannot be evaluated without appreciating its applicability and practicality. Truth may appear as lies, analogies, or through parables, and vice versa.

All decisions and actions have possibility of fallibility. They require resources that may seem conflicting. Prudence is considered by many to be only the avoidance of risk and extremes. It requires discretion. Even dropping the first atomic bomb as a weapon apparently saved life. If not, the war of attrition was projected to result in greater deaths.

The Visconti card, *Il Tempo* (Time), shows a bearded old man (Saturn) holding a sandglass in his right hand, and a staff in his left hand. In later traditional decks, a lantern replaces the sandglass. Otherwise, the basic design remains the same. The Marseilles card, *VIIII L'Hermite*, has the number and title included. The Wirth Tarot is *VIIII l'Ermite*. It has a small upright serpent at the base of the staff. The Rider / Waite card, IX The Hermit, is austere. The change from the sandglass to the lantern makes knowledge, light, more apparent. The substitution of knowledge for time implies truth will ultimately prevail through experience.

On the traditional tarot card, the Hermit carries knowledge in his lantern. It is his guides to decision-making and action. The text in Liber CCXXXI implies this knowledge is not readily available to all. When an initiate hears the message, he may not yet be prepared to perceive or understand it. He may remain ignorant. He may misinterpret it. He may consider it illusion.

The Hermit dominates the Thoth card assigned to Virgo. In the center, he holds the golden sun that correlates to the spermatozoon. It is the Yod. It is earthly and natural, shown by grain in the background.

Casuistry is the application of ethics and morals to decisions and actions. Specifically, it uses subtle reasoning to justify something, or mislead someone. It can involve narrow mindedness, strict definition, redirection, or hidden agendas. They appear outwardly prudent but are dangerous when applied without understanding the practical results or the side effects.

Yod in Cosmos

Yod (יוד) of Yod Heh (יוד הי) is the Father of Tetragrammaton. It encompasses space and time. It is the basis for the Hebrew alphabet and all communication.

The qliphothic sigil shows an inversion of the mercuric lamp. It is an outline of the lamp turned inward and inverted. The light is hidden but not lost. The borders of ignorance are always eroding as the flame of the lamp invades the dark.

The oil, the secret and potential fire (סוד, פור) within the lamp, is its reservoir of unrevealed Truth and Nature.

Wisdom, even though incomplete, derives from universal truth. The message of the Hermit is growth in wisdom and experience. They are asymptotic. No one attains total truth.

Yod in Initiation

The hand-held oil lamp goes back thousands of years as a symbol for knowledge. The oil represents truth and fact. The flame represents revealed knowledge. Revealed truth is often veiled. Knowledge is not always perceived, assimilated, or appreciated. How often have ideas been considered ahead of their time (the truth is too bright), or ideas challenged and denied, ahead of their time because of expectation, bias, or prejudice?

The mercuric sigil has an erect cross emerging from the lamp. It represents revealed knowledge. In the sigil, the cross has the hilt of a sword, the symbol of discrimination.

The clear message of the initiation process is often missed the first time during its rituals. Later experience and meditation enhance revelation, appreciation and applicability — sometimes quite suddenly. Then revelation and transformation occur. The hidden seed from the phallus transmits information within the microcosm. It takes circumstance and time, and suitable environment, for it to develop into an adult organism.

Table of Letter Comparisons

Yod (י) compares to Mem (מ)

Understanding truth (י) is the prime objective of initiation. The path of Mem (מ) opens the aspirant to spiritual knowledge and his soul. The path summarizes knowledge throughout life and initiation.

Both sigils can be interpreted as disinformation and ignorance needing to be purged. The mercuric sigils, with crosses indicating a sword of justice, keep the path of truth open. Knowledge of spirit is indicated by the Golden Dawn symbol. Symbolically, light comes from the east as the morning sun rises.

Genii

Qliphoth — Yamatu

The Source

a	יא	Origin of unity (truth)
ma	מא	Mother
tu	תו	Root or source

Mercurii — Iehuvahȝ anɛ θatan

Restriction by the Satan

Iehuvah	יהוה	Jehovah
Ich-	יה	Manifestation of restriction
vaha	ואהא	Barking, roaring
St	ȝ	Spirit
Tsatan	צאתא	Satan, the Serpent

Arcana 231

Merlin is the magician of Arthurian legend. He inherited many occult powers of past and present. According to one story, his virgin mother was mortal. His father was a demon. Part of his heritage is dark sided. He was baptized at birth to separate him from his demonic inheritance. His prophetic knowledge of the future came from God after his baptism. He is an old guard wizard representing past knowledge, magic, mystery, and tradition.

Merlin is described wearing a ragged coat, wild hair, and a large beard. He is a reported shape-shifter. He was beautiful. In old age, he was a hunchbacked ugly herder, driving animals, and carrying a club. The details of the myths and stories are not consistent. In this drawing, he appears as the longhaired, bearded magician or hermit. He was the wizard advisor to the king. The winged dragon indicates his dark side. He maneuvered the birth of King Arthur through magic.

King Arthur is closely associated with the legends of the Holy Grail. The story begins with the sword Excalibur, which could be removed from its mounting stone only by the true king. He is looking to the future. The image shows him holding the sword symbolizing knowledge and discrimination and the serpent of knowledge.

The required characteristics for Grail seekers in the court of King Arthur was purity, innocence and will. This is the initiate on his journey. His siege perilous while seeking the Grail is a trial analogous to the paths from Death to The Tower.

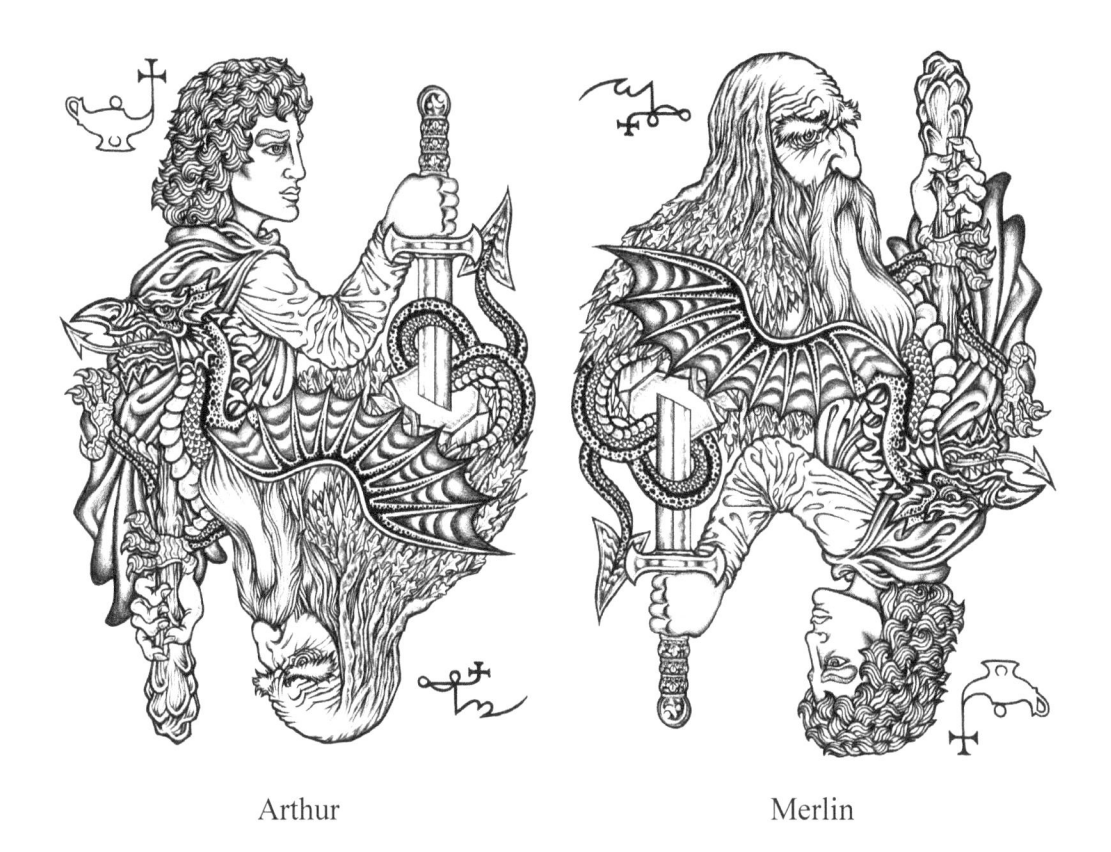

Arthur   Merlin

כ

Wheel of Fortune — Life, Experience

Jupiter (♃) — Karma

10. Now then the Father of all
issued as a mighty wheel;
the Sphinx, and the dog-headed god, and Typhon,
were bound on his circumference.

Domus Mercurii　　　　　　　Carcer Qliphoth

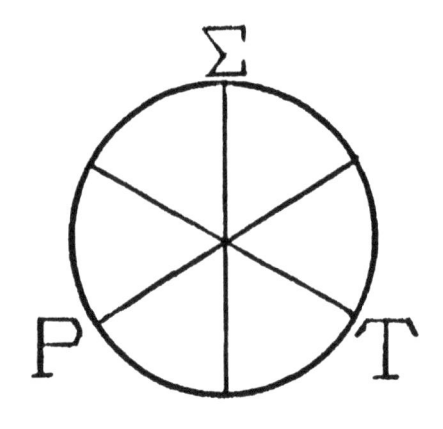

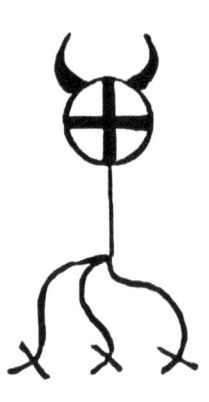

Kerugunaviel　　　　　　　Kurgasiax

Kaph (כ) compares to Vau (ו)

The eleventh path is Kaph (כ), 10. The Wheel of Fortune. It has a numerical value of twenty (20). It attributes to the planet Jupiter (♃). The path relates to the external aspects of life, experience, and time.

The path shows stability and change. It encompasses the experience throughout life. It represents the cycle of life from birth to old age.

The axis of the wheel is the center of a circle. While the axis rotates, there is no apparent change in its position. The circumference of the wheel also seems not to change, though each point on it moves through the entire 360 degrees in each rotation. The former represents static, the latter represents kinetic, equilibrium. The turning of the wheel is relentless, the course of nature and life.

The qliphothic sigil shows the wheel in stasis. The three gunas all unite at its bottom, locking it in position. The internal cross also is in a fixed upright and erect position. The horns suggest a primeval dark state. That cosmic state is before time and is without change. The cycle includes creation, preservation, and destruction.

In the mercuric sigil, the forces are active. The mercuric sigil is a circle with six radii. The Greek letters are Rho (P Rajas), Sigma (Σ Sattvas) and Tau (T Tamas). Rajas represents light and active aspects. Sattvas represents balanced and preservative aspects. Tamas represents dark and destructive aspects. Their interaction determines the character and progress of the individual.

The parallel Hermanubis, Sphinx, and Typhon often occur in their stead. The dog-headed god Hermanubis pulls counterclockwise in a constructive sense. At the top, the Sphinx represents purity, balance, and stabilization. Typhon is the monster that pulls clockwise. It represents the force of destruction, a plague to men.

The Visconti Tarot shows a blindfolded woman inside a circle. On its perimeter are page-princes at the right and left. Above is a mature ruler holding an orb. Below is a crawling old man in white robe holding up the wheel. The scroll indicates the ages of man as: *regnabo, regno, regnavi* and *Ego sum sine regno*. The Marseilles *X La Roue de Fortune* has three guna-like animals on the rim of a wheel. This is a major change of design. The Wirth card, *X la Roue de Fortune*, follows the same pattern. The base holding the wheel is an upright post with circle and crescent (sun and moon) and two serpents twisted around it (caduceus). The figure on the right is Hermanubis, on the left is Leviathan, and on top, the Sphinx. The handle at the top of the post suggests the wheel is capable of being turned by an external force.

The Thoth card, The Wheel, has guna animals as symbols.

Kaph in Cosmos

The basic formula of the universe is 0 = 1 or Nothing equals everything. Expanded, it becomes 0 = 1 = 2 (manifest). The numbers 120 and 210 also describe it. Activity is expressed through *Solve et Coagula*. The cosmic process has three stages — creation, preservation, and destruction. The god Shiva has the trident to symbolize three aspects. It is also the wheel showing the interaction or equilibrium created by the three gunas.

Kaph in Initiation

The cycle of creation, preservation and destruction applies not only to universal activity, but also to the life of an individual. It represents time and experience. It is the record of life and its resultant karma.

The three gunas, as qualities of nature, are indicated by Greek capital letters.

P	Rajas	Movement (Positive) reflects desire, anxiety, ambition, competition, power, and fame.
Σ	Sattvas	Equilibrium, balance (Neutral) reflects purity, wisdom, and kindness.
T	Tamas	Stagnation (Negative), expresses impurity, anger, delusion, envy.

Table of Letter Comparisons

Kaph (כ) compares to Vau (ו)

Qliphothic sigils have similar bases. The Vau sigil has an upper active part, the message brought to the lower. The Kaph sigil summarizes the life of a Fool.

The mercuric sigils are both circles. Vau is the messenger and identifies the grades of initiation in the New Æon. Kaph relates the message to the cycle of life to a man awaiting enlightenment.

Genii

Qliphoth — Kurgasiax

Guardian of Life

Kurg	Κερξ	The keryx guards the temple. He watches over the candidate and leads him through the rituals.
asiax	ασιας	East. The light arising from the dark (at dawn)

Mercurii — Kerugunaviel

Guardian of change and Karma

Kerug	Κερυξ	A variant of Kurg (see above).
guna	γυνα	A fundamental force of nature. The three are RST (above).
aviel	ἄνιελ	Haniel, האניאל. The archangel of Netzach. Guardian of change or karma.

(The English v is a blind for ν, the lower-case Nu in Greek.)

Arcana 231

Janus   Fortuna

The Wheel of Fortune summarizes change in life. It also signifies celestial motion. Seven wheels related to the motion of the planets against the backgrounds of the zodiac of stars. The zodiac appears to move constantly, affecting fate and fortune.

The central figure is a three-dimensional gyroscope. The outer circle represents the zodiac. The inner wheels are the planets in their orbits. The earth appears to be rotating at the middle like the axle of the wheel. This is the viewpoint of man at the center interpreting the universe. They show the archetypal and cosmological aspects of stability and change. Separation is change measured as time.

Work is considered virtuous. Idleness is not. Luck constantly changes. Those who lack virtue invite misfortune.

describe the reign of a king — left, I shall reign; top, I reign; right, I have reigned; and bottom, I have no kingdom.

Fortuna is the Roman goddess of luck and fate, good or bad. She is veiled and blind, without the scales of justice, and impartial. Like Jupiter, she could be bounteous, indicated by the overflowing cornucopia. She is the rudder and prow of a ship sailing steadfastly between safe water and dangerous shoals.

Janus is the Roman god of time, gates (thresholds), beginnings, transitions, and ends. He symbolizes the new and the old years. His two faces look back to the past and forward to the future. He also presided over war and peace, planting, and harvest. He holds keys as the god of gates and arrivals and protects the community.

The formula illustrated here is IRE, Latin *to go*. Spermatozoa are the means of propagation from one generation to the next. Janus holds the keys. The prow of the ship is at his right.

(Note that in a circular model, the linear sequence of the cards has the Ten of Discs adjacent to The Fool, following the traditional sequence. On the Tree of Life, having Kether in Malkuth and vice versa results in a similar iterated arrangement of sephiroth.)

ל

Justice — Equilibrium

Libra (♎) — Balance, Adjustment

11. Also the lady Maat
with her feather and her sword
For Fate was already established.

Domus Mercurii　　　　　Carcer Qliphoth

Lusanaherandraton　　　Lafcursiax

Lamed (ל) compares to Samech (ס)

The twelfth path is XI. Justice. It attributes to Lamed (ל), meaning Ox Goad and to Libra (♎), evaluation in the zodiac. It has the numerical value of thirty (30).

The scales measure justice and equilibrium. It is the state of Nature interpreted by man as the virtue concerning balance. It follows from the 0 = 1 fundamental formula of identity and contrast. Nature is exact overall but has local imbalance and inequality. Equilibrium is a process of return toward the ideal state in cosmic Nature. The scales tip from side to side. For man, the virtue justice incorporates ethical, moral, and legal concepts based on rights, duty and responsibility. Some view it as settlement of debt. Debt implies inequality. Ethically, balance implies fairness, integrity, adjustment, and responsibility.

Justice purports to give each man his right and due. The principle of justice is the resolution of imbalance. It is independent of good and evil, which qualities man imposes on facts and contrasts. Justice, a platonic virtue, is closer to truth than the other virtues. (Is this why Justice precedes Fortitude in the Marseilles Tarot sequence?). Plotinus (Enneads I: 2, 6) calls it doing one's own work and fulfilling one's task. How much this sounds like the process of initiation! See Liber Librae, the Book of Balance.

The *Arcanorum* text is straightforward. Maat is the Egyptian goddess of Justice. The feather is her symbol. In the Book of the Dead, the heart of the dead is weighed against the feather. The sword divides. The fulcrum measures the imbalance between the two pans. The last line says that karma resulting from the past life is the ultimate object measured.

The role of a leader is to make and guide decision. Nothing affects his success in exercising power more than his sense of justice and delegating powers. Mercy without justice is destructive. Justice without mercy is cruelty. Emotion and prejudice sully objectivity and equanimity.

Justice in the New Æon derives from Liber XXXI, I: page 1 (verses 3, 4), a statement of inherent equality:

> Every man and every woman is a star.
> Every number is infinite: there is no difference.

As virtue, Justice involves the interaction between the individual and members of his community, singly or collectively. Family interactions mostly involve morals and ethics. Community interactions involve law, compensation, and restitution. Inequality, debt and sin are factors to consider.

Righteousness is a quality derived from the application of virtue, ethics and morals to life. Liber CXXVII vel OZ begins with Man has the right to…. This is a statement of belief and value. The Will of one individual should not forcibly bend the will of another. Justice aims for prudent resolution of differences. It requires knowledge and respect, fortitude and dignity, severity, and mercy. Injustice, bias, and disequilibrium are counterproductive.

The qliphothic sigil shows an unbalanced state. The scales (balances) are in disarray. The figure holds the letter Lamed (ל) balance in the left hand, and the pans of justice in the right. The sword of Justice, the discriminating fulcrum, is disconnected. Man is juxtaposed in the disequilibrium, between knowledge and will. He looks to the pans and sword to reestablish balance.

The mercuric sigil provides one of the few representations of a 2-d Tree of Life model in Liber CCXXXI. The model is inverted relative to its standard projection including the Ain (origin at bottom) and Ain Soph. Path assignments on the TL are non-specific. The feather of Maat at the top is the indicator of Malkuth, equilibration and universal balance. Bilateral symmetry indicates manifestation, contrast, and duality.

Going from the bottom up, the dot in the sigil represents Ain, Ineffable. The cup-shape represents the dimensions of Existence, the Ain Soph. The central structure only includes Positive Existence, like the Tree of Life model. It begins with the central path, the separation of Ineffable and Universe. The three triads of columns are Upper (branching), Middle (three dots), and Lower (rectilinear, three armed). Below the longer central path is a triple junction, from which the feather extends as a measure of balance.

The Grigonnier Justice card shows a seated woman holding a sword and balances. The Visconti card, *La Giustizia* (Justice), shows a woman holding a sword and balances. Above her is a knight in shining armor riding a white horse. He also carries a sword. He is a symbol for ideal and truth. The Marseilles card is *VIII La Justice*. A seated and crowned woman holds a sword and scales. The Wirth card is similar. It is attributed to *VIII la Justice* and the letter Cheth (ח). The Rider / Waite follows the Marseilles design and calls it XI. Justice.

The Thoth Tarot, VIII. Adjustment is assigned to Lamed (ל) and Libra (♎). The woman, Maat, holds a sword in both hands. The scales hang from the headdress of Maat. She is the crux. The Alpha and Omega are balanced in the pans of the scales. Crowley calls this card an expression of Love is the law, love under Will.

The numbering and sequence of the tarot paths for Strength and Justice are discussed in the introduction.

Lamed in Cosmos

The Ain (0, None, Ineffable) emanates to produce a dualistic universe. It establishes contrast. They exist as reflections of one another. They are neither good nor evil, right nor wrong. For every action, there is an equal and opposite reaction. Its end reduces entropy and returns to unity.

The sequence of paths in Liber CCXXXI relates to the Hebrew, the alphabet letters in the *Sepher Yetzirah* and other Class A libers.

Lamed in Initiation

The mercuric sigil progresses upward to manifestation and final judgment, measured by the feather of Maat.

Equilibrium moves inequality toward balance. The mind of man superimposes quality and value but does not change truth. The feather of Maat evaluates the life of the aspirant. In that sense, it reflects karma from previous actions.

Table of Letter Comparisons

Lamed (ל) compares to Samech (ס)

The virtues of Justice and Temperance are closely related. Fairness results from wise action applied in a practical way and without prejudice.

The qliphothic sigil for Lamed has the forces unbalanced, while the one for Samech shows cyclical forces in operation with the aspirant balanced in the center.

The mercuric sigils are more comparable. The sigil for Samech shows the lower triads of the Tree, the part below the traditional Abyss. The sigil for Lamed extends to the esoteric level.

Genii

Qliphoth — Lafcursiax

Revealer of Imbalance

Laf	λαφ	Gluttony (excess)
kur	κυρ	From κυρεω — to master, to attain
siax	σιαξ	From the east (revelation from darkness)

Mercurii — Lusanaherandraton

Ease of Civility and Order

Lus	λὐ	From λυω — to loosen or abolish
anaher	αναειρ	From αναειρω — to lift or raise
andr	ανηρ	Man
aton	ατον	Without exertion

Arcana 231

This path is the symbolic evaluation of a person's life in the Egyptian Book of the Dead. Ammit and Maat are two gods in the old Egyptian ritual passage known as the weighing of the soul. The weighing includes a declaration of innocence. Plate 3a of the Papyrus of Ani pictures the ritual. Ammit sits behind Thoth. He is the devourer of hearts that fail the weighing. The 42 declarations occur on Plate 31b.

Thoth oversees the balance of the Scales and makes final judgment. He expresses knowledge. In the evaluation, the soul is challenged 42 times. In the New Æon, the Troa and Pyramidos (Liber DCLXXI, rituals of Thelemic initiation) have a parallel sequence. Much is modeled after that ritual. Instead of 42 declarations, 22 paths follow Hebrew alphabetic order. (See also the First Æthyr in Liber CDXVIII, the Vision and the Voice). Each is followed by the declaration that He is under the shadow of the wings. He who succeeds rises in the end. This is justice evaluating the overall success and lifestyle of an individual.

Ammit is a funerary deity, the devourer of the dead or eater of hearts. She is part hippopotamus, part leopard with spots, with the head of a crocodile. On the papyrus of Ani, she sits in the Duat in the Hall of Truth (Maat) behind the scale of justice and Thoth in the Egyptian underworld. In the Hall of Two Truths, the heart of a person is weighed against the ostrich feather of Maat. The feather is often pictured in the headdress of Maat. If the heart is judged not pure, Ammit devours it. That person undergoing judgment does not continue to immortality. Once Ammit swallows the heart, the soul was believed to become restless forever; this was called 'to die a second time'. Ammit was also sometimes said to stand by a lake of fire. The unworthy hearts were destroyed, cast into the fiery lake. Ammit and the lake represent destruction.

To the Egyptian mind, Maat bound all things together into indestructible unity. The universe, the natural world, the state, and the individual were all seen as parts of the wide order generated by Maat. She represented the normal and basic values that formed the backdrop for justice carried out in truth and fairness. Maat is the exemplar of the virtue, Justice. Her feather was the sensitive standard by which a soul (considered to reside in the heart) was pure enough to reach paradise. In an abstract sense, Maat was divine order (the laws of Nature) established at creation and reconstituted at the accession of each new Pharaoh. She evaluated truth, loyalty, universal balance, and divine order. She was key to ethical behavior for the living, and judge of their souls after death. She is often paired with Thoth, associating experience and wisdom to ethics during life. Thelemites perceive many similarities to Nuit.

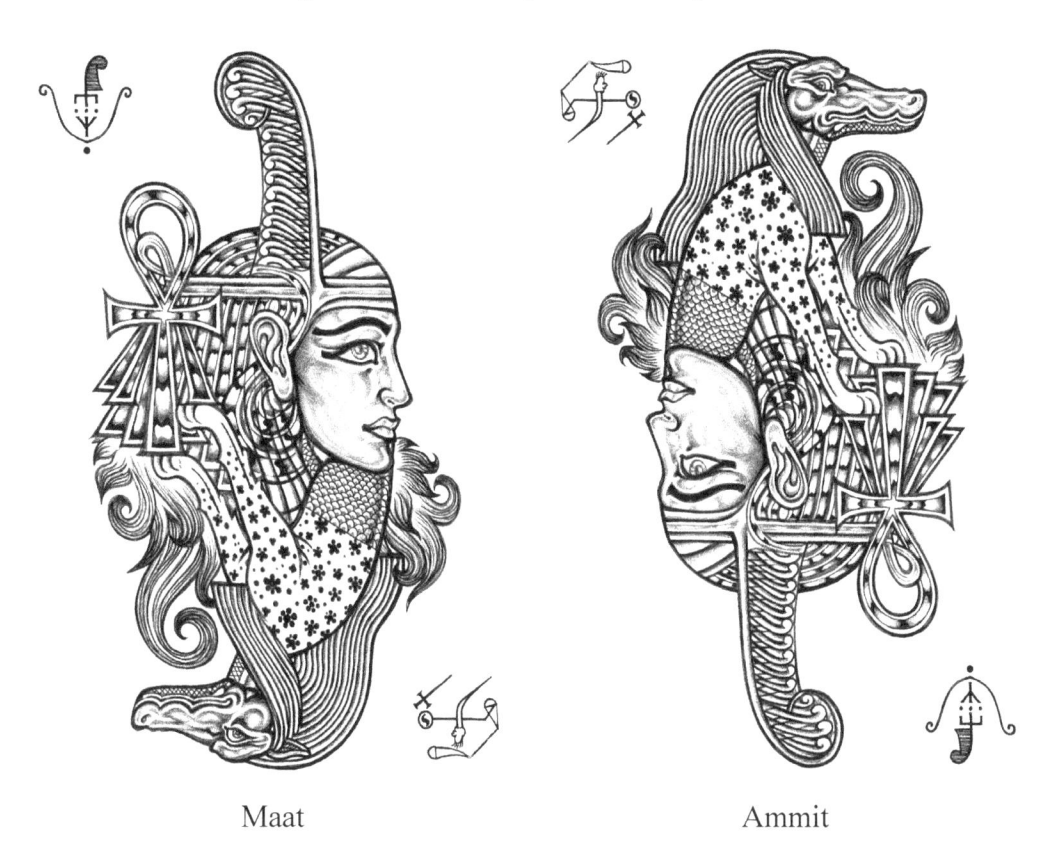

Maat

Ammit

מ

Hanged Man — Baptism

Water (▽) — Lustration, Rebirth

12. Then the holy one appeared
in the great water of the North;
as a golden dawn did he appear,
bringing benediction to the fallen universe.

Domus Mercurii　　　　　　　Carcer Qliphoth

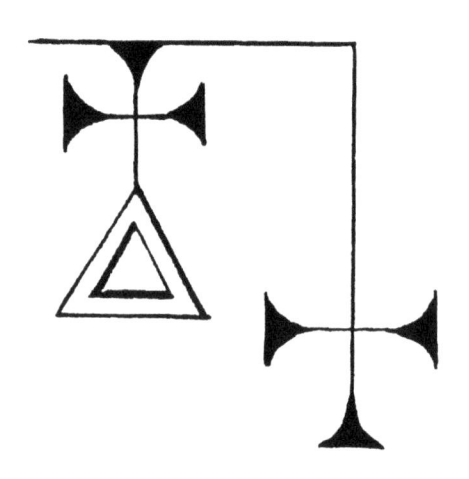

Malai　　　　　　　Malkunofat

Mem (מ) compares to Samech (ס)

The thirteenth path is Mem (מ), XII. The Hanged Man. It symbolizes a significant event in the life of the initiate. It has a numerical value of forty (40). It attributes to the element water (▽). While the previous paths relate to the exoteric body, the following paths describe the journey of a concurrent inner body or esoteric self. The culmination of the former is the path of the Wheel of Fortune (כ); that for the latter is the Sun (ר). The Fool and the Hanged Man are complementary aspects of the initiate. They exist in parallel rather than in serial or consecutive sequence.

This path introduces renewal, rebirth, and baptism. As an elemental path, it begins the stages for becoming an Adept. It is a ritual of consecration. In such rituals, consciousness changes. The inner self emerges as distinct. In cosmic terms, it increases the awareness of god.

The exoteric man contains elements of spirituality. Baptism activates the spiritual life beyond the material side. It empowers spiritual growth. Both aspects progress simultaneously, subject to law, love, liberty, and life.

Previously, the path of Mem was viewed as sacrifice. Here it is seen as consecrating, cleansing, renewal, and promise.

In baptism, the holy one appears from above. Its symbol was the descent of the dove at the baptism of Jesus at the Jordan River. Air and water come together. Spirit enters manifestation. Light and knowledge come from the North [origin, darkness, ignorance], but first appear in the East [golden dawn]. The light counters darkness and ignorance.

This path indicates the role of the anointed Christ, distinct from Jesus. It is ritual relating to the lesser mysteries of John, at the summer solstice. It contrasts with the dying god of the greater mysteries of the Christ, the resurrected god at the winter solstice. The dagger and the disk complement the wand and the cup.

The qliphothic sigil alludes to the biblical Deluge or world cleansing. An image of God appears as a cloud, the source of the rain. The line of the mouth suggests water. The visage shows concern, sadness, but also hope. The biblical Deluge was world scale baptism. Its end meant promise. NVH spells Noah. It has a qabalistic value of 61, Ain, Nothing. Destruction occurs before renewal.

The mercuric sigil for Mem shows the symbol of the Golden Dawn suspended from a scaffold, a bent sword of division. Its shape, Daleth (ד), is the symbol for a gate. The Fool traverses the journey toward initiation. The Light from the east [the Golden Dawn] now directs his inner path. He seeks truth.

The Visconti *L'Appeso* (The Hanged Man) shows a figure hanging upside down by one foot. It shows the punishment especially applied to debtors. It has been referred to Judas. The Marseilles card, *XII Le Pendu*, is similar. The Wirth card, *XII le Pendu*, adds the association with Lamed (ל). On the Rider / Waite card, XII The Hanged Man suspends from T-shaped gallows. The distinction is the addition of a radiant halo around his head. In all the cards, the figure has similar configuration.

The Thoth Tarot, XII The Hanged Man, is attributed to Mem (מ) and water (▽). The figure, as a cross above a triangle, hangs from an ankh. A snake connects them. His hands and foot are nailed (? ≈ sacrifice). Above is light; below is water. It marks a change from the Old Æon. In the darkness below, the serpent begins to stir.

Mem in Cosmos

The Old Testament God became dissatisfied with his creation. Something needed change. It required renewal or replacement. Noah had favor with God. God warned him of coming destruction and gave directions to build an ark [salvation by means of water] to save Noah's family. The ark was engulfed in water. Survival resulted through God's will and action, and Noah's faith and obedience. The old, fallen state was replaced with a new one. Genesis, Chapters 6 to 9 record it, as do some other ancient traditions, *e.g.*, the Epic of Gilgamesh.

On the qliphothic sigil, the downward arrow indicates the act of God. NVH (נוה) is Noah. It destroys (נ = 50) the sacred (ו = 6) and secular (ה = 5). Noah became a savior for the world. The renewed world begins from NVH, 61, Nothing. The experience in the ark was Noah's test of faith, his path of the Devil experience.

In the Old Testament account, the dove brought sign of renewal and promise of worldly regeneration. The forty days signified Mem, water, the Deluge — the death that brought life. The rainbow signified benediction. God would not destroy the world again. In the New Testament, the birth, baptism (water and dove) and 40-day temptation of Jesus in the desert, and his message, are striking parallels. Here the dove symbolizes renewal of the presence of God. By his baptism, Jesus becomes recognized as Christ, anointed one.

Mem in Initiation

In the New Æon, Hoor (ה) rules dominion. See the sigils for Heh (ה) and Vau (ו). Ra-Hoor rises in the east as ruler and initiator.

The initiate realizes a further aspect of life through baptism or rebirth. He progresses through renewal, temptation, and trial in succeeding paths. In rituals such as the Star Ruby and Reguli, pentagrams define his microcosm. The hexagram connects him to the macrocosm. His goal is their union.

Water is more prominent in the original manuscript drawing of *Liber CCXXXI* than in the published version. The historic aspect of sacrifice or punishment is superseded by baptism. Crowley emphasized that this is not a path of sacrifice. It represents the descent of the spirit into the individual. It is more like the corresponding Golden Dawn card, and his original drawing of the sigil.

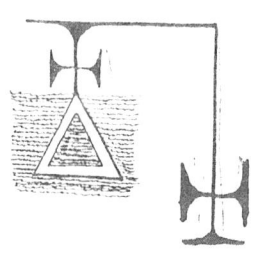

Table of Correspondences

Mem (מ) compares to Samech (ס)

The qliphothic sigil for Samech has SKRZ, Sanctus Kreutz, or Holy Rosenkreutz. The center has the Hanged Man. A rising phoenix is at the left. The outer frame is the cycle, *Solve et Coagula*.

The mercuric counterpart shows the Hanged Man as an initiate represented by the Golden Dawn symbol. The sword is a gate or divider between initiation grades.

The cloud representing The Deluge in qliphothic Mem implies a potential rainbow, QST, קשת. This is the promise in its mercuric counterpart. The model shows the cleansed world that follows.

Genii

Qliphoth — Malkunofat

Saved by water

Ma	מאה	Water, fluidity
Mul	מל	Continuity, plentitude
kun	חונו	Difficult and painful action, trial
o	ע	Crooked, false, bad
fat	פת	A Fool or simpleton

Mercurii — Malai

This is the Latin equivalent for Protection or Care (or Sacrifice). The pelican symbolizes it. Now the aspirant looks ahead.

Arcana 231

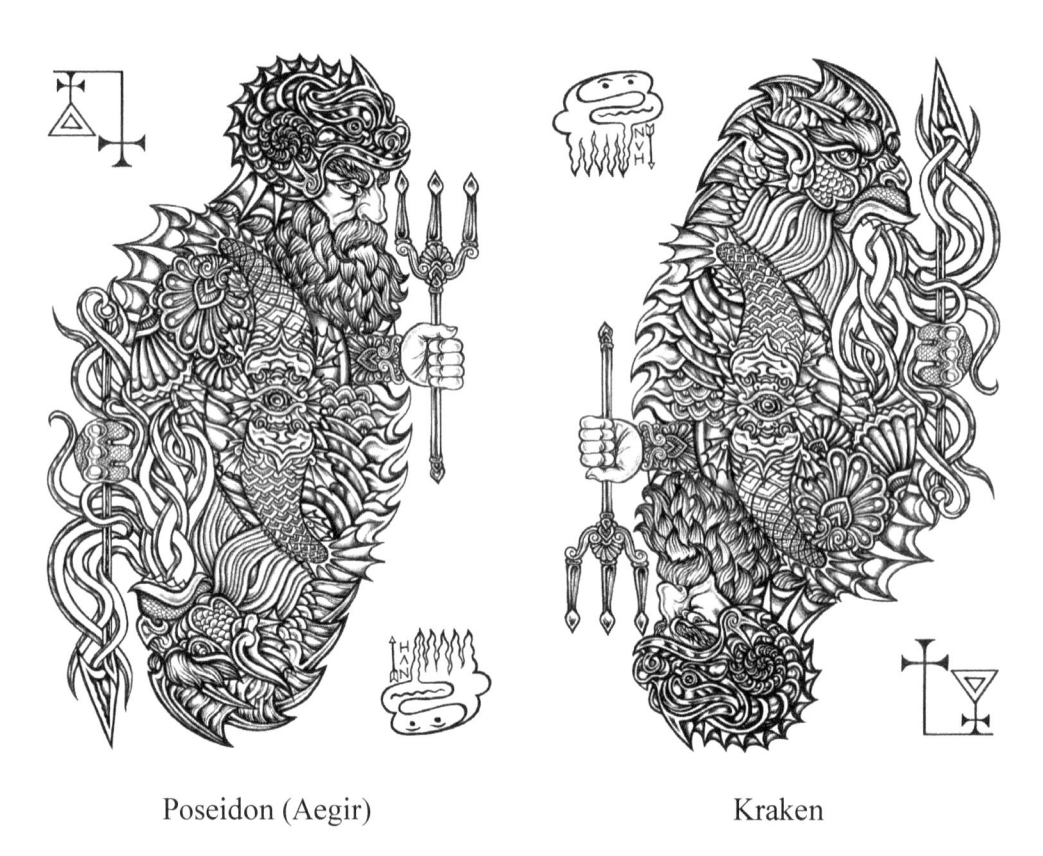

Poseidon (Aegir)　　　　　　　　Kraken

The shells and fish scales radiating from a central focus emphasize water. The image refers to both destructive and beneficial aspects, personified here as Kraken and Poseidon. Destruction is not evil or disadvantageous, but also a precursor to construction or renewal. All is the neutral expression of the laws of Nature.

The Kraken is a sea monster. It represents the Deluge engulfing the world, destroying mankind. In Norse mythology, there are two sea monsters — a huge whale (Lyngbakr) and a sea monster (Hafgufa). The Hafgufa links to the Kraken. It is huge and can swallow men and ships. This also relates to the story of Jonah, relating to water and the dying god. The image draws from early representations of a giant squid with tentacles enwrapping a ship. The harpoon, destroyer of the destroyer, is held among the arms of the monster.

Aegir is the Norse god of the sea. Poseidon is his Greek counterpart, as is Roman Neptune, god of the sea and earthquakes. He forms a triumvirate among the Olympians with Zeus (sky, air), Poseidon (sea, water) and Hades (underworld, fire). These are parallel to grades indicated by the paths of Aleph, Mem and Shin.

Poseidon is depicted as an old, bearded male with curly hair. He created new islands and calm seas. In contrast, by striking the ground with his trident he caused earthquakes, rough seas, shipwrecks, and drowning. He could also save ships at sea, or destroy them, by controlling the weather. In the Book of Thoth, Crowley notes that self-sacrifice and chastity should be replaced. Certainty should replace faith. Ecstasy should replace chastity. Baptism expresses mercy and promise. It activates the spiritual aspect to individual life.

נ

Death

Scorpio (♏) — Mortality

13.   Also Asar was hidden in Amennti;
and the Lords of Time swept over him
with the sickle of death.

Domus Mercurii   Carcer Qliphoth

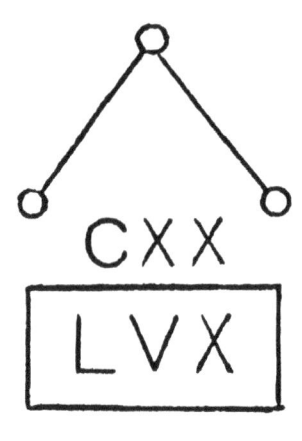

Nadimraphoroiozεθalai   Niantiel

Nun (נ) compares to Shin (ש)

The fourteenth path is Nun (נ), XIII. Death. It has a numerical value of fifty (50) and attributes to Scorpio (♏) in the zodiac. As the final act of physical existence, it is a necessary aspect to renewal and recycling. Death separates the living from their soul. The paths from Mem (XII) through Peh (XVI) are joined into what Thelemites generally associate with crossing the Abyss. The paths of Nun, Ayin and Peh compare to the dark night of the soul of St. John. These paths break down a complex process. They integrate profound spiritual change that man can experience. They define qualification for spiritual advancement. For the non-initiate it is the coda after the Wheel. For an initiate it is death of the ego.

Death, the Devil, and the Tower are three paths that encompass Ordeal x. Compared to attaining an advanced academic degree, the path of The Hanged Man is his matriculation. Death is his qualifying examination. The Devil is his course of study, the challenge demonstrating attainment and mastery. The Tower is his final examination before the successful scholar emerges. The student proceeds as an independent research scholar or doctor. With his inner self in hand, the initiate proceeds as an established adept, a Star.

Thirteen (13) has historical association with Death. Traditionally, the number is imbued with darkness, misfortune, and evil — very human perceptions. Bowing to such beliefs and contemporary culture, some historic tarot cards omit the number 13 or XIII from the card. Exempting the path is unrealistic!

The text says that the dark lord Asar (Osiris, Death is the crown of all) rules Amennti, the Underworld. The qualifications and internal advancement are judged. Those who fail die. The tarot paths related to the adept are open.

The rectangle in the mercuric sigil shows the tomb of Christian Rosenkreutz. It indicates the return to life after 120 years. It implies death but with rebirth — ON.

The qliphothic sigil shows a crowned Osiris, king of the underworld. Osiris is a dark god. The Grim Reaper is Death. He is holding a scythe with a cross at the handle, and a rose-cross near the tip of the cutting blade — the sign of renewal.

The Visconti Tarot *La Morte* (Death) shows a human skeleton holding a bow in its left hand and an arrow in its right. The untitled Marseilles card, *XIII La Morte*, shows a skeleton wielding a sickle over a field of body parts. The same is true for the Wirth card. The Rider/Waite card, XIII Death, is very different. The armored death is riding the apocalyptic white horse.

The Thoth Tarot, XIII Death, is attributed to Nun (נ) and Scorpio (♏). It shows the eagle, snake, and scorpion, the three aspects of that zodiacal sign. The Osiris-crowned skeleton is reaping. His scythe is creating new forms of life as it reaps.

Nun in Cosmos

Saturn, Father Time, the Grim Reaper, is one of the Titans. He is described symbolically as eating his children (time, memory) to stop change. He is an elder god overthrown by the Olympian ones but is still included in many New Year celebrations as a symbol of the passing year. The scythe of death erases memory, so renewal may occur. It has an analogy to the Hanged Man at its point. The rose-cross implies reawakening. It is renewal as the eternal cycle repeats itself.

The child of the New Year becomes an old man Saturn at its end. Here is the cycle of Kaph expressed in cosmic and initiatory terms. The cycle is expressed in the Eleusinian mysteries. Pluto is the god of the underworld. His capture of Persephone to be queen of the underworld and her return is reflected in the annual cycle. Her mother, Demeter, pursued Persephone until she was returned for part of the year. As the stem of wheat holds seeds with potential for life, so death carries the seed for renewed activated life. They also reflect the annual cycle.

Nun in Initiation

The rectangle in the mercuric sigil represents the tomb of Christian Rosenkreutz. The sigil shows aspects of that medieval tradition. The arch above is the vault of the chamber. He has the light of life, LVX, knowledge, enclosed within his tomb. The CXX represents the 120 years of his years before re-awakening. This 120 is also the formula for the cycle of universal existence — 120 in light LVX or 210 in dark aspect NOX. From an initiatory perspective the story includes inherent rebirth. On the tomb was written, *Non patebo*, I await return. See the qliphothic sigil for Shin. The process compares to the pupal stage in butterfly metamorphosis.

Table of Letter Comparisons

Nun (נ) compares to Shin (ש)

These two paths represent different levels of transition, of death and change. The former separates the external from the internal. The latter involves the threshold between unity and duality. It is the final and eternal abyss.

The qliphothic sigils relate the individual to Rosenkreutz going through spiritual metamorphosis. The mercuric sigils show the vaulted chamber as a unit, then as part of the pyramid. They show the subsequent stages within the cycle. Death divides life from life.

Death (נ) and Judgment (ש) are junctions during the journey. The first separates the non-initiate from the initiate, relating body and inner self as separate aspects of life. The second crowns spiritual growth for an initiate and offers options for continuation.

Genii

Qliphoth — Niantiel

Angel of youth and nothingness

Ni	ני	Connect being and nothingness
an	אנ	Ain, Nothing
nt	נתה	Parceling out
iel	יאל	Angel or spirit

Mercurii — Nadimraphoroiozξ θalai

Regenerated youth. The name has many elements relating to life.

Na	נא	Youth
di	די	Fertility, fecundity
m	מ	Developing in space
raph	רפ	Regenerating movement
or	ער	Passion, exciting fire
oz	עז	Persistence, vigor, generative support
o	ע	Void, also perverse, false
thalai	טל	That which covers or shelters

The qliphothic sigil considers Death as male, a Grim Reaper with several aspects. He is the skeleton, the most enduring remains of an individual. He carries a scythe, a tool for harvesting. He carries an orb to show material aspects, but also the universality of existence. He is mortal. He appears to a victim and brings death. He represents finality for individuals not on the path of initiation. He also is an end of the year symbol, Father Time, Saturn. The Thoth card shows the scythe reaping life forms, suggesting rebirth.

On the mercuric side, Coatlicue is the Aztec mother goddess, creator and destroyer. Two fanged serpents replace her decapitated head. Combined, they appear to be a front view of her face. They represent flowing blood. Her necklace has hands, hearts, and a skull pendant. She is Goddess of Fertility, Goddess of Life, Death, and Rebirth. She is womb and grave. She is usually perceived as a devouring mother. She is the mother of the moon, stars, and the god of the sun and of war. She is the goddess of childbirth and wrongful behavior. Her deadly aspect shows that earth is mother and destroyer of all life.

Arcana 231

Coatlicue, Creator   Holy Death, Grim Reaper

Coatlicue was first the mother of many stellar deities, the *tzitzimime*. She could only give birth once. While at Mt. Coatepec (Snake Mountain), she was later impregnated by a feather and gave birth to Huitzilopochtli, the god of the Sun and War. Coyolxauhqui, her oldest daughter led a rebellion with her brothers. Coatlicue died as she was born. With the serpent's help, he immediately murdered the *tzitzimime*. The beheaded Coyolxauhqui lies in a deep mountain gorge. The beheading of Coatlicue is not explained.

The Aztec Templo Mayor pyramid at Tenochtitlan [now Mexico City] had a stone at its base to commemorate this battle. Death is the gateway to life.

The qliphothic illustration shows female skull with long hair, holding a scythe and globe, a counterpart to Mictlantecahtli. She is Holy death, Lady of the Land of the Dead, a modern personification of the Mexica god Mictlantechihuatl. They are like husband and wife, like the devil and death. She is the protector of souls and goddess of peaceful death and childbirth.

All mortals die. Death is a state between stages of life. The planted seed can germinate. The scythe finishes life at death. The globe represents universality, the death that is experienced by all and the earth to which all return. Death takes the aspects of decay and yields regeneration, rebirth, and resurrection.

ס

Temperance —Self-restraint, Control

Sagittarius (♐) — Practice, Peace

14.　　And a mighty angel appeared as a woman,
pouring vials of woe upon the flames,
lighting the pure stream with her brand of cursing.
And the iniquity was very great.

Domus Mercurii　　　　　　　Carcer Qliphoth

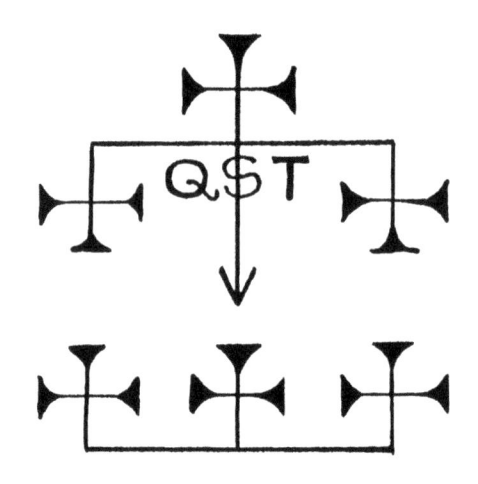

Salaθlala-amrodnaθεiʒ　　　Saksaksalim

Samech (ס) compares to Zain (ז)

The fifteenth path is XIV. Temperance, the fourth of the virtues. It attributes to Samech (ס) and Sagittarius (♐) in the zodiac. It has a numerical value sixty (60). The letter means a prop. Temperance is the fourth cardinal virtue. It may be considered a higher expression of the archetype of Zain (ז), the Lovers or Love. It is the application of the three other virtues to life.

The king and queen mix a container of extreme and evil woe. The heat combines them. The resulting pure stream is a tempered result of union — the elixir, or Vitriol.

The expression of Temperance is expressed Will. Iniquities are the negative aspects of this virtue. As virtue, the path also relates to fertility — *Solve et Coagula*. Self-restraint is paramount. Applying outer restraint is not necessary. Tolerance appreciates that differences exist, though not necessarily acceptable within the limits of True Will.

Temperance uses action, attack, and even force for change. It requires knowledgeable appreciation of opposing influences. Temperance involves Will. It incorporates wisdom, self-restraint, calmness, and diplomacy. It is often tested by fire. It controls excess, such as anger, sexual desire, and other impulses. He who uses temperance responds to the feelings and ideas of others. Experience may require drastic action, attack, and even forced change. Words and actions are subject to criticism and may rebound with disadvantage.

Freedom, the lack of external restriction, challenges tradition. Temperance involves perception. It is classic in goal, limitless in application.

Do not these qualities embody the classic virtues — Wisdom (י), Fortitude (ט), Justice (ל) and Temperance (ס) — define persona? Do not Death (נ), Devil (ע) and Tower (פ), test the life (כ) and virtues of the Hanged Man (מ)?

The Liber CCXXXI text effectively describes Babalon or the Scarlet Woman operating seemingly in contrast to traditional temperance. Rather, she is integrating, recombining to produce renewal and revolution. Iniquity is unjust morality. The formula VITRIOL applies.

Visita interiora terrae rectificando invenies occultum lapidem.

Visit the interior of the earth, by redress you will find the hidden stone.

The interior of the earth represents the mind of man. The hidden stone is the elixir of life, the flux, the azoth of successful initiation.

Within consciousness, the adept resolves objectives of life as he accomplishes his initiation. The Liber XXXI and Liber CCXXXI texts use the Woman and the Beast as prototypes for action. The path of Teth (ט) emphasizes sexual and material aspects of life. Samech emphasizes inner aspects of magic. Freedom from external restriction requires focused Will and Nuit. The word of sin is restriction. Are these not a central principle of life?

The Visconti card, *La Temperanza* (Temperance), shows a woman pouring water from an upper to a lower urn. At the bottom is a green field and mountains. The Marseilles card, *XIIII Temperance*, adds wings to the woman. The Wirth card, *XIIII la Tempérance*, adds Nun (נ) by the name. The Rider / Waite card, XIV Temperance, has the angel with a sun on its forehead and יהוה and the square and triangle septenary on its breast that combines the material and conscious natures.

The Thoth card, XIV Art, is attributed to Samech (ס) and Sagittarius (♐). The background has the formula for Vitriol prominent. The royal marriage is symbolized by a mixed figure stirring a hot cauldron. The White Lion and Red Eagle represent fertility. A stream rises to form two rainbows. It is the consummation of the Royal Marriage, symbol of the Great Work.

Samech in Cosmos

The qliphothic sigil shows the cycle of death and rebirth, complementing Mem and Nun. The central figure is like the Hanged Man of Mem. This is his Inner Self of an initiate. The phoenix at the left signifies renewal and consecration. On the right, the four letters, SKRZ, stand for RosenKReutZ, or Sanctus KReutZ. He is a mystic initiate waiting to arise. The latter is Holy Cross, a symbol of death prior to resurrection.

Samech in Initiation

The mercuric sigil shows a pattern of a Tree of Life below a traditional abyss. It is inverted, as in the sigil for Lamed. The crosses represent sephiroth. QST (קשת), the Hebrew word for rainbow, connects it to traditional paths on the Tree of Life. This parallels the promise to Noah after the Deluge. It is the promise of light, and the union of air and water. The arrow on the central path of Samech and pointing downward in the sigil is a symbol for Will.

Table of Letter Comparisons

Samech (ס) compares to Zain (ז)

The paths of Zain and Samech have dual character. Samech is often interpreted as a higher expression of Zain ז), the Lovers. Virtues function as guides at all levels for both the external and internal self.

The mercuric sigils of the two suggest a similarity to an inverted Tree of Life leading to the spiritual ordeal. The elements pair as follows:

Zain	Samech
Arrow	Arrow
Moon	QST and crosses

Temperance is the practical application of virtues in life. It can be considered as a key to resolution.

The Lower triad is unbalanced in the qliphoth. The rainbow of promise after cosmic baptism or the Deluge (מ) and entering rebirth shows the return of balance on the mercuric side.

The Middle triad qliphothic sigil illustrates the legend of KRZ and the Phoenix. It represents success and renewal.

Genii

Qliphoth — Saksaksalim

Reciprocal Movement (up and down)

Sak	סכ	Turning, upside down. Reciprocal movement (doubled)
sulam	סלמ	Ladder of Jacob's dream. Path between lower and upper
im	מה	Plural ending

Mercurii — Salaqlala-amrodnaqεiẓ

Spirit of Reciprocity

This genius name is two parted — the origin of reciprocity

Sal	סל	Movement which moves or takes away
at	את	Sympathy and reciprocity
lala	לאלא	Circular or reciprocal movement
am	אמ	Mother, origin, nation, rule
rod	רד	Movement, as in a wheel
nat	נת	Offshoot
iẓ	עיז	Genius designation

Arcana 231

Adam kasya / Hawwa   Samael / Lilith

The central motif is the seven-pointed star of Babalon with the formula of VITRIOL between its points. This expresses the *summum bonum* of alchemical initiation. The seven letters of VITRIOL alternate with the seven points of the star of Babalon. In the New Æon, initiation is unto Nuit!

The figures of mercuric Adam and Eve and qliphothic Samael and Lilith relate to opposites and their union.

The qliphothic aspect shows light and knowledge (the lightning flash and the serpent) related to vitriol, the Stone of the Wise. The interpretations relate to Lucifer as light-bringer with his serpent (≈ Messiah) and owl (wisdom) rather than as evil and tempter.

The mercuric aspect shows the eagle and the lion.

The illustration is Gnostic. Mandaeans recognize a dualistic view with a World of Dark and a World of Light. The former comes from original Chaos. Contrast comes with creation through the demiurge. Knowledge is recognized through duality. Dark and light, death and life, are inherent expressions of creation. Good and bad are evaluations by dualistic man. The Lord of Darkness rules the World of Darkness. The

Lord of Life or the Great Mind rules the World of Light. Their interaction produces the salvation of souls.

Adam and Eve represent duality. In mercuric aspect, the dark view of Adam has a bright radiance that activates his World of Light. His wife, Hawwa is looking away. His forehead has a sun. Hers has a moon. They are crowned by air and water respectively. Adam has a dark wing and a lion-serpent on his shoulder. Hawwa has a light angel wing, and an owl (wisdom) on hers. She is his redeeming light, the initial He (ה) of Tetragrammaton יהוה). A displaying peacock, air (△) also symbolizes the rainbow. It speaks the truth of the colors of the vitriolic formula.

On the mercuric side, radiance surrounds the heads of Adam and Hawwa as a royal pair. They are looking straight ahead. He bears the scepter of rule in his right hand. Under his chin is a medallion with a (red) eagle. She holds the orb signifying worldly domain in her left hand. The medallion under her chin shows the (white) lion. They represent alchemical elements and wedding. Between them, the resultant crowned serpent of gnosis rises from the Secret Stone.

ע

Devil — Temptation

Capricorn (♑) — Trial, Challenge

15.   Then the Lord Khem arose,
He who is holy among the highest,
and set up his crowned staff
for to redeem the universe.

Domus Mercurii   Carcer Qliphoth

Oaoaaaoooε-iʒ   A'ano'nin

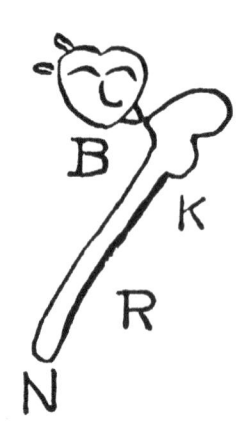

Ayin (ע) compares to Peh (פ)

The sixteenth path is Ayin (ע), XV. The Devil. Its value is seventy (70). It means eye. It attributes to Capricorn (♑) in the zodiac.

The Devil is the adversary. His action is temptation and trial. He tests the veracity and dedication of the initiate. He tests resistance to adversity. He sharpens the value and application of the virtues. He emphasizes polarity and opposites that derive from universal principles — As above, so below; and *Solve et Coagula*; and 2 = 1 = 0. He challenges wisdom, justice, fortitude and temperance — the virtues of life. Challenge of self is inherent. The greatest challenge occurs at the dark night of the soul, as Jesus' 40 days trial in the wilderness followed his baptism.

The Lord Khem is the ruler of darkness. Here it refers to Set / Osiris. Set is the dark god of the south. He is also the Black God of the underworld. Khem also refers to the productive dark soil of the valley and delta of the Nile. Osiris is the god of the underworld.

The qliphothic sigil combines symbols of these results. It symbolizes the result of conflict between Set and Osiris.

The mercuric sigil shows a base of Σ (Sofia) and E (Eros), wisdom and love, or reason and emotion. The Devil uses these in temptation. The sigil shows an erect phallus penetrating a circle (vulva) with its seed. It indicates the continuity of life. But every union is not successful.

The Visconti card has not survived. The Marseilles card, *XV Le Diable*, shows a winged and horned hermaphroditic figure holding a club. Beside his feet are naked male and female demons chained to a pedestal. The Wirth card, *XV le Diable*, is similar. It shows characters like Levi's Baphomet, including *Solve* and *Coagula* on its arms. It is assigned to Samech (ס). The Rider / Waite card, XV The Devil, follows the same basic pattern.

On the Thoth card, the goat is the symbol for Baphomet. It stands in front of a tree that illustrates the biological process of life — *Solve et Coagula*. The tree equates to the caduceus in Levi original design. He called it the Goat of Mendes, an Egyptian god of fertility.

Ayin in Cosmos

The qliphothic sigil represents the conflict between external dark and light, and internal good and evil. In their conflict, Horus emasculated Set and Set tore out the left eye of Osiris. The face in the sigil is blind. The phallus is separate. The words for blind (עור) and eye (עין) each begin with Ayin.

The BKRN (בכרנ) may be the wiles of the Devil applied to life. Broken is the attempt of the Devil.

Beth (ב)   In the Beginning, בראשית; Blessing, ברכה; Birthright, בכורה

Kaph (כ)   Wheel of Fortune, culmination of exoteric life

Resh (ר)   Sun, fulfillment of esoteric life, Will

Nun (נ)   Death, the Crown of All

Ayin in Initiation

The Devil is an adversary, neither evil nor good. He explores contrast. His mode of operation is challenge. He tempts and presents alternatives for evaluation. These make the initiate think, decide, and grow in understanding. His final success is based on the character (*virtus*) and their application to his life.

Chapter 15, The Gun-Barrel, in The Book of Lies equates The Devil with Pan. It equates phallus with the pyramid of fire — φαλλος = πυρμις = 671, and phallus with Will. These relationships relate to the mercuric sigil in Liber CCXXXI, and the Thoth card.

Table of Letter Comparisons

Ayin (ע) compares to Peh (פ)

Ayin (ע) and Peh (פ) are part of the Ordeal of any Soul. They are analogous to the weighing of the heart and passing through Ammenti in ancient Egypt. It is crossing the abyss in Thelema. See Liber CDXVIII, 10th Æthyr. They relate to the paths of Law, Love, Liberty (ethics, virtues) and Life (wheel) of The Fool.

The sigil is like the Thoth card for The Devil. Baphomet the Goat is in front of the tree whose roots show meiotic gamete formation and whose trunk and crown show union.

Genii

Qliphoth — A'ano'nin

Nothingness is manifest

A'	א	Void, Ain, Ineffable
ano	ענא	Pain, sorrow, agony
nin	נן	Continuous manifestation

Mercurii — Oaoaaaoooε-iʒ

Nothing is All

Oa	עא	Unity in contrast, 0 = 1.
o	ע	Nothingness or void, singular with dark implication.
aaa	אאא	All, 111, Aleph (The Fool, and none by the book)
ooo	עעע	Nothing, 210, NOX
ε	טע	Obstinance, evil material persistence
-iʒ		Genius designation

Arcana 231

Baphomet | Saturn

Saturn has bat-like wings. The down-curved horns on Saturn (≈ Chronos, as Time) indicate his dark nature. He is shown three-faced, each one eating a child. Saturn conquered his father Uranus, the chief Titan god who ate his own children as they were born, so that they would not replace him. However, his last son, Jupiter, survived and ultimately overpowered all the Titan and replaced him. Thus, Chronos represents aspects of past, present and future, necessary for change and creation.

The Baphomet image includes resemblance to the classic illustration by Eliphas Levi. The central firebrand, the symbol of light, indicates him as Lucifer who counteracts the dark. The spiral horns reflect the spiral (helical) character inherent in nature — from DNA to galaxies. Crowned lion-serpents represent Azoth as the vital force of nature.

The message of Ayin is challenge and trial. Failure means dying in darkness. In an academic sense, this is the research background thesis and conclusions, *i.e.*, the course of study and demonstration of mastery. It is resolved by trial and testing.

Crowley's ritual experience is recorded in the Tenth Æthyr of the Vision and the Voice. The wiles that followed are temptations and seductions. A series of bouts between the scribe and the demon follow. They describe the form and actions of Choronzon following a Satanic invocation.

פ

The Tower — House of God

Mars (♂) — Annihilation, Enlightening

16.   He smote the towers of wailing;
he brake them in pieces in the fire of his anger,
so that he alone did escape from the ruin thereof.

Domus Mercurii   Carcer Qliphoth

Puraθmetai-apηmetai   Parfaxitas

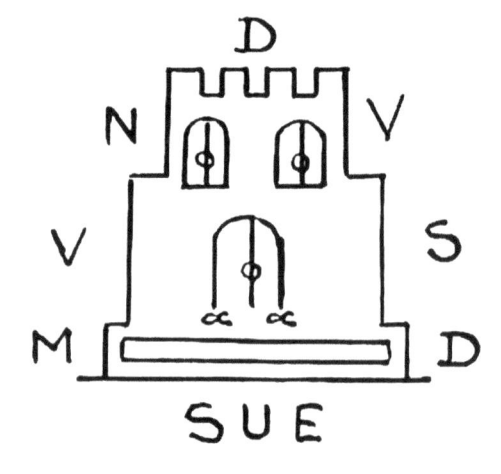

Peh (פ) compares to Qoph (ק)

The seventeenth path is Peh (פ), XVI. The Tower. It is also known as The House of God or the Lightning Struck Tower. Its numerical value is eighty (80) and means mouth. It is attributed to Mars (♂) in the zodiac.

The message is annihilation, the destruction necessary for progress and renewal of the inner self. It completes a process also known as crossing a spiritual divide or experiencing the dark night of the soul. The paths from Nun to Peh (נ to פ) compare going from Chesed to Binah on the Tree of Life model.

In the text, the initial He refers to the Lord Khem, the Dark Lord of the previous verse. The towers of wailing represent the old state being replaced. The fire of his anger is the new knowledge of the lightning flash. The successful inner self emerges. Truth becomes evident.

This final stage in the ordeal changes the Hanged Man (מ) into a true initiate (צ). He survives Death (נ). He conquers the Devil and temptations (ע) to stray from his Will. In the Tower, Peh (פ), his ego is finally annihilated. He accepts Pure Will and Truth as his guide and goal. The Fool discards the baggage of his knapsack. His innocence is recognized. The confident new Star (צ, Adept) emerges.

The Visconti tarot card, *Casa di Dio* (The House of God, or of the Devil), has not survived. The Marseilles tarot card, *XVI La Maison Dieu*, shows the crown on the tower separated by lightning. A man falls from it, one crawls out the bottom. The Wirth card, *XVI la Maison Dieu*, is similar, and assigned to Ayin (ע). The lightning originates at the Sun. The Rider / Waite card, XVI The Tower, has lightning setting fire to the tower. Two persons fall from it.

The Thoth card shows the broken tower with the open eye of Shiva, destroyer emanating rays from above. They are analogs of the lightning. The dove and lion-serpent, symbolize energies from above. Distorted bodies fall from The Tower. The fire of destruction attacks the base of the tower.

The text of Liber XXXI, Chapter One describes different views of the Dove (Mu, מ), serpent (Satan, ע), and the Fortress or House of God (destruction, enlightenment, פ).

Peh in Cosmos

In the path of Mem (מ), the cosmic Deluge purifies and consecrates the earth by water. The path of Peh (פ) purifies by fire.

Instead of a Tower, the qliphothic sigil shows a crenellated building, a fortress. The letters MVNDVS DEUS form an alternative name of the path as the World (≈ House) of God. The central door shows a Hanged Man, trapped within, who will be freed to continue his journey when the outer building is destroyed. It indicates a traditional state before annihilation. To conquer an empire, the *coup de grace* requires demolition of sites of worship, temples, images of gods, principles — the core values that define it. The overall action is dire. The base is prepared for renewal. Herein is the mystery of the House of God (פ) in Liber XXXI, I: 57. The defense of the aspirant is found there. Then follows the mystery of Tzaddi (צ).

> Invoke me under my stars. Love is the law, love under will. Nor let the fool mistake love; for there are love and love. There is the dove and there is the serpent. Choose ye well! He, my prophet, hath chosen, knowing the law of the fortress and the great mystery of the House of God.

Peh in Initiation

The lightning flash adds further truth to knowledge. It is simultaneously destructive and creative. Each hypothesis is tested. Science explores natural law through its method. Its results determine fact. Explanations can be preserved or be replaced on the evidence of a single contradictory fact. Religion is similar but is limited by dogma within its system overruling unbreakable natural law.

The mercuric sigil has three vertical units that position it. Ayin, 70, The Devil at the bottom is temptation. The branching symbol in the center represents 80, the decision. It indicates the choice or fork in the road, the choice. The upper one is the Greek symbol Koppa (ϙ) for the number 90, the emergent, successful Star. The 80 positions the path of Peh between Ayin and Tzaddi, between the Devil and the Adept.

Table of Letter Comparisons

Peh (פ) compares to Qoph (ק)

The path of Peh clears the way for the inner self to emerge as a cleansed and consecrated Star. The lightning flash increases new awareness and introduces truth. The Moon, (ק), is the period of development as he grows toward maturity.

Genii

Qliphoth — Parfaxitas

Liberation through fire

Par	פר	Fertility, fecundity, product of any sort
Fax	פצ	Diffusion, liberation, easing
it	ית	Essence
as	אש	Fire

Mercurii — Puraθmetai-apηmetai

Light the fire at the Tower. Let the destruction begin.

Pur	πυρ	Fire
Puraθ	πυραθ	πυργος, a Tower or fortification
metai	μετα + αιρεω	To take beyond by force
apη	αρη	Ares, god of war.
αρηπαιθω		To light a watchfire

The three ordeals of initiation, Death, Devil and Tower are in Liber AL, Chapter One. What follows is the progress of the Adept as Star, in the star system, in the universe. The Mystery of the House of God continues along the esoteric, initiatory path, ultimately preparing for the final Abyss.

Arcana 231

Tower of Babel — House of God

The central figure shows Peh as a mouth relating the destruction of the Tower of Babalon, and diversifying language. The motivation for its construction was Nimrod. The meaning of Nimrod has now devolved to a style of mindless life.

In the qliphothic view, the Pyramid or House of God represent established tradition. The towering bastions are destroyed by fire. Each state destroys and replaces the institutions of the preceding establishment. Pyramids are built over the bases of pyramids.

The center shows the mouth of Peh, devouring destruction and annihilation. The ingested food (experience) becomes the source of renewed life.

This is stability and change. The pyramids are among the oldest surviving physical remnants of earlier civilizations. The institution of religion is also enduring. Mankind builds on the shoulders of giants. These giants are replaced when major changes occur. Religions superimpose their monuments on the sites of earlier ones. The Spanish conquistadores leveled those of the Aztecs and Incans. Yet, traditions and influence survived even though overlain by new culture. This is predicted for the New Æon as well in Liber XXXI, III: 34.

The mercuric view shows the Tower of Babel (Genesis, Ch. 11). The biblical monarch Nimrod was a hunter. He was the great-grandson of Noah and king of Babalon (Gen. 10: 10) and other cities in Shinar (now in Iraq), Mesopotamia. Non-biblical sources are unable to connect him to any historical figure. Myths relate him to a tall tower-temple built by the city to reach the gods. The gods, jealous of their unity and power, destroyed it. As builder of that tower, he became a symbolic rebel against the gods.

The tower-temple north of the temple of Marduk at Babylon may be the basis for the myth. The Babylonians called it Bab-ilu, the Gate to God. The Hebrews called it Babel, similar in sound to בלבול, meaning confusion.

The face at the right is Mesopotamian in character (≈ Nimrod). On the left is a fiery caduceus of twisted lion-serpents representing constructive force. The tower resembles a stepped pyramid of fire. Thunderbolts and lighting strike from the central eye (of Horus) at the top. The central flash, in form like one on a Tree of Life model, descends to a mouth. The many lightning flashes and peripheral droops of water indicate renewed life. Love death therefore, and long eagerly for it.

This is the scarab, Kheph-ra, the Egyptian God of Midnight who carries the (Black) sun through the Underworld. This ordeal from Nun to Peh brings the consecrated Hanged Man (the inner self of The Fool) to clarified awareness.

צ

The Star — Awakening

Aquarius (♒) — Emergence

17. Transformed, the holy virgin
appeared as a fluidic fire,
making her beauty into a thunderbolt.

Domus Mercurii   Carcer Qliphoth

Xanθaƺeraneϲϱ-iƺ   Tzuflifu
[ϲϱ = sh, q]

Tzaddi (צ) compares to Aleph (א)

The eighteenth path is Tzaddi (צ) XVII. The Star. Its numerical value is ninety (90) and is attributed to Aquarius (♒) in the zodiac. Other symbols for Tzaddi are the fish-hook and thunderbolt. The underlying meaning of Tzaddi is righteousness.

This is the path of an emergent Star as an adept initiate. He sees the One Star in Sight as his goal ahead.

The Initiate is a proven enhanced complement to The Fool. He enters the path as an enlightened Star following the lightning flash in Peh. The Class A description of the Star is found in Liber VII vel Lapis Lazuli, Chapter V: 5, where it matches the Marseilles Tarot image, and states:

> Only one fish-hook can draw me out;
> It is a woman kneeling by the bank of the stream.
> It is she that pours the bright dew over herself,
> and into the sand so that the river gushes forth.

This identification is reinforced by Crowley's comment to the last verse in Κεφαλη NE (55), The Drooping Sunflower, in The Book of Lies, reiterates the description.

> The number 90 in the last paragraph is not merely fact, but symbolism; 90 being the number of Tzaddi, the Star, looked at in its exoteric sense, as a naked woman, playing by a stream, surrounded by birds and butterflies.

The Liber CCXXXI text describes a woman, transformed. She has passed through the paths of Death, Devil and The Tower to emerge as a Star. Her soul is activated. She appears as a thunderbolt, a symbol for Tzaddi (צ). Tzaddi IS the Star. She is the metamorphosed emerging butterfly.

The original Visconti card shows a woman holding an eight-pointed star upraised in her left hand. The card, *XVII L'Etoile,* in the Marseilles Tarot and its derivatives has traditional eight-pointed stars of initiation, though a few seven-pointed ones also occur. The Wirth card, *XVII les Etoiles* (The Stars), is distinctive with its multiple star name. It is assigned to Peh (פ) because that sequence starts with The Magus, rather than The Fool. The Star is pouring two urns directly into the water, signifying temperance. The Rider / Waite card, XVII The Star, is parallel to the Wirth design.

The Thoth card, XVII The Star, shows the same basic image, though Crowley assigned the Hebrew letter Heh (ה) to it. The star in the upper left is the seven-pointed star of Babalon. A globe forms the background. Crowley relates the figure to the manifestation of Nuit. His distinctive assignment to Heh is based on interpretation of the glyph (ﺻ) clause in Liber XXXI, I: page 18.

The paths from Tzaddi to Resh (צ to ר) describe subsequent development of the inner, esoteric self. The paths of Shin and Tau (ש and ת) complete the journey. Referring to the original manuscript, the text of Liber XXXI, III: 39 says: for in it is the word secret & not only in the English.

This further clarifies the blind at the end of the riddle in Liber XXXI, Chapter Two, verse 76.

$$RP\text{-}ST\text{-}OV\text{-}AL \approx RP\text{-}ST\text{-}\mathbf{OV}\text{-}AL \approx RP\text{-}ST\text{-}ON\text{-}AL$$

The Initiate emerges as a Star at Tzaddi (צ). He recognizes the polarity and contrast of RP (≈ קר, by chance shape) represented by the Sun and Moon. He will experience Judgment and resolution on the paths ST (תש), 700, The Veil of the Holy, the esoteric level in initiation. He relates to the Universe (ON = עז = 120, the expanded 0 = 1) in his Great Work and unites with Ineffable, (Not = AL= LA = 31) — all key formulas of the New Æon.

Liber XI vel Nu is a way to express this in ritual. It deals with the two goals of initiation — external certainty (Truth, Light) and internal resolution (wisdom and peace). The initiate uses Liber XXXI, Chapter I as a base grimoire to produce the ritual. He takes the role of Had, as Priest, and unites directly with Nu as the Universe or Nature. This produces the ecstasy of the Great Work, 5 + 6 = 11.

Tzaddi in Cosmos

Throughout the biological world the processes of meiosis and mitosis, of gamete formation and union, haploidy and diploidy are fundamental to continuing life. Compare stages in the life cycle of a butterfly — egg, larva, pupa, and imago.

The qliphothic sigil shows a face with a phallus-like extension upward. It represents Babalon (or the Scarlet Woman) as the Star, the Tzaddi connection between Netzach and Yesod described in Liber VII, V: 5. The phallus represents the Beast. This is the hidden path connection from Geburah to Yesod.

Even the stars of the cosmos reflect fusion and division. The shards of a Nova recombine to form new celestial objects. Even atoms (and their sub-atomic particles) involve the same processes through radioactivity and fission.

Tzaddi in Initiation

The mercuric sigil is a glyph of the initiation process. The swastika is an analog to Alpha (α, A). At each corner is a K, referring to the path of Kaph (כ) representing its stages of life. Each K represents an alchemical element or cherub. Each arm of the swastika is in the form of an L (ל), so it is a symbol of AL.

Among the arms of the swastika is the lightning flash. This is extension of new knowledge and power. Different combinations of the three letters, O, B, N, with AL, spell familiar words of initiation, and BABALON.

Table of Letter Comparisons

Tzaddi (צ) compares to Aleph (א)

These two paths represent beginnings, but at different levels. Aleph is the Fool, or Man of Earth beginning his eternal journey. He starts on the path of life, innocent and inexperienced. His character expands when he is reborn and undergoes life and ordeals leading to becoming an Adept. Tzaddi is the path where his esoteric self emerges as an Adept.

The two mercuric sigils are based on swastikas, showing the initiatory nature of each path.

The interpretation of the qliphothic sigils shows contrast. In Aleph, the sigil shows creation by division, *Solve*. Creation begins with emanation of the Universe from Ineffable. The Tzaddi qliphothic sigil has a face with an extended head as phallus. In Tzaddi, the sigil shows perfected magical union, *Coagula*.

Genii

Qliphoth — Tzuflifu

Mystery

Tzu	צו	Order, direction
fli	פלי	Emphasis, mystery
fu	פו	Apparent, strikes at first sight

Mercurii — Xanθaζeranϵϙ-iζ

Genius of the Golden Star (? of Dawn, Enlightenment, Peace)

Xanth	Ξαντθ	Golden
aζer	Αστηρ	Star
anϵϙ	anshq	Form may suggest ankh
-iζ	-ist	Genius designation

Arcana 231

Ishtar, Venus   Psyche

The center motif is a star of initiation, the sun. Two eight-pointed stars indicate its dark and light source. Around the star is a 16-petal flower. It is a symbol for Ishtar (≈ Venus, Aphrodite, Babalon). It relates to knowledge on the human plane. It is symbolic of purity and purification. It expands awareness of the universe, including antimatter. In the Hindu tradition, it is like the crescent at the apex of the stupa (significant Buddhist shrine).

The qliphothic figure shows a naked Psyche. Psyche is the Greek soul (≈ inner self, Roman, *Anima*) and butterfly. She symbolizes higher consciousness. She becomes the wife of Cupid (≈ Eros).

Apuleius tells the story of Cupid and Psyche in The Golden Ass. Psyche is the archetypal character for a soul going through a major transition or crisis.

Psyche was a mortal princess of great beauty who received the attention of many men. This raised the jealousy of Venus, who commanded Cupid to cast a spell on her. She was to fall in love with a most hideous man, a monster. Instead, Cupid fell in love with her. At his palace, he always came to her between sunset and sunrise. She was not permitted to see his face. One night, at the provocation of her sisters (woe and sorrow), she came with a knife (discrimination) and lamp to see his face. He turned out to be the beautiful Cupid. She wounded herself with one of Cupid's arrows. Startled, she spilled oil from the lamp and woke him up. He fled. She followed but failed. Seeking Cupid, she eventually served Venus, who gave her several tasks, including a visit to the Underworld.

For the first task, she had to sort out a large mass of mixed grain. A sympathetic ant assembled a crew of ants to sort it while she was elsewhere. That appeared to satisfy Venus. The ants demonstrated compensation — Justice.

For the second task, she had to sort wool from some violent sheep. A spindle gathered the wool left on the briers while they fought. She learned ingenuity and how to overcome danger — Temperance.

For the third task, she had to fill a crystal flask with water from the source of the river Styx. An eagle (Zeus) took the flask to the source and filled it for her. She learned cooperation in solving problems — Wisdom.

For the fourth task, she went to the underworld to get a box of beauty ointment from Persephone. She is told not to open it. She learned the importance of preparation and distraction — Strength, Force, Fortitude.

To go to the underworld meant to die. Psyche went to a tower to jump off. The tower told her another way to go and how to prepare for the trip. She went to the underworld, got the box, and returned to the upper world. She wanted to be beautiful and have Cupid return. She opened the box and she fell into deep sleep. During this time, Cupid left the palace of Venus. He found Psyche, awakened her from sleep. He put sleep back in the box. He brought them back to Venus.

Cupid sought the approval of Jupiter for his marriage to Psyche. Jupiter announced his approval of the marriage to Psyche (love conquers all!). He gives Psyche ambrosia to drink, so the pair may be joined as immortal gods — love and soul. Their child is *Voluptas* (Pleasure, Joy). They lived happily ever after.

The myth describes the whole history of an evolving soul. Seen here, Psyche emerges as a Star in the tarot sequence (צ). Her tasks represent the developing soul, the illusion of the path of the Moon (ק). Her marriage to Cupid is the path of the Sun (ר). The paths of Shin (ש) and Tau (ת) describe the result. The myths of both Psyche and Ishtar contain visits to the underworld and the subsequent restoration of life. They share commonality with Venus.

The mercuric drawing shows Ishtar, Aphrodite, or Venus. She was queen of the Universe; the ultimate deity of early Greece, carrying scepter and universal orb. She is Nuit, the ultimate feminine goddess of Thelema. She was the Mesopotamian goddess of love, beauty, fertility, and war. Her symbol is an 8- or 16-pointed star within a circle. Her images are often winged. Her war-like symbol was the lion. Lion-serpents decorated the ceremonial entrance gate of Babalon. She protected prostitutes of both sexes and drinkers. When her husband Tammuz died, she descended into the underworld to find him. While there, Ea created an intersex being Asu-shu-namir to retrieve them so fertility could be restored on earth. Ishtar personified the planet Venus, the morning and evening star.

ק

The Moon — Illusion

Pisces (♓) — Development, Perception

18. By her spells she invoked the Scarab,
the Lord Kheph-Ra,
so that the waters were cloven
and the illusion of the towers was destroyed.

Domus Mercurii   Carcer Qliphoth

QaniΔnayx–ipamai   Qulielfi

Qoph (ק) compares to Peh (פ)

The nineteenth path is Qoph (ק), XVIII. The Moon. It has a numerical value of one hundred (100). It means back of the head. It is attributed to Pisces (♓) in the zodiac. It associates midnight with Khephra, the Scarab beetle.

The path relates to the developing inner self. It includes growth, change, illusion, and doubt. The initiate faces his demons continuously. He must recognize their challenge and master them.

The text refers to an Adept recognizing the forces that guide his journey. The Scarab, Lord Kephra, carries the midnight Sun, the symbolic source of new knowledge. Details are obscure at first. With increasing light, the images become more distinct and clearer. The Adept improves his awareness and knowledge.

The path also relates to science. The scientific method only applies to hypotheses or phenomena that are repeatable. It explores natural law. Any formulation or conclusion always may contain uncertainty or doubt. The interpretation of every experiment is fallible. Reinforcement by further experimentation reduces uncertainty. Levels of increased surety are described as theories or laws but are still subject to challenge and correction. Only relative truth is attained. Absolute truth is approached asymptotically. The laws of Nature are not completely known, recognized, or understood. They operate independently of the mind of man. They do not require his recognition, definition or understanding. Yet, their known limited application has allowed man to reach or understand planets and stars. Science eschews dogma. Its goal is a clearer understanding of nature.

By contrast, every religion is based on faith. Each religion should have consistency within its dogma. Each can profess absolute truth and even include an Ineffable. But this truth is not the truth of Nature. It is illusion created within the mind of man. The paradox of the blind men and the elephant illustrates the multiplicity of beliefs.

The qliphothic sigil shows the sun at bottom center. The sun radiates light onto the moons above. Its phases occur in rows of three, seven and twelve. The arrangement follows the letters of the Hebrew alphabet — three elementals, seven double letters (planetary), and twelve single zodiacal letters. They reflect true light, but their light is not original. They indicate shades and subtleties of meaning and aspects of illumination.

The mercuric sigil has the same basic pattern as the Thoth card. Like the traditional tarot card, its path passes between Anubis jackals and towers. The shaded moon in the arms of the sun illuminates the scene. The path connects Pisces to Aries, to the beginning of the next cycle. The eclipse is passing. The base shows the watery nature of the path, its fluidity and change. The towers of Peh fade. The lightning flash increases. Truth is revealed as the adept proceeds along the path. He approaches dawn over the hill as the cycle continues.

The Visconti card, *La Luna* (The Moon), has a standing woman holding a crescent moon in her left hand. In her right hand, she holds a long thread, used to distinguish night from day. The Marseilles card, *XVIII La Lune*, shows a major shift in pattern. At the top is the moon in the arms of the sun, radiating to the scene below. Paired towers and jackals mark the path. They are dark and light. Below is a large expanse of water with a crustacean at the center. The Wirth card, *XVIII la Lune*, has a similar pattern. The path going to the horizon is distinct. It is assigned to Tzaddi (sic). The Rider / Waite card, XVIII The Moon, follows the same pattern, but there is more emphasis on the sun / moon, and less on the water below.

The Thoth card, XVIII The Moon, is assigned to Qoph (ק) and Pisces (♓). The two towers and two jackals guard the path. Between, the path seems to go over a pass from Pisces to Aries, indicating a new cycle, to a sun / moon at the horizon. The bottom quarter shows water with a water beetle carrying the Sun in front of cyclical waves. It shows the path going toward the rising sun, or a path to the new zodiacal annual cycle.

Qoph in Cosmos

The cosmic view relates to science, defined by its method. Relatively few hypotheses survive to become scientific laws as originally proposed or accepted as truth. They may seem to be truth but are still fallible. They are the best explanations in the mind of man at the time. They are always subject to challenge, change and reinterpretation.

Qoph in Initiation

The initiate on his journey is seeking truth, but still is learning. Demons (doubts, delusion, and disaster) challenge him. Light and truth come from the dark. Knowledge has an element of confusion and uncertainty. Some is received before it can be understood or appreciated. Yet, by continuing his path, he hopes to dissipate illusion and perceive the pure light.

From a psychological view, the unconscious is inherent in this path. Unconscious realization increases. Understanding may be illusion at first — hypnagogic or dreamlike. This is where demons need to be challenged.

Table of Letter Comparisons

Qoph (ק) compares to Peh (פ)

The path of Qoph is more revealing than that of Peh. Both seem certain. Each has aspects of uncertainty and manifest illusion. The paths purify and define the progress of the Adept.

Genii

Qliphoth — Qulielfi

Genius of the Night and Moon

Qu	קל	Light, attenuated dark
liel	ליל	Night, circular motion, cycles
fi	פי	Manifest appearance

Mercurii — QaniΔnayx–ipamai

Illusion and the Moon

Qani	παινω	To scatter
Δ	Δ	Change (Delta)
nayx	ναυξ	Ship
nux	νυξ	Night
-ipamai	επι + ιημι	To put into motion

Arcana 231

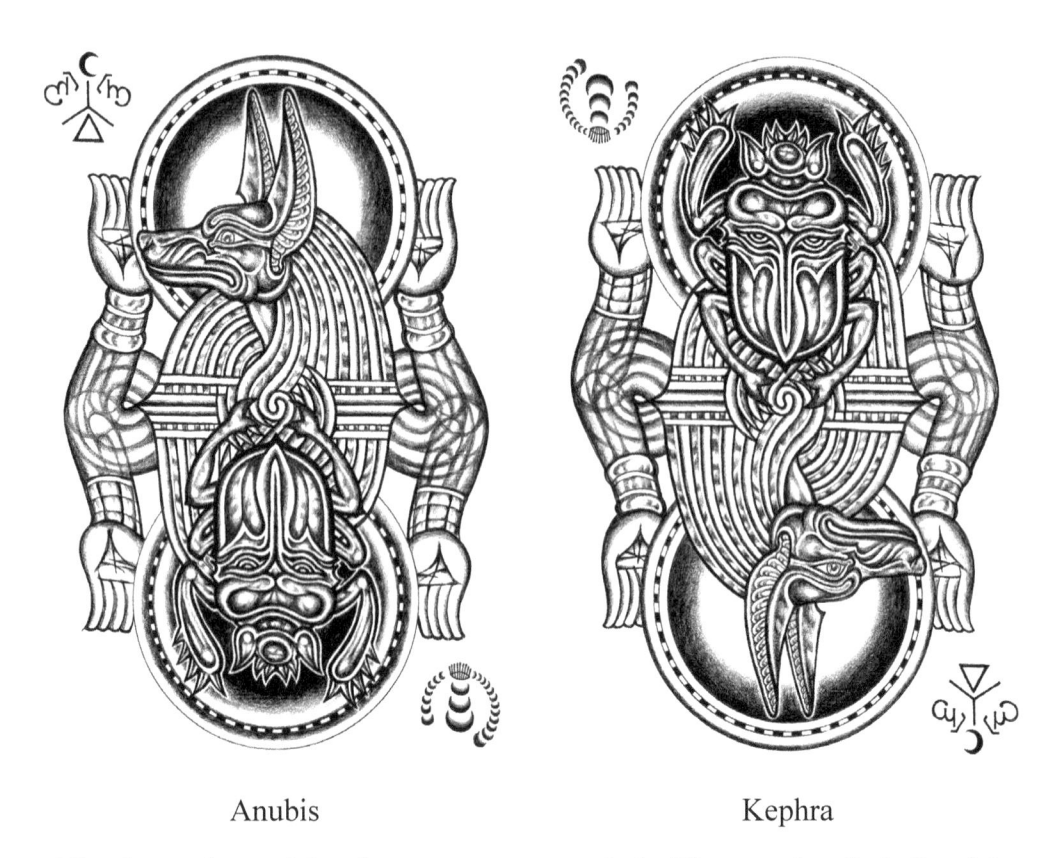

Anubis · Kephra

Khephra and scarab beetles are cognate symbols. The scarab rolls balls of dung across the ground like the sun rolls across the heavens in its orbit. The dung (dark) provides nourishment for the beetles that develop and emerge from eggs within it. Therefore, the scarab became a symbol of rebirth, creation and the rising sun.

Ra-Hoor is the Sun God for the æon. Kephra is his personification at midnight. It carries the Sun through the underworld from midnight to dawn. It represents dark leading to light. The Sun at midnight relates to consciousness through the symbol of Qoph (ק), the back of the head. It relates to the dark source of light and knowledge.

Anubis guarded the scales during the weighing of the soul in Ammenta. He was the god who protected the dead and guided them in the afterlife. He was portrayed as a jackal. Anubis has the color of a mummy. He is also a symbol for beginning and rebirth.

ר

The Sun — Enlightenment

Resh (☉) — Truth, Clarity

19.   Then the sun did appear unclouded,
and the mouth of Asi was on the mouth of Asar.

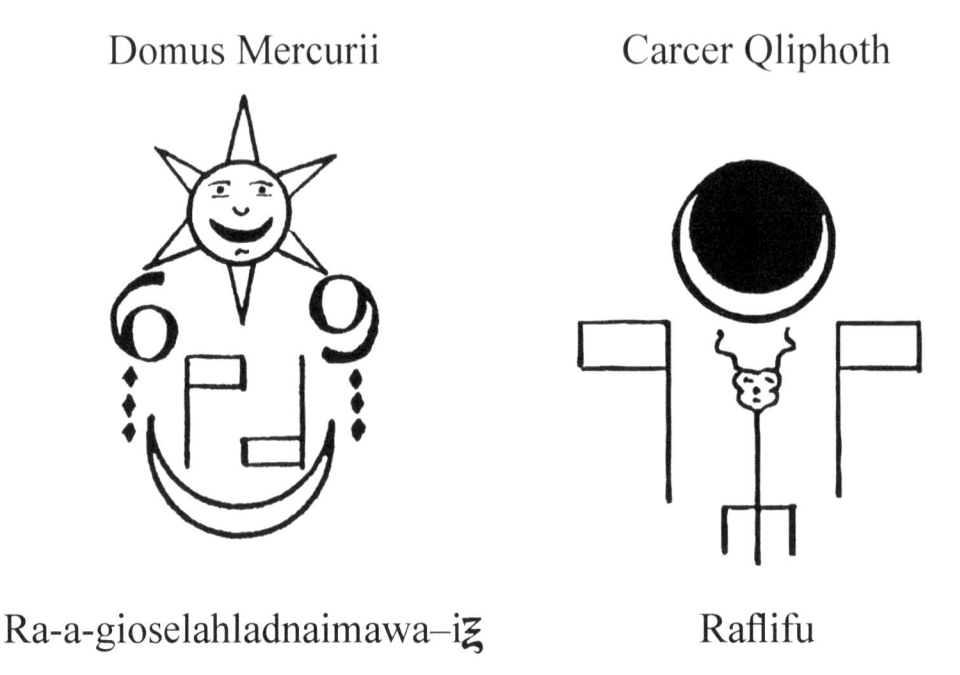

Domus Mercurii   Carcer Qliphoth

Ra-a-gioselahladnaimawa–iʒ   Raflifu

Resh (ר) compares to Zain (ז)

The twentieth path is Resh (ר), XIX. The Sun signifies enlightenment It has a numerical value of two hundred (200) and is attributed to the Sun (☉).

The path is the culmination of enlightenment, revelation, or gnosis. As the initiate traverses this path, clouds of darkness and ignorance dissipate. They displace illusion, the reflected message of the Moon. Light is direct and reaches its maximum intensity and purity. Certainty appears. The full Sun symbolizes Truth.

The text presents the unclouded sun as an analogy for truth. The adept reaches the climax of his inner journey. He attains his goal.

The qliphothic sigil shows an occluded Sun, i.e., with an image of the Moon hiding some of its surface. During his journey, the aspirant has learned much. He enters the path hoping to achieve understanding of truth. Some facts will not be appreciated. Knowledge will always be incomplete.

Below is a static horned figure with two upright neters beside it. The horns imply darkness. The static neters imply the absolute truth of the gods and nature that do not vary.

The mercuric sigil shows a bright six-rayed Sun. The bright sun is above the moon. It reiterates the universal formula of duality. Truth becomes evident. The image has the macro- above micro-cosm. The dots and 69 indicate action, reciprocity, and interchange. The neters indicate the presence of gods. The sigil shows how the mystery of life involves through the universal formula *Solve et Coagula*.

The 69 and neters reflect the message of Κεφαλη ΞΘ (69), for Cheth in The Book of Lies. The first three paragraphs describe the interaction of the triangles in the hexagram revealing the truth from above, and the aspiration from below. It represents the received and perceived light of the Sun.

> This is the Holy Hexagram.
> Plunge from the height, O Man, and interlock with Man!
> Plunge from the height, O Man, and interlock with the Beast!
> The Red Triangle is the descending tongue of grace;
> The Blue Triangle is the ascending tongue of prayer.

The Visconti card, *Il Sole* (The Sun), has a naked putto (a cherub) holding a mask of the Sun above his head. A long ribbon is around his body. He is standing on a blue cloud. A green landscape is at the bottom of the card. The Marseilles Tarot shows an eight-pointed radiating Sun with two figures standing in water below. The Wirth Tarot, *XVIIII le Soleil*, has a 24-point sun with alternate red and yellow rays. A male and female stand in a green circle below. The Rider / Waite card, XIX The Sun, also has a 24-rayed sun. Below is a boy riding a white horse. He has a red banner in his left hand. The banner leads the procession from the manifest world toward the world to come.

The Thoth Tarot shows two figures dancing below. They are analogous to the figures at the bottom of earlier tarot cards.

Resh in Cosmos

On cosmic scale, the Sun is a universal symbol for truth. The Brothers or Lovers, below, show different relationships as neters in the sigils. Here is truth, harmony, and love. Ra-Hoor-Khuit, the solar god, rules the æon. His message is truth. The distinction among RHK, Aiwass, HPK, Tarot and Wisdom can be found in Liber CDXVIII, Eighth Æthyr.

Resh in Initiation

This is the climax for the Adept on his journey — the revelation of truth, clear and free of illusion. Hoor-Paar-Kraat is the silent authority behind *The Book of the Law* (Liber XXXI), transmitted through Aiwass. He realizes its truth. His inner self achieves the understanding of nature, and his duality. He may abandon all to traverse the uttermost Abyss into unity with Ineffable.

Table of Letter Comparisons

Resh (ר) compares to Zain (ז)

The comparison of the paths relates particularly to the neters at the bottom of the sigils. They refer to figures on the Tarot. The qliphothic sigils each have a compromised moon. The bilaterally symmetrical lower half implies balance and possibly static equilibrium. The mercuric sigils show balanced moon symbols. The bottom halves show different neter positions, suggesting circular and dynamic movement.

Genii

Qliphoth — Raflifu

The Sun is the source of mystery and truth

Ra	רא	Ra, the Egyptian Sun God
fli	פל	Wonderful, mystery, miracle,
fu	פו	Breath, source, mouth

Mercurii — Ra-a-gioselahladnaimawa-iẓ

Holy Ra, Genius of Adonai, the One Great Ineffable Lord

Ra-	רא	Ra, the Egyptian Sun god
a-	א-	Equivalent to definitive ה
gio(s)	אגיו	Holy, άγιος
selah	סלה	Pause, Comma
l	ל	To
adnai	אדני	Adonai, the Lord
ma	מא	Mother or source, All
wa	הוא	Hua, The Great God
-iẓ	-st	Genius, Spirit

The syllables outside the hyphens say Holy Ra (represented as the Sun) is the superior Spirit Genius of God. The syllables between are an attempt to describe the ultimate Ineffable Unity of God. The surah emphasizes the unity of God, contrasting to the polytheistic gods of the time.

Selah is undefined connector or indicator of change. It functions as a transition between groups of verses, from which many connotations may be implied.

Surah 112: قُلْ هُوَ ٱللَّهُ أَحَدٌ Say: He is Allah, He is One.

For Thelemites, the Surah is used as a preface to *Liber 813 vel Ararita*. It presents the nature of Ineffable. The Hebrew Adonai is added among the relationships. In the Ritual Pyramidos, the God Hua is given homage immediately after the Secret Word:

> For from the Silence of the Wand,
> Unto the Speaking of the Sword,
> And back again to the Beyond,
> This is the toil and the reward,
> This is the Path of Hua — Ho!
> This is the Path of IAO.

Arcana 231

Hoor-Paar-Kraat　　　　　　　　　Sobek-Ra

The central motif is a sun radiating arrows of fire in all directions. Its complexity is involved and evolving as revelation and knowledge It is the Logos.

The crocodile, Sobek or Sebek, surrounds that core as a symbolic force of creation. Its nature relates to original Chaos, creation and destruction, and knowledge. Sebek symbolizes the agent that carries the prophets and delivers the Logos from æon to æon. Sobek-Ra ferries the prophets of the æons so the Logos is delivered safely across the rivers.

The qliphothic crocodile unites with Horus-Ra and the solar deity Sobek-Ra. It wears the solar disk and horn headdress of Amun-Ra. The qliphothic view shows it. The diadem on its forehead has the sun in the arms of the moon held by scarab-like forelegs. The symbol implies contrast, light and dark, both of which are necessary for revelation to be recognized. It is the achievement of the Great Work.

The mercuric side shows Hoor-Paar-Kraat or (= Gr.) Harpocrates, the silent, dark aspect of Heru-Ra-Ha. He has his finger at his mouth, indicating silence. He holds the tail of the serpent, wisdom, in his left hand. He transmitted the Book of the Law through his messenger, Aiwass in (Liber XXXI, I: page 1 (verse 7). Ra-Hoor-Khuit, the active aspect is the ruler of the æon. See the path of Heh, the Emperor, earlier for this basis.

The God of Silence is Horus the Child. In the New Comment to Liber AL, he is also the Higher Self. As a babe, he identifies with the birth of the New Æon.

The Thoth Tarot card shows Ra-Hoor-Khuit in an egg superimposed on Hoor-Paar-Kraat. The voice in the third paragraph of the Eighth Æthyr in Liber CDXVIII says that Harpocrates wrote the secrets of truth in The Book of the Law. The silence is the rapture of things to come.

The crocodile is an ancient animal. It symbolizes creation and destruction. It protects knowledge and assists in the transmission of the Word by the prophet. This path presents new knowledge and wisdom. In it is the ultimate revelation for an initiate in the macrocosm.

שׁ

Judgment, Choice, The Abyss

Fire (△) — Translation, Rebirth

20. Then also the Pyramid was builded
so that the Initiation might be complete.

Domus Mercurii   Carcer Qliphoth

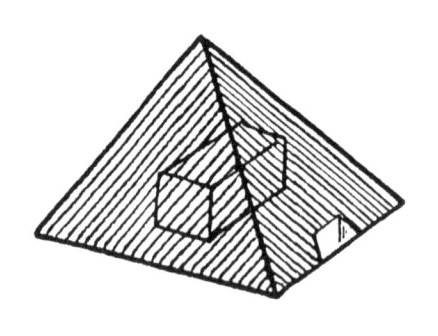

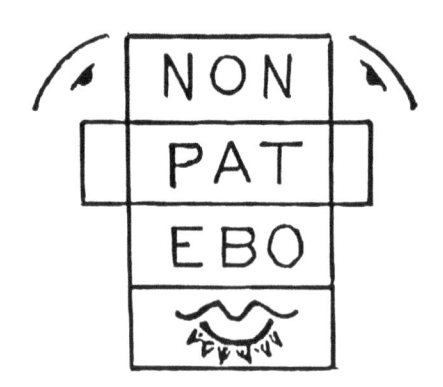

Shabnax-odobor   Shalicu

Shin (שׁ) compares to Mem (מ)

The twenty-first path is Shin (ש), XX. Judgement, The Abyss. It has a numerical value of three hundred (300) and is attributed to the element Fire (△).

The path relates to choice before the Abyss. Some consider it as the apocalypse or final judgment of the Inner Self. It is entered after completing the paths of Kaph (exoteric) and Resh (esoteric).

The pyramid is a symbol of achievement and initiation. The text compares the process of initiation to building a Pyramid. The pyramid is a symbol of fire and light. When the capstone is put in place, the process is complete. For the initiate the path of Resh means coming to the realization of pure light, Truth. This is the climax of initiation. Shin is the entrance path to the level of Spirit. It is final judgment, final transformation. At this decision fork of his journey, the adept opts to continue in duality, or chooses to unite with the universe (1 = 0). Accordingly, the path separates fire from spirit.

The qliphothic sigil is a representation of the pastos of Rosenkreutz with the face of god. The formula, NON PATEBO, means "I will not be exposed, or will not be under the power (of death)". The bottom rectangle includes the mouth of god or a dark sun below the horizon. It is the hidden light, the Word, and awareness of Ineffable beyond.

The mercuric sigil shows the Great Pyramid [≈ Giza in Egypt], whose entrance is on the north and the King's Chamber east-west. Creation begins at the north, symbolized by darkness, midnight, and ignorance. Many cycles begin there symbolically. Its King's Chamber is now believed to be an initiation site rather than a tomb. It is in this main chamber that the Pharaoh achieves final identity as Osiris. This is the symbolic portal of the Abyss, upward toward the capstone, Tau (ת). Manifest initiation proceeds eastward, the direction to the next Pharaoh or prophet who carries the Word in the next generation.

Traditional tarot cards often illustrate the apocalypse of biblical Revelations, the rapture. The Visconti card, *XX Il Giudizio* (The Last Judgment), has a crowned Almighty God holding the discriminating sword at the top. Below are two angels with trumpets. At the bottom are three persons in an open tomb awaiting resurrection. The Marseilles card, *XX Le Jugement*, has just a single angel with a trumpet above, and three persons in the tomb below. The Wirth card, *XX le Jugement*, is assigned to Resh (ר). Above, the angel has a trumpet with a flag. Only one of the three persons at the bottom is standing in the tomb. The others are outside in the grass. The dead, roused by the trumpet, await their destiny. The weighing of the souls determines the result.

The Thoth tarot card, renamed the Æon, has Hoor-Paar-Kraat and Ra-Hoor-Khut aligned under the arch of Nuit. It represents the current New Æon. Shin (ש) is at the bottom center. The Child, Horus, manifest as the ruler of the Æon and under the arch of Nuit, dominates the center. Falling into Nuit at the edge of the cliff, the climax (cremnophobia) of the ritual. Liber XI vel Nu is a foretaste of such an abyssal experience. One may simulate this by aligning microcosm and macrocosm in the ritual of Liber V vel Reguli.

Shin in Cosmos

The qliphothic sigil indicates transition. The face of the god represents the Word carried by a reincarnated prophet. Tradition follows that Rosenkreutz arises after 120 years. Two options are possible.

1). Absorption into unity. This is return to Nothing. It is the annihilation of an Adept. He has given his last drop of blood to Babalon. He becomes non-manifest and anonymous. There is no further indication of his existence in Ineffable.

2). Remaining in duality. Here the Initiate is an enlightened Fool with an evolved soul. He is experienced and wise, beyond innocence. He becomes a Magus, a mentor to Fools. He opens their eyes to the knowledge of life. The question mark is the unanswered state at the beginning of The Book of Lies. The Magus may decide his final answer, the exclamation point. Alternatively, he may reincarnate.

Shin in Initiation

The Pyramid is a significant symbol of initiation in three dimensions. Its etymology derives from fire (πυρ), whose form and symbol are △. Spirit is an aspect of Fire when four instead of five elements are considered. Pyramids around the world are among the largest, most enduring structures built by man. Their bases are foursquare. The universe is built on an expansion of the number four, reflecting manifestation. The capstone represents the quintessential spirit (ש), alluded to by the eye of God.

Here is final decision, the Abyss for a completed initiate. He chooses his continuance in duality, or translation into unity. The decision is his alone.

The Collect for the end in the Gnostic Mass, Liber XV, makes clear the options. The Deacon says:

> Unto them from whose eyes the veil of life hath fallen may they be granted the accomplishment of their true Wills; whether they will absorption in the Infinite, or to be united with their chosen and preferred, or to be in contemplation, or to be at peace, or to achieve the labour and heroism of incarnation on this planet or another, or in any Star, or aught else, unto them may there be granted the accomplishment of their will.

The secrets of Liber CCXXXI are evident here. The initiatory cycle is like a comet. Some comets appear once and have a path that disappears into infinite space. Other comets return for succeeding incarnations. Some adepts choose to become one with the Infinite and pass into unity. Others choose the path of a Bodhisattva, a reincarnate lama, Magus, or prophet. They maintain duality and return to serve as guides or mentors, sharing their experience and wisdom with succeeding generations.

Table of Letter Comparisons

Shin (שׁ) compares to Mem (מ)

These paths mark the end and beginning of the initiatory cycle of the inner self. Mem and Shin connect the paths of inner consecration and transformation. The intermediate paths detail development of life as the preceding paths did for his external life.

Qliphothic Samech shows the Hanged Man as part of the KRZ life cycle. The pastos is the place of transition. The pastos is analogous to Noah's ark during the Deluge. It and the Pyramid represent places of challenge and transformation. The sarcophagus in the Kings' Chamber in the Great Pyramid at Giza is analogous to a transitory tomb. They each have the potential of life to return.

Genii

Qliphoth — Shalicu

Choice, Action

Sha	שׁא	Movement related to power
li	לי	Restrained utterance
cu	כו	Restraining force

Mercurii — Shabnax-odobor

Rest in the dark, awake to eternal light

Shab	שׁאב	Sabbath, rest (from שׁבת)
nax	נאצ	Dark, NOX
od	עד	Eternity
ob	עב	Awake
or	אר	Light

Arcana 231

Solomon   Beelzebul

This path is the last judgment option — crossing of the ultimate Abyss. It offers the option of duality or unity. The drawing contrasts the symbolism of the darkness of Beelzebub to the light and wisdom of Solomon. Yet, each carry both good and evil.

Beelzebub is a demon prince of the underworld. He is shown here as Lord of the Flies. The crown indicates his rank. He incites conflict and chaos. He is an important fallen angel representing the dark side and decay but also helped in the building of the Temple with the assistance of demons. His left hand connects to an inverted pentagram, implying evil, destruction, or idolatry. Whether specific destruction is constructive depends on viewpoint. The tops of the columns are shattered or disorganized. They represent return toward chaos. Beelzebub tempted men through pride. He is a distinct counterpart to Solomon.

Solomon contrasts to Beelzebub. His contribution is the building of the temple in Jerusalem and a worshipper of IHVH (יהוה). These show in his image and crown. The ring on the left hand of Solomon controlled the demons. He holds the firebrand of truth. The pillar Boaz on the left shows the strength of God. The lily at its top indicates its sacred, universal aspect. The pillar Jachin on the right, the secular side, alludes to the establishment of God in the world.

The crown of Solomon shows the tablets of Moses, the law. They were the main objects in the ark in the Holy of Holies in the Temple. Below them is the formula for God, IHVH (יהוה). His beard indicates age and experience, the precursors of wisdom. His right hand holds the torch of enlightenment, of challenge and war. Here he represents wisdom. For all his wisdom and dominion, Solomon was also sybaritic, a seeker of luxury, who levied excessive taxation for many architectural monuments.

The traditional interpretation of the apocalypse implies judgment between good and evil. It includes the role of human hubris. The character of Solomon and Beelzebub personify it. They also reflect the paths of Kaph and Resh — exoteric and esoteric.

The contrast is between the light (Solomon) and the dark (Beelzebub). Both represent the duality of manifestation. In contrast, Solomon represents the aspect that crosses the Abyss. he combines with Ineffable and unites with it. As such, they cancel and become indistinguishable. Beelzebub fails to cross the abyss and wreaks his influence in the world.

ת

Universe — Options

Saturn (♄) — Attainment

21. And in the heart of the Sphinx
danced the Lord Adonai,
in His garlands of roses and pearls
making glad the concourse of things;
yea, making glad the concourse of things.

Domus Mercurii

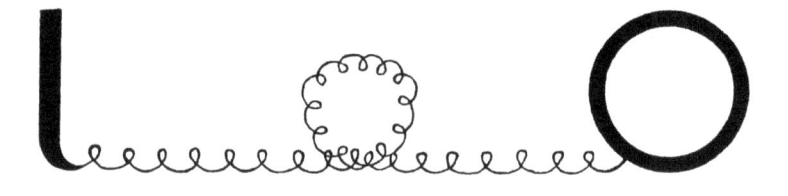

Thath'th'thitɛhthuth-thiʒ

Carcer Qliphoth

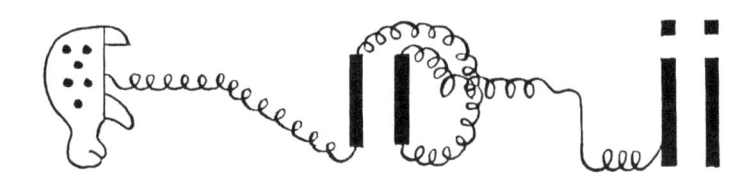

Thantifaxath

Tau (ת) compares to Beth (ב)

The twenty-second final path is Tau (ת), XXI. The Universe. It has a numerical value of four hundred (400). It is attributed to Saturn (♄). The sigils for the path of Tau are three columns wide in contrast to the others. The tripartite symbol is important to a broad understanding of Nature.

This path presents is the final expression of Pure Will. Upon reaching the completion of both exoteric and esoteric attainment, the Adept Initiate must act on his final option.

The text is just one sentence. It expresses the joy of the Lord celebrating union with the enlightened initiate in a dance. The roses symbolize perfection. The pearls indicate purity. Together they identify the perfect result. The final Collect in Liber XV, the Gnostic Mass, spells them out.

If the adept chooses to become one with the universe (1 = 0), he crosses the ultimate Abyss. Absorption is complete. No evidence or even evidence of evidence remains. For him, there is only silence — the final power of the Sphinx — the Ineffable Not — the absolute perfection.

If the adept chooses to continue in duality, he may reincarnate as a Man or Magus, ת = ב. He may return to continue his initiation. His rewards and burden are spreading knowledge, understanding, and wisdom to future generations.

The qliphothic sigil indicates duality. It is nature of Nature, as emanation of the incomprehensible Ineffable. At the left is a turtle, a symbol of origin. On its carapace is the geomantic figure *Aquisitio*, meaning gain or manifestation. It signals good fortune. At the center and right are two double figures. They have looped connections.

The mercuric sigil indicates unity. The I and O are singular and directly connected. They suggest $1 \approx 0$ or $0 = \infty$. Every number is infinite; there is no difference. Contrast!

The Visconti card, *Il Mondo* (The World), is an upper circle held by two naked winged putti. Inside the circle is a walled city, possibly the idealized celestial Jerusalem, the true world. The Marseilles Tarot, *XXI Le Monde*, has a central wreath analogous to the universal Ouroboros with a dancing figure inside. The four cherubs are in the corners. The Wirth card, *XXI le Monde*, adds a Tau (ת). It is similar, more colorful, and the wreath is green. The Rider / Waite card, XXI The World, follows the Marseilles pattern.

The Thoth card has a circle of zodiac stars for the wreath. The dancing figure has its foot on the head of a serpent. The circle of stars and the snake combined form the Tai Chi. The four alchemical cherubs are in the corners of all the cards.

Tau in Cosmos

Nothing can be said about unity (≈ Heaven, Ineffable) beyond the ultimate Abyss. Truth is Silence — without form, void and dark — incomprehensible, incommunicable. It is the beginning and the end, About duality (≈ Nature, Universe, Man), illusions and analogies are expressed as idealized and glorified visions of the world.

Tau in Initiation

The Initiate faces a choice facing the ultimate Abyss on his initiatory journey. His options are presented in Shin. The results are described in the path of Tau — reincarnation or transcendence.

Table of Letter Comparisons

Tau (ת) compares to Beth (ב)

The Adept reached his highest level of initiation at Resh. He completed the spiritual journey started at Mem. The perfected individual — exoteric and esoteric — faces finality. Some adepts cross the abyss into the unity of the universe. Some remain in the duality of the world.

The Adept sees the options of his journey in Tau (ת). The alternative explains why the Magus card is assigned to Beth, and immediately follows The Fool. It expresses the power inherent in the Fool expressed through the Magus. Both illustrate IAO. The Magus (I) becomes The Fool (0). The Fool becomes the Magus (I = 0). The A (= א) is the transform between.

The paired letters support a circular instead of a linear path. This was indicated by Crowley on the original manuscript, though he never followed through on the topic. The Hebrew alphabet sequence can connect א to ת, forming a circle. The qliphothic story and the initiatory story then coincide, rather than follow in the opposite direction of a reciprocal (Tree of Life) model.

Genii

Qliphoth — Thantifaxath

Gift of manifestation

Than	תנ	Gift
ti	תא	Determination, limits
fax	פצ	Confusion, giving liberty
ath	אתפ	Manifest, real, substantial

The option to reincarnate as a Magus is the alternative to Unity. The Magus returns as prophet, mentor, or student for a succeeding generation.

Mercurii — Thath'th'thithϵthuth-thiȝ

Tath te tith toth tuth – tiȝ (ȝ = st = שת)

The 'א ה י ע ו' are between Taus. They may express creation of the world as the sound of God. These are the vowel-like consonants in Hebrew. The ending designates a genius or speaker. It suggests communication from beyond the ultimate Abyss, unity.

166　　ARCANA ARCANORUM

Arcana 231

Unity
Joy
The Daughter of Fortitude

Duality
Sorrow
"It is the veil of the modest woman;
it is the veil of sorrow"

The central motif is held by contrasting female figures. They are interpreted here as the Shekinah and the Shekinah in Exile, the feminine counterpart of Ineffable. The younger female figure is the Daughter of Fortitude from a vision of John Dee and Edward Kelley.

The central motif represents a visualization of the Universe. The Ouroboros surrounding it is an ancient icon, the serpent (or dragon) eating its own tail. It symbolizes the cycle of creating, sustaining, and destroying. Unity is transcendent, crossing the Abyss, union with Ineffable, anonymity. Duality is return to the world, reunion with Man, contrast.

The green line: *Linea viridis gyrat universa* of Liber LXV, III: 2 is Ouroboros.

As an alchemical serpent, part light and dark, it indicates contrast. As with Yin-Yang, the parts are complementary and not antagonistic. The Ouroborus is the celestial Milky Way, the serpent of light extending across the sky. It symbolizes the perimeter of the Universe.

Within the Ouroboros are two semi-circles showing contrasting results. The dark one relates to Peh, The Tower. The turret windows show the light to come. This is destruction bringing enlightenment and renewal.

The light semi-circle reflects the traditional design for the path of Resh, The Sun. The multi-rayed Sun fills the central background. Below is the green mountain. The two figures are dancing, as stated in the Liber CCXXXI text. They represent the joy and satisfaction of accomplishment, the idealism of roses and pearls. They are man's interpretation of the heavenly Jerusalem and the Universe.

In the Hebrew tradition, the Shekinah is the manifestation of God who descended to dwell among men. She is considered an intermediary between God and the world. The female figures that surround the central motif are dark and light, sorrow and joy. The qliphothic one is sorrow, the manifest counterpart of Ineffable on earth. She is separated from God as the Shekinah in exile. The mercuric Shekinah is joy, a heavenly counterpart who resides with Ineffable, not in exile.

Liber CDXVIII, First Æthyr. Equinox I (5): Supplement, page 172, refers to the Prophet and those who achieve success in initiation. It characterizes the god Horus inviting him into a manifest Royal Palace. The alternative, the Cubical Altar of the Universe, is manifestation. The analogy is in human terms.

This is the formula of the Æon, and with that the voice of LIL, that is the Lamp of the Invisible Light, is ended. Amen.

Nothing is a secret key of this law.

Chapter Six

Summary

The paths in Class A *Liber CCXXXI vel Arcanorum* help explain mysteries in *Liber XXXI vel AL*. Together, they expose the understanding of an Aspirant by providing approaches, analogies, and subjects for meditation. Liber Trigrammaton and Liber Arcanorum are examples of universal models. They apply to the Tarot and the Quantum Tree of Life as Thelemic models.

Universal unity is incomprehensible and Ineffable. Nature is the emanated Word of Ineffable which existed before time and space. It operates through unbreakable laws. Nature sees duality and contrast. Creation determines it, $0 = 1$. Nothing and everything are different views of its identity. Contrast sees light as waves or particles and hears sound as pulses or harmonics. The measurer is an inherent part of the measurement.

The expanded formula $0 = 1 = 2$ expresses duality. With it comes dark and light, ignorance and knowledge, female and male. Nature is the even-numbered feminine side (Shekinah). She may exist in unity with Ineffable or may be in exile as the Universe or Nature. Energy is the odd-numbered masculine side. The operation of nature follows the cycle of creation, maintenance, and destruction. The alchemical formula *Solve et Coagula*, divide and unite, represents this expression as love. The goal of an initiate is knowledge of self and union with Nature. Evil and good are interpretations of quality from the perspective of the interpreter.

The paths of Liber CCXXXI use Tarot trump to illustrate cosmic evolution and individual initiation. Cosmic evolution is external. It occurs outside the mind of man. Man uses light and truth as ways to label and describe it.

Human acceptance and interpretation of Nature during initiation may result in wisdom and peace. The Liber CCXXXI model recognizes three aspects in the life of an individual — external, internal, and spiritual (body, mind, soul). The elemental letters of the Hebrew Alphabet, Aleph (א), Mem (מ) and Shin (ש) index them.

Liber CCXXXI follows the cosmology of Liber XXXI vel AL and other Class A libers to express relationships. It portrays the universe as the stellar, feminine Nuit, with all power and paired with masculine Hadit. The unity of Heru-Ra-Ha becomes the silent Hoor-Paar-Kraat and the active Ra-Hoor-Khuit. The latter is the ruler of the current Æon. Their manifest equivalents are Nu, Had, and Ra-Hoor-Khu.

The paths of the outer or exoteric life represent aspects of the study of Nature:

Light — Path of Initiation

The Fool, א, the Student or Initiate.

The Magus, ב, the Teacher or Prophet.

The High Priestess, ג, Nature, the Object of study and worship.

Law — The rules of operation

Natural (Empress, ד) — Unbreakable, *Solve et Coagula*.

Secular (Emperor, ה) — Government statutes and regulations.

Sacred (Hierophant, ו) — Dogmata of religions.

Love — Relationships

Φιλεω Brotherly love, (The Brothers or Lovers, ז).

Ἀγαπη Sacred Love, (The Chariot, ח).

Ἔρος Secular Love (Strength, ט).

Life — Cycle of the Exoteric

Wheel of Fortune (כ) — Birth, Life, Death, and Rebirth.

Virtue applies to both exoteric and esoteric aspects of life. They occur at the Middle Triad of the Quantum Tree of Life and so are relevant to both the exo- and eso-teric life.

Fortitude	Fidelity, consistency (Strength, ט).
Wisdom	Knowledge based (Hermit, י).
Justice	Adjustment, Equilibrium (Balance, ל).
Temperance	Self-restraint, practical application (Art, ס).

The inner or esoteric life occurs simultaneous with the exoteric, though it may not seem as evident or as developed. The paths include:

Consecration —

Hanged Man, Baptism (מ). The Adept, Esoteric initiation.

Purification through Ordeal —

    Death (נ) — Distinction between exoteric and esoteric.

    Devil (ע) — Advocacy and temptation.

Annihilation and enlightenment —

    Tower (פ) — Annihilation and Trial, Refinement.

Emergence as an Adept —

    Star (צ) — The Star revealed.

    Moon (ק) — Uncertainty and Illusion, Subconscious.

    Sun (ר) — Culmination of Enlightenment, Revelation.

    Will and Decision — Duality vs. Unity.

    Judgement (ש) — Decision, Resurrection, the Final Abyss.

    Universe (ת) — Duality or Unity.

    The paths of Shin and Tau describe the spiritual aspects.

The path of Shin is the final Abyss. There the adept chooses between duality and unity. He may choose to reincarnate as a Fool or Magus or may choose to join Ineffable across the Abyss. With the latter choice he become anonymous and synonymous with Ineffable. He leaves no trace. Unity is the greatest unanswered mystery of all. We can only perceive and know duality.

Circular model

Part of the original Liber CCXXXI manuscript is still extant. It includes a note indicating the trumps can be arranged in either a circular or pillar format. Crowley never published further information about the circular arrangement.

The information in *Arcanorum* correlates paths by the Hebrew alphabet sequence and Tarot trumps. The repetition of a linear sequence end to end, where Aleph is adjacent to Tau iterates the same way as a circular arrangement. It orders both cosmic evolution and individual initiation evolution from Aleph to Tau. The Class A libers of Thelema are consistent.

The circular model shows cosmic evolution and initiation to be parallel, not reciprocating. Fuller, who prepared the diagrams for Liber CCXXXI in Equinox I (7), later tried some unpublished attempts using the circular model and the Thoth tarot images. His torus model needs further study and evaluation.

Each model takes a particular view. Its components divide the universe into labelled units. When successfully integrated, they improve understanding. They provide gateways for meditation and bases for magical ritual and individual growth. Success requires a receptive and critical mind, the willingness to explore new ventures, to ask new questions, and to separate fact from interpretation. Facts are timeless, they express the laws of Nature.

The paths on the journey are facets and qualities of life. This study emphasizes facts over individual interpretations. The Aspirant must question all and draw his own conclusions. It omits any discussion of divination.

? and !

Literature Cited

Bible. King James version.
     n.d.   London: Oxford University Press.

Chajes, J. H.
     2022   The Kabbalistic Tree האילן הקבלי. University Park: Pennsylvania State University Press.

Crowley, Aleister
     1899   Note by H. Fra on the R.O.T.A. by the Qabalah of Nine Chambers. In: Equinox I: 7, p. 74. (See Appendix One).

     1907   The Works of Aleister Crowley, Vol. III.
Foyers: Society for the Propagation of Religious Truth.

     1909   ΘΕΛΗΜΑ, The Holy Books. 3 vols. Privately published.

     1909   777 vel Prolegomena Symbolica. London: Walter Scott Publishing.

     1919   Equinox III: 1.
          XV. The Gnostic Mass.
          CL. A Sandal. De Lege Libellum L_L_L_L_L.

     1944   The Book of Thoth. Privately Published.

     1962   The Book of Lies. Ilfracome, Devon: Hadyn Press.

     1983   Equinox III: 9. The Holy Books of Thelema.
York Beach, Maine: Samuel Weiser.
          II. Liber Magus.
          VII. Liber Lapidus Lazuli.
          XXVII. Liber Trigrammaton.
          XXXI. Liber AL (holographic manuscript).
          CCXX. Liber AL (typeset edition).
          CCXXXI. Liber Arcanorum ton Tahuti.
          DCCCXIII. Liber Ararita.

     1986.   Equinox III: 10. NY: Thelema Publications.
DCCLXXVII. OZ: The Rights of Mankind.

     1991   Liber Aleph (Revised edition). New York: 93 Publishing.

De Mellet, M. le C.
    1781   Recherches sur les Tarots et sur la Divination par les Cartes des Tarot.
Le Monde Primitiv, vol 8, tom. 1. Facsimile in: 1983. Court de Gébelin.
Le Monde Primitiv. Paris: Berg International Editions.

Kaplan, Aryeh.
    1990   Sepher Yetzirah. The Book of Creation. York Beach: Weiser.

Kircher, Athaneus.
    1652   Oedipus Aegyptiacus. Rome: Mascardi.

Kuntz, Darcy
    1990   The Complete Golden Dawn Cipher Manuscript. Edmonds, WA: Holmes Publishing Group.

Levi, Eliphas. (trans. A.C.)
    1959   The Key of the Mysteries. London: Rider and Company.

Runyan, Carroll.
    2009   Secrets of the Golden Dawn Cipher Manuscript. Silverado, CA: Church of Hermetic Sciences.

Stein, Robert C.
    1990   Liber DCLXVI vel Troa, vel Pyramidos. Buffalo: Pyramid Lodge.

    2014   Thelema. Re: Al Arcanorum. Tonawanda NY: Privately Published.

    2015   Mystery of the Letters and the Tree of Life. York Beach ME: Black Jackal Press.

Tarot Decks

(XV Cent) 1975 Visconti-Sforza Tarocchi Deck. Stamford CT: U. S. Games Systems.

(XV Cent) 1984 Cary-Yale Visconti Tarocchi Deck, XVC. Stamford CT: U.S. Games Systems.

(XV Cent) 2004 Golden Tarot of Renaissance. Torino: Lo Scarabeo. Tarot of Charles, Grigonnier.

(1650) 2007 Tarot de Marseille. Jean Noblet. Paris: Editions Le Tarot.

(1650) 2012 Tarot de Jacques Vieville. Paris: Editions Le Tarot.

(1701) 2009 Tarot de Marseille Jean Dodal Lyon. Paris: Editions Le Tarot.

(1761) n.d. Tarot de Marseille, ed. Nicolas Conver. Heron S. A

(1889) 1976 Tarot Oswald Wirth. Switzerland: AGM Urania.

(1909) 1971 Rider/Waite Tarot Deck. Stamford CT: U. S. Games Systems.

(1944) n.d. Thoth Tarot Cards — New York: Samuel Weiser.

Appendix One

LIBER ARCANORUM tωn ATV tou TAHVTI

Class A

from

Equinox I (7): pages 69 to 74

Including:

Note by H. Fra. P. 4 = 7 (1899) on the R.O.T.A. by the Qabalah of Nine Chambers

LIBER
ARCANORVM τῶν
ATV τοῦ TAHVTI
QUAS VIDIT
ASAR IN
AMENNTI
SVB FIGVRÂ
CCXXXI

LIBER
CARCERORVM τῶν
QLIPHOTH
CVM SVIS
GENIIS

ADDVNTVR SIGILLA ET
NOMINA EORVM

A∴A∴
Publication in Class A.
Imprimatur:
N. Fra A∴A∴

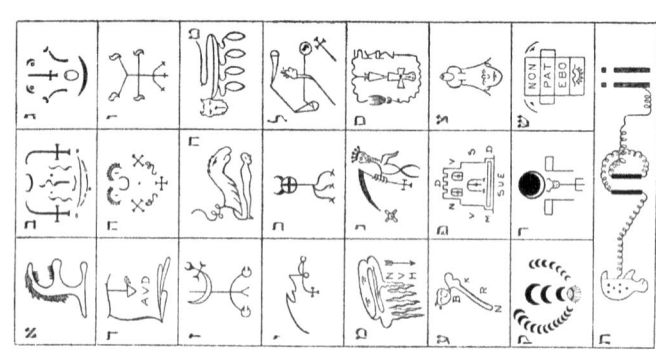

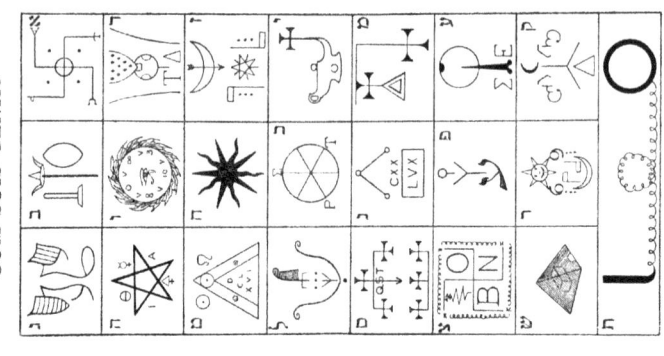

180 · ARCANA ARCANORUM

LIBER CCXXXI

(This book is true up to the grade of Adeptus Exemptus. V.V.V.V.V. 8°, 3°.)

0. A, the heart of IAO, dwelleth in ecstasy in the secret place of the thunders. Between Asar and Asi he abideth in joy.

1. The lightnings increased and the Lord Tahuti stood forth. The Voice came from the Silence. Then the One ran and returned.

2. Now hath Nuit veiled herself, that she may open the gate of her sister.

3. The Virgin of God is enthroned upon an oyster-shell; she is like a pearl, and seeketh Seventy to her Four. In her heart is Hadit the invisible glory.

4. Now riseth Ra-Hoor-Khuit, and dominion is established in the Star of the Flame.

5. Also is the Star of the Flame exalted, bringing benediction to the universe.

6. Here then beneath the winged Eros is youth, delighting in the one and the other.

He is Asar between Asi and Nephthi; he cometh forth from the veil.

7. He rideth upon the chariot of eternity; the white and the black are harnessed to his car. Therefore he reflecteth the Fool, and the sevenfold veil is reveiled.

THE EQUINOX

8. Also came forth mother Earth with her lion, even Sekhet, the lady of Asi.

9. Also the Priest veiled himself, lest his glory be profaned, lest his word be lost in the multitude.

10. Now then the Father of all issued as a mighty wheel; the Sphinx, and the dog-headed god, and Typhon, were bound on his circumference.

11. Also the lady Maat with her feather and her sword abode to judge the righteous.

For Fate was already established.

12. Then the holy one appeared in the great water of the North; as a golden dawn did he appear, bringing benediction to the fallen universe.

13. Also Asar was hidden in Amennti; and the Lords of Time swept over him with the sickle of death.

14. And a mighty angel appeared as a woman, pouring vials of woe upon the flames, lighting the pure stream with her brand of cursing. And the iniquity was very great.

15. Then the Lord Khem arose, He who is holy among the highest, and set up his crowned staff for to redeem the universe.

16. He smote the towers of wailing; he brake them in pieces in the fire of his anger, so that he alone did escape from the ruin thereof.

17. Transformed, the holy virgin appeared as a fluidic fire, making her beauty into a thunderbolt.

18. By her spells she invoked the Scarab, the Lord Kheph-Ra, so that the waters were cloven and the illusion of the towers was destroyed.

LIBER

19. Then the sun did appear unclouded, and the mouth of Asi was on the mouth of Asar.

20. Then also the Pyramid was builded so that the Initiation might be complete.

21. And in the heart of the Sphinx danced the Lord Adonai, in His garlands of roses and pearls making glad the concourse of things; yea, making glad the concourse of things.

THE GENII OF THE 22 SCALES OF THE SERPENT AND OF THE QLIPHOTH

א	Aϱu-iao-uϱa[ϱ=ν]	Amprodias
ב	Beϱθaoooabitom	Baratchial
ג	Gitωnosapφωllois	Gargophias
ד	Dηnaχartarωθ [χ=st]	Dagdagiel
ה	Hoo-oorω-iχ	Hemethterith
ו	Vuaretza—[a secret name follows]	Uriens
ז	Zooωasar	Zamradiel
ח	Chiva-abrahadabra-cadaxviii	Characith
ט	θalϱχer-ā-dekerval	Temphioth
י	Iehuvahaχanϱθatan	Yamatu
כ	Kerugunaviel	Kurgasiax
ל	Lusanaherandraton	Lafcursiax
מ	Malai	Malkunofat
נ	Nadimraphoroiozϱθalai	Niantiel
ס	Salaθlala-amrodnaθϱiχ	Saksaksalim
ע	Oaoaaaoooϱ-iχ	A'ano'nin
פ	Puraθmetai-apηmetai	Parfaxitas
צ	Xanθaχeranϛʔ-iχ [ϛʔ=sh, q]	Tzuflifu
ק	QaniΔnayx-ipamai	Qulielfi
ר	Ra-a-gioselahladnaimawa-iχ	Raflifu
ש	Shabnax-odobor	Shalicu
ת	Thath'th'thithϱthuth-thiχ	Thantifaxath

THE EQUINOX

NOTE BY H. FRA. P. $4°=7^{\square}$ (1899) ON THE R.O.T.A. BY THE QABALAH OF NINE CHAMBERS

Units are divine—The upright Triangle.
Tens reflected—The averse Triangle.
Hundreds equilibrated—The Hexagram their combination.

1. *Light.*—[Here can be no evil.] א The hidden light—the "wisdom of God foolishness with men."
    י The Adept bearing Light.
    ק The Light in darkness and illusion.
    [Khephra about to rise.]

2. *Action.*—ב Active and Passive—dual current, etc.—the Alternating Forces in Harmony.
    כ The Contending Forces—fluctuation of earth-life.
    ר The Twins embracing — eventual glory of harmonised life under ☉.

3. *The Way.*—[Here also no evil.] ג The Higher Self.
    ל The severe discipline of the Path.
    ש The judgment and resurrection
    [$0°=0^{\square}$ and $5°=6^{\square}$ rituals.]

4. *Life.*—ד The Mother of God. Aima.
    מ The Son Slain.
    ת The Bride.

5. *Force* (Purification).—ה The Supernal Sulphur purifying by fire.
    נ The Infernal Water ♏ purifying by putrefaction.
    This work is not complete; therefore is there no equilibration.

6. *Harmony.*—ו The Reconciler [ו of יהוה] above.
    ס The Reconciler below [lion and eagle, etc.].
    This work also unfinished.

7. *Birth.*—ז The Powers of Spiritual Regeneration.
    [The Z.A.M. as Osiris risen between Isis and Nephthys. The path of ג, Diana, above his head.]
    ע The gross powers of generation.

8. *Rule.*—ח The Orderly Ruling of diverse forces.
    פ The Ruin of the Unbalanced Forces.

9. *Stability.*—ט The Force that represses evil.
    צ The Force that restores the world ruined by evil.

Appendix Two

LIBER TRIGRAMMATON

Class A

from

ΘΕΛΗΜΑ (part 3): pages 39 to 48

LIBER TRIGRAMMATON

SVB FIGVRÂ XXVII

BEING

THE BOOK OF THE TRIGRAMS OF THE MUTATIONS OF THE TAO WITH THE YIN AND THE YANG

PUBLICATION IN CLASS A

IMPRIMATUR. V. V. V. V. V. Pro Coll. Summ.

D. D. S.
O. M. } Pro Coll. Int.

V. N.
P. } Pro Coll. Ext.
P. A.

O. S. V.

Imp.

THE BOOK OF THE TRIGRAMS OF THE MUTATIONS OF THE TAO WITH THE YIN AND THE YANG

•
•
•

Here is Nothing under its three forms. It is not, yet informeth all things.

•
•
———

Now cometh the glory of the Single One, as an imperfection and stain.

•
———
•
———

But by the Weak One the Mother was it equilibrated.

•
———
•

Also the purity was divided by Strength, the force of the Demiurge.

·
─┼─
·

And the Cross was formulated in the Universe that as yet was not.

───
·
·

But now the Imperfection became manifest, presiding over the fading of perfection.

── ──
·
·

Also the Woman arose, and veiled the Upper Heaven with her body of stars.

·
══

Now then a giant arose, of terrible strength; and asserted the Spirit in a secret rite.

·
══
── ──

And the Master of the Temple balancing all things arose; his stature was above the Heaven and below Earth and Hell.

☰̇

Against him the Brothers of the Left-hand Path, confusing the symbols. They concealed their horror [in this symbol]; for in truth they were ☰̣

☰̇

The master flamed forth as a star and set a guard of Water in every Abyss.

☰̇

Also certain secret ones concealed the Light of Purity in themselves, protecting it from the Persecutions.

☰̇

Likewise also did certain sons and daughters of Hermes and of Aphrodite, more openly

☰̇

But the Enemy confused them. They pretended to conceal that Light, that they might betray it, and profane it.

43

Yet certain holy nuns concealed the secret in songs upon the lyre.

Now did the Horror of Time pervert all things, hiding the Purity with a loathsome thing, a thing unnameable.

Yea, and there arose sensualists upon the firmament, as a foul stain of storm upon the sky.

And the Black Brothers raised their heads; yea, they unveiled themselves without shame or fear.

Also there rose up a soul of filth and of weakness, and it corrupted all the rule of the Tao.

☰

Then only was Heaven established to bear sway; for only in the lowest corruption is form manifest.

☱

Also did Heaven manifest in violent light,

☲

And in soft light.

☳

Then were the waters gathered together from the heaven,

☴

And a crust of earth concealed the core of flame.

☵

Around the globe gathered the wide air,

☷

And men began to light fires upon the earth.

45

⚏

Therefore was the end of it sorrow; yet in that sorrow a sixfold star of glory whereby they might see to return unto the stainless Abode; yea, unto the Stainless Abode.

The full knowledge of the interpretation of this book is concealed from all.

The Practicus must nevertheless acquire a copy, thoroughly acquaint himself with the contents, and commit them to memory.

This copy belongs to

By authority of V. V. V. V. V. this book is published and issued.

The Price, one Guinea, is to be remitted to the Treasurer through the Philosophus introducing.

Appendix Three

ARCANA231

by Barry William Hale

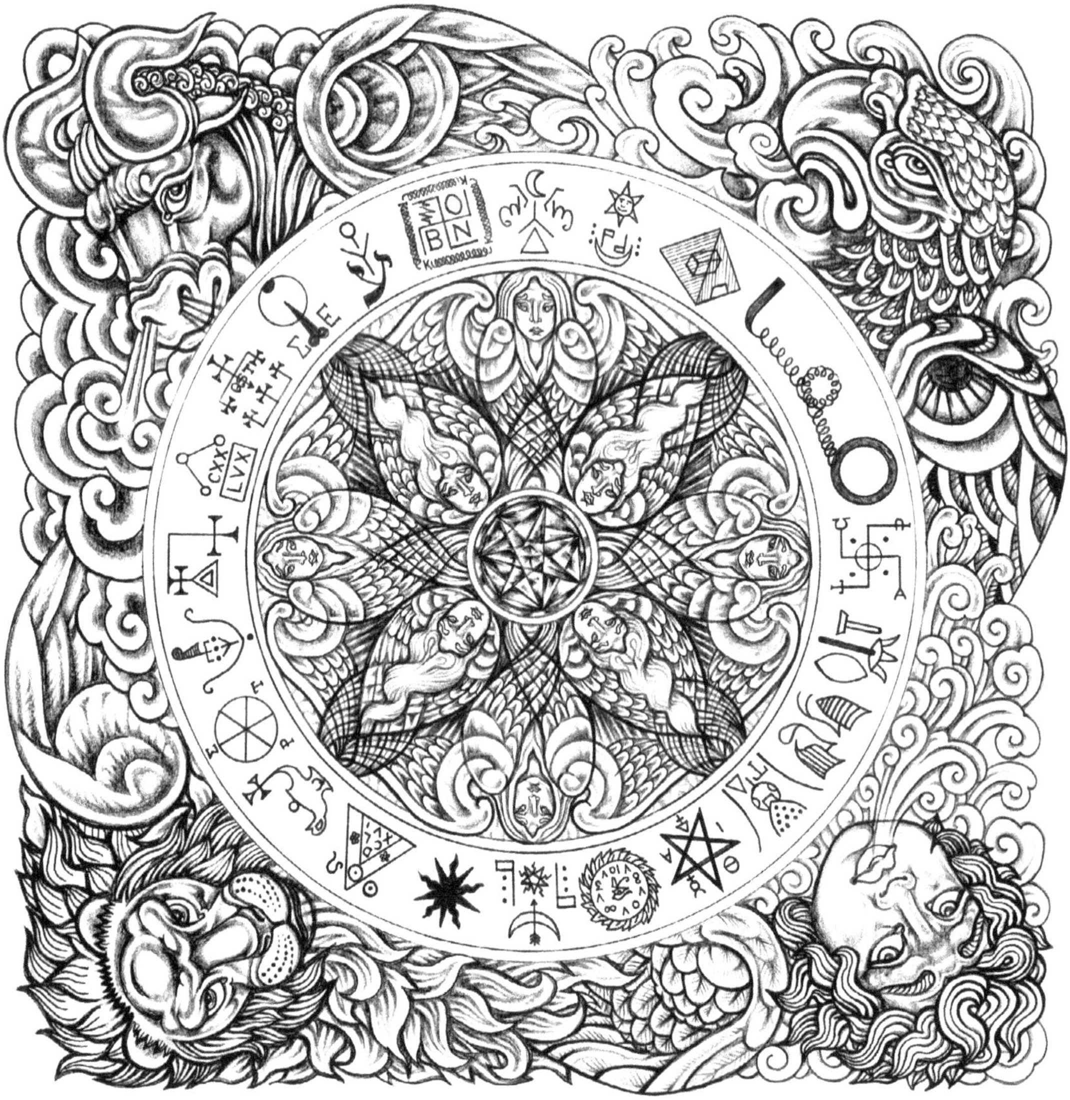
CXX
LVX

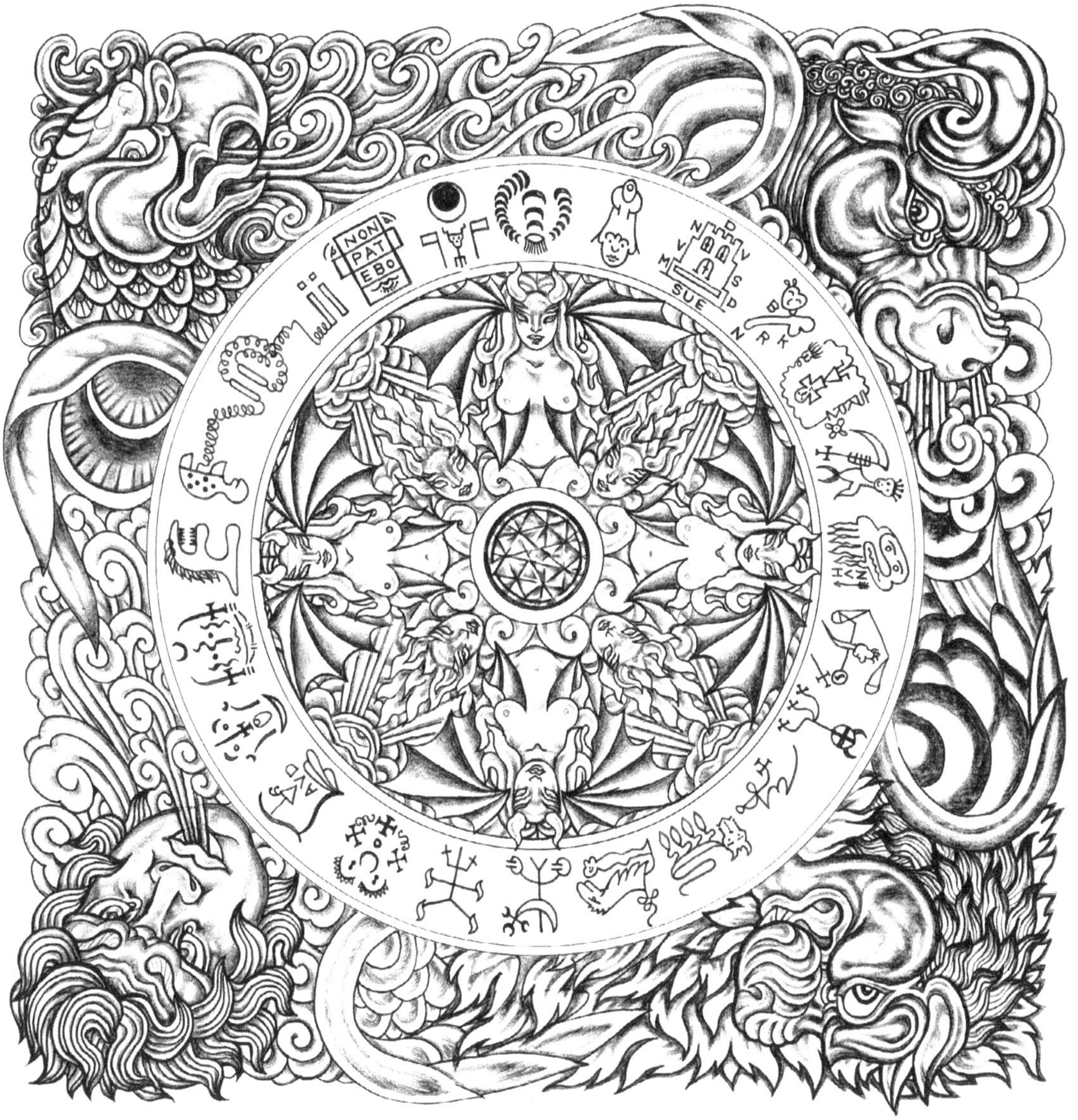
NON
PAT
EBO
SUE

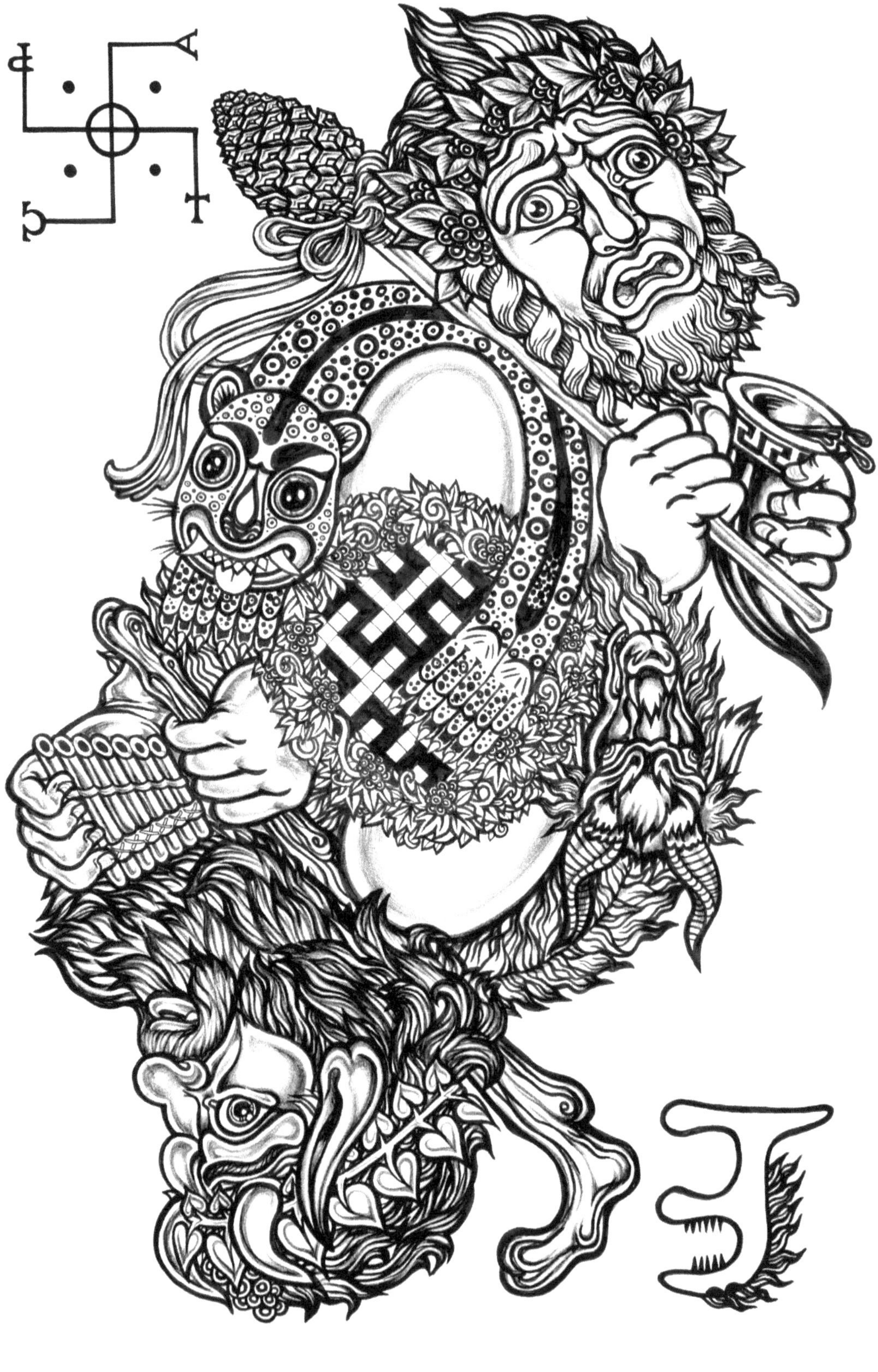

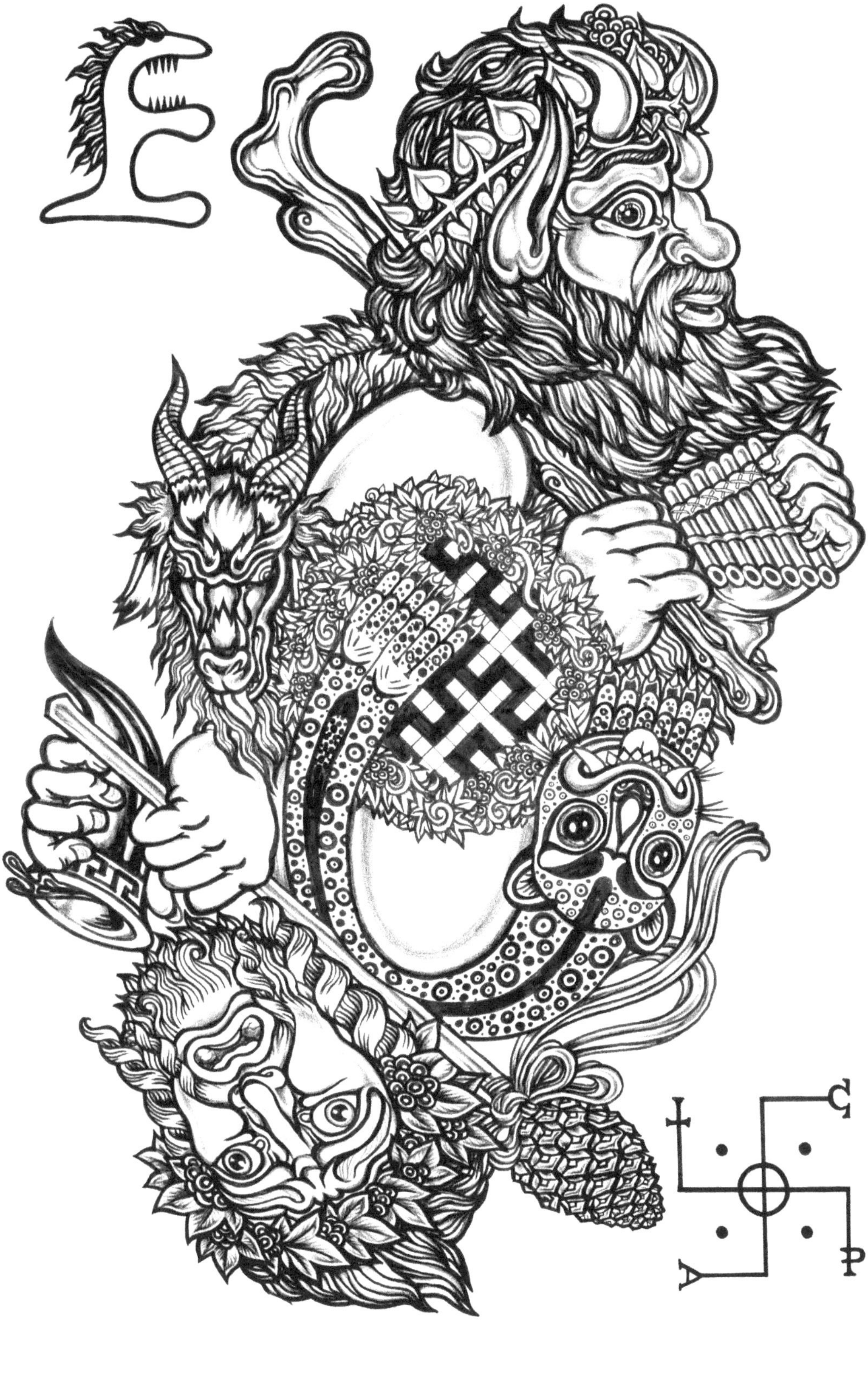

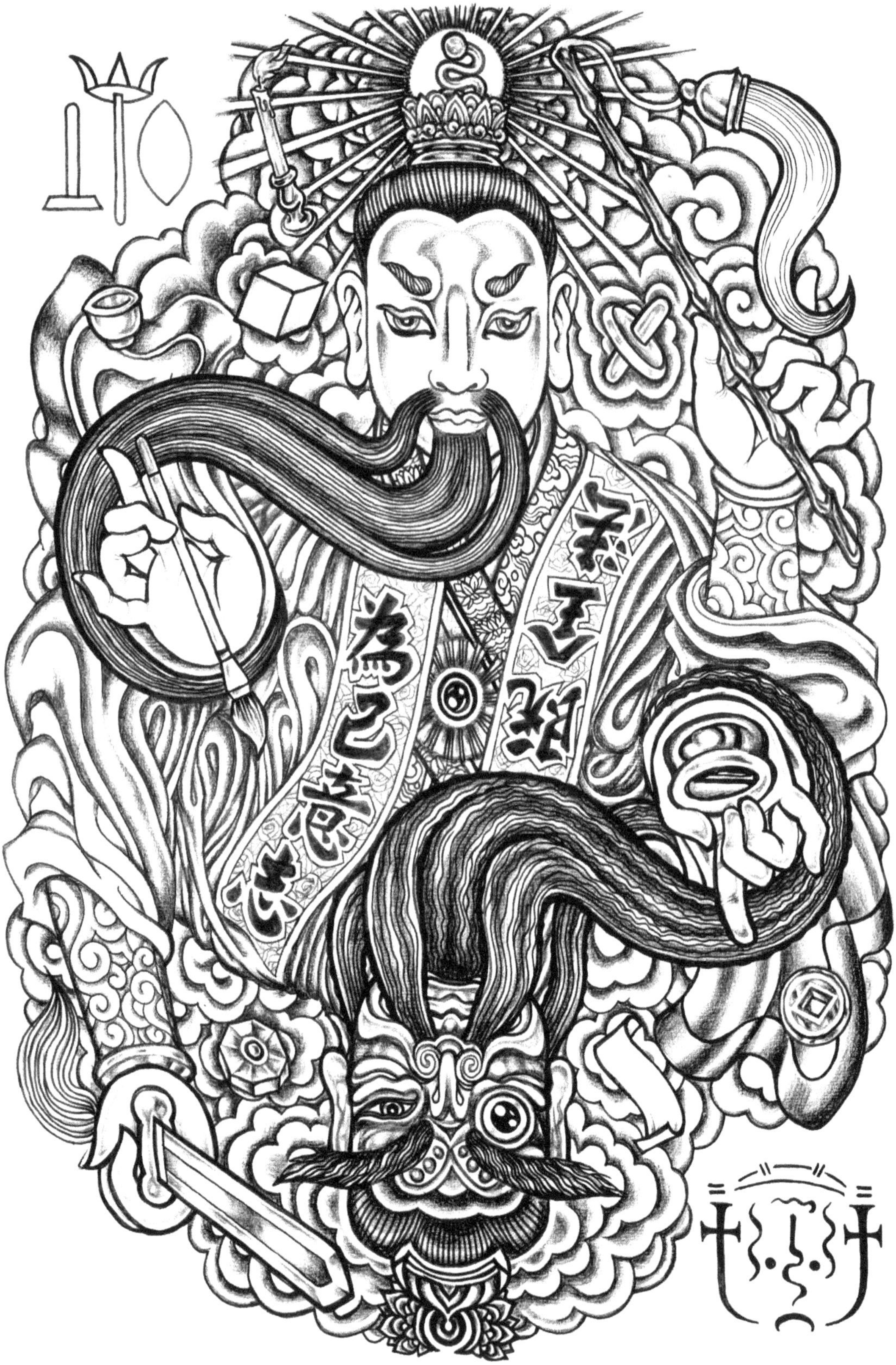

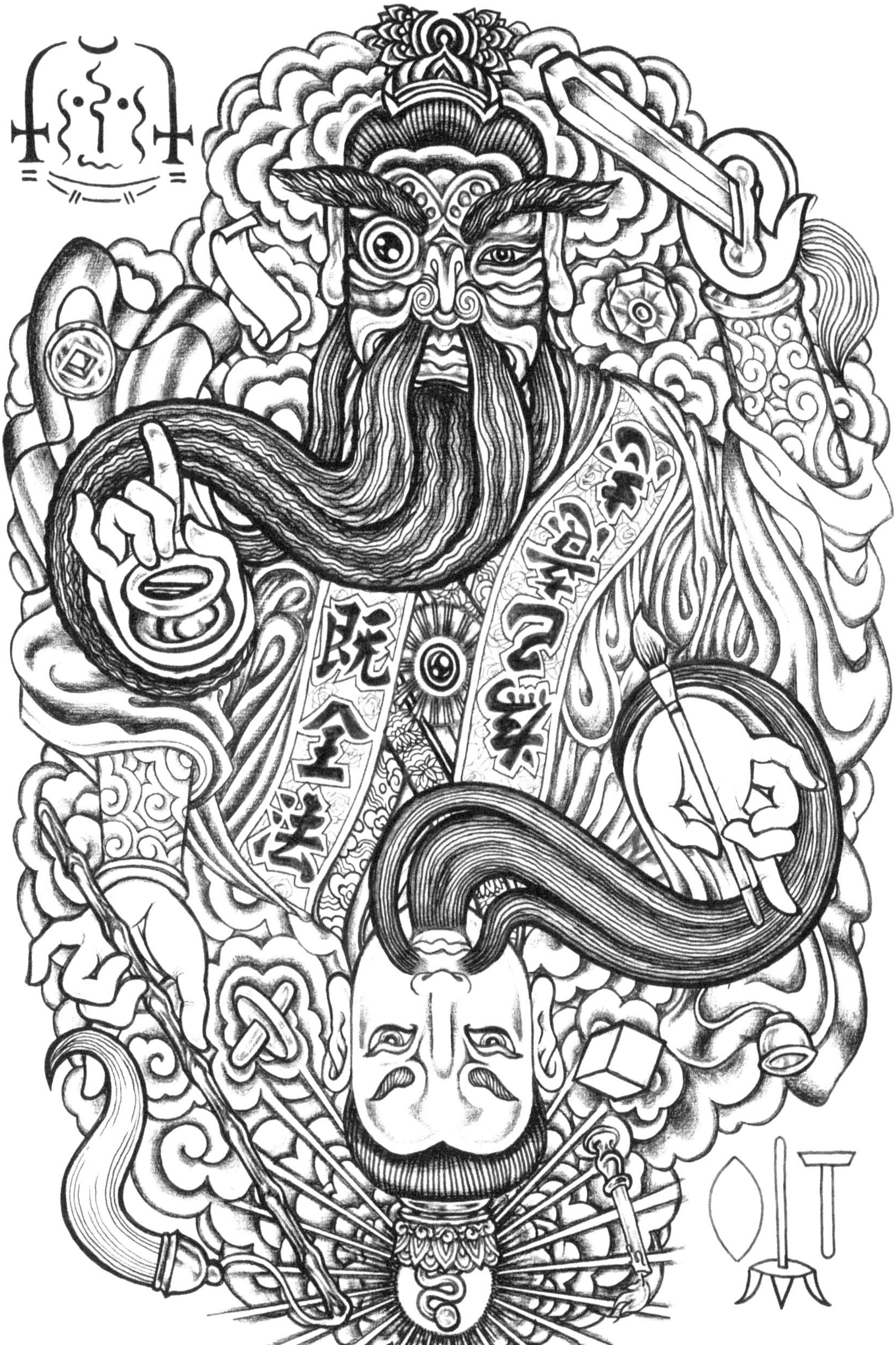

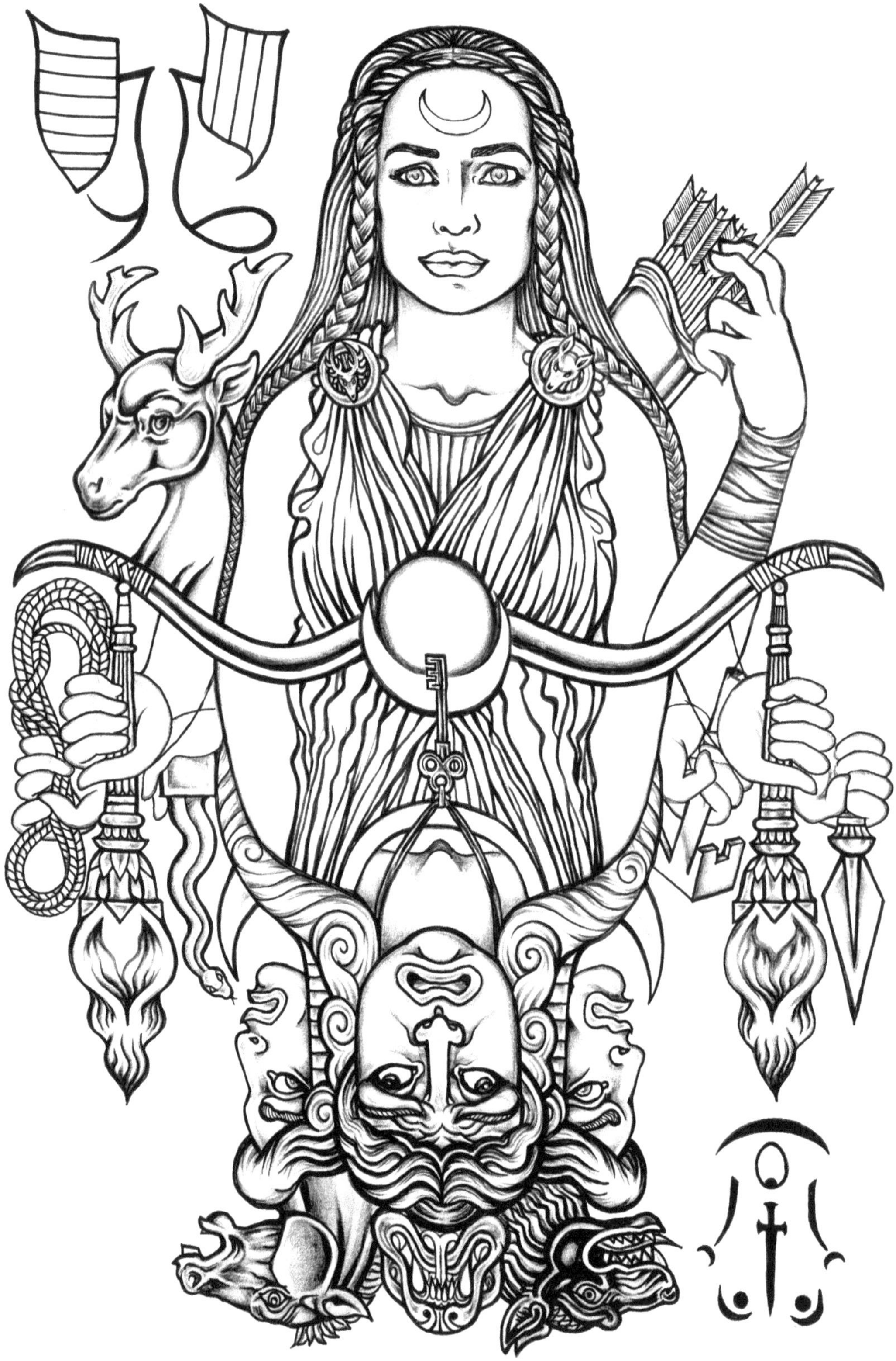

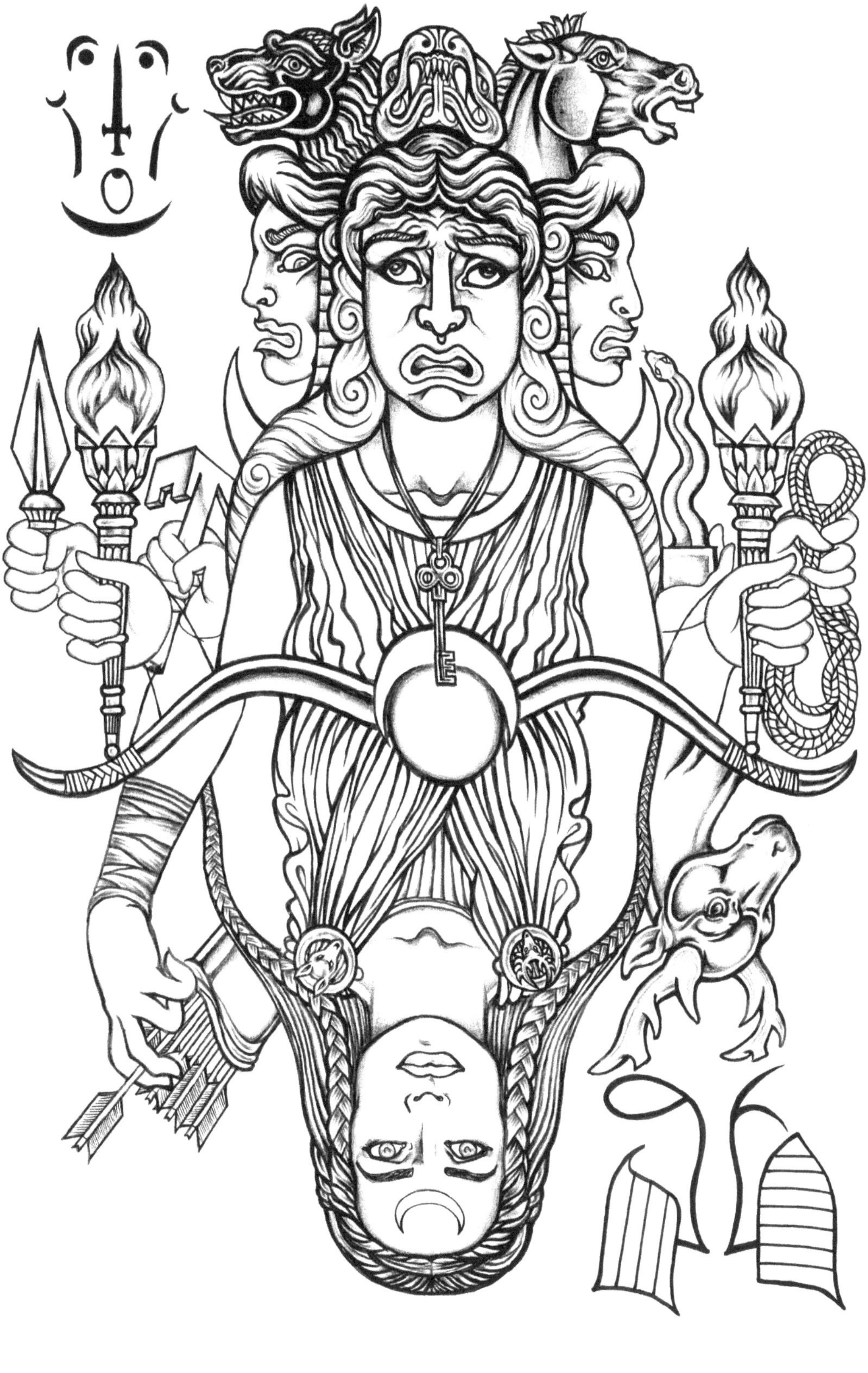

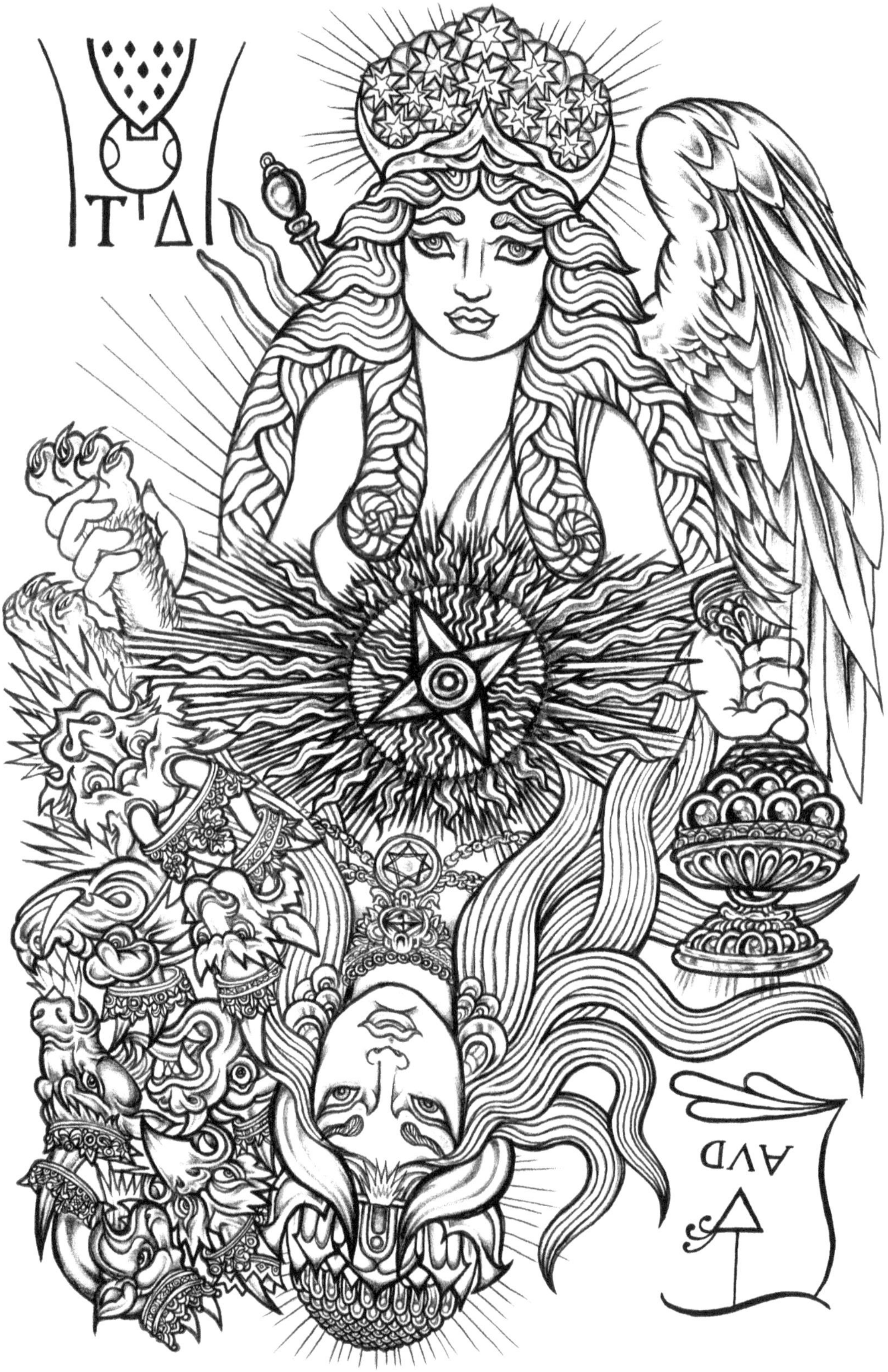

TΔ
AVD

AVD

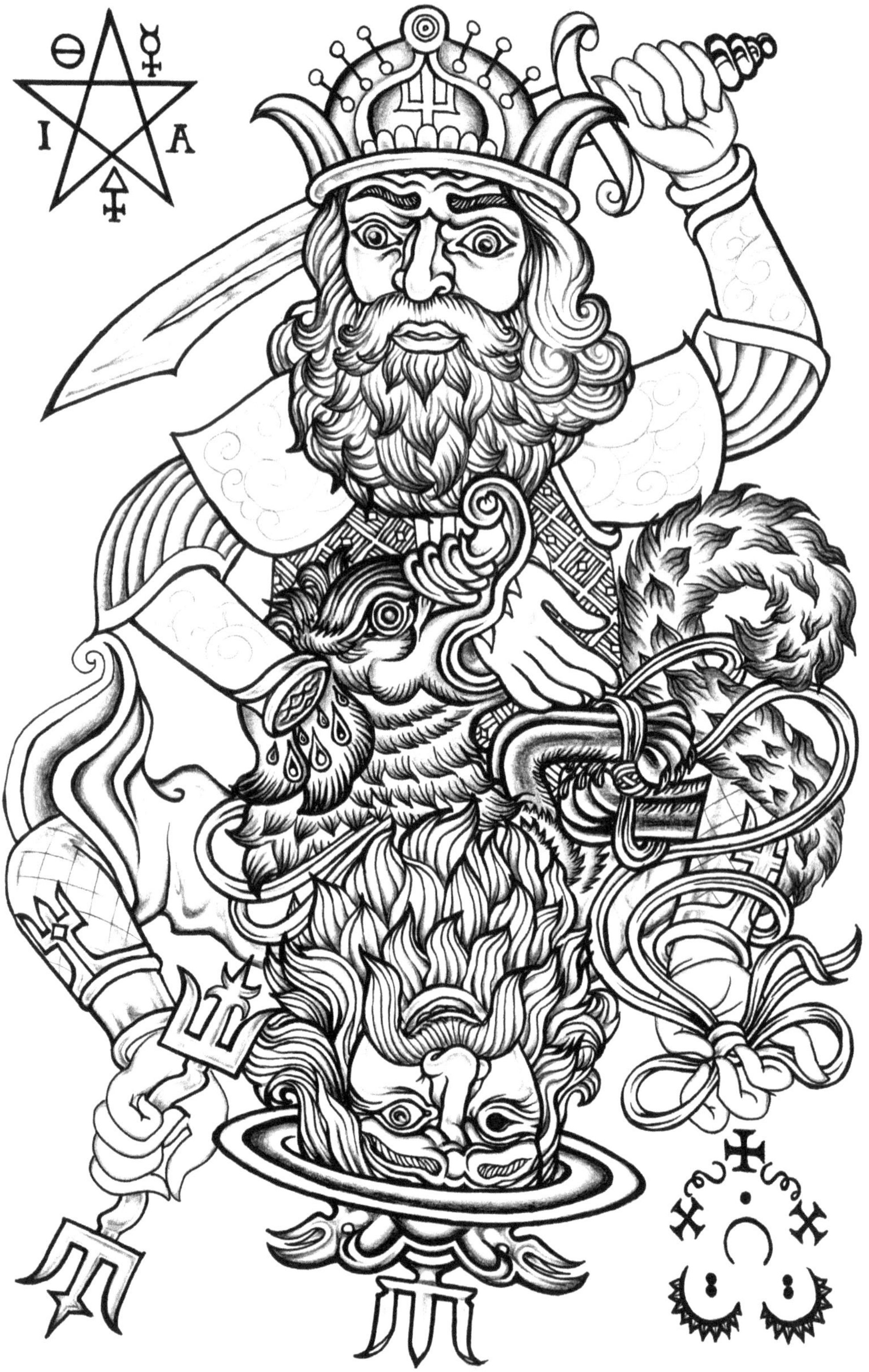

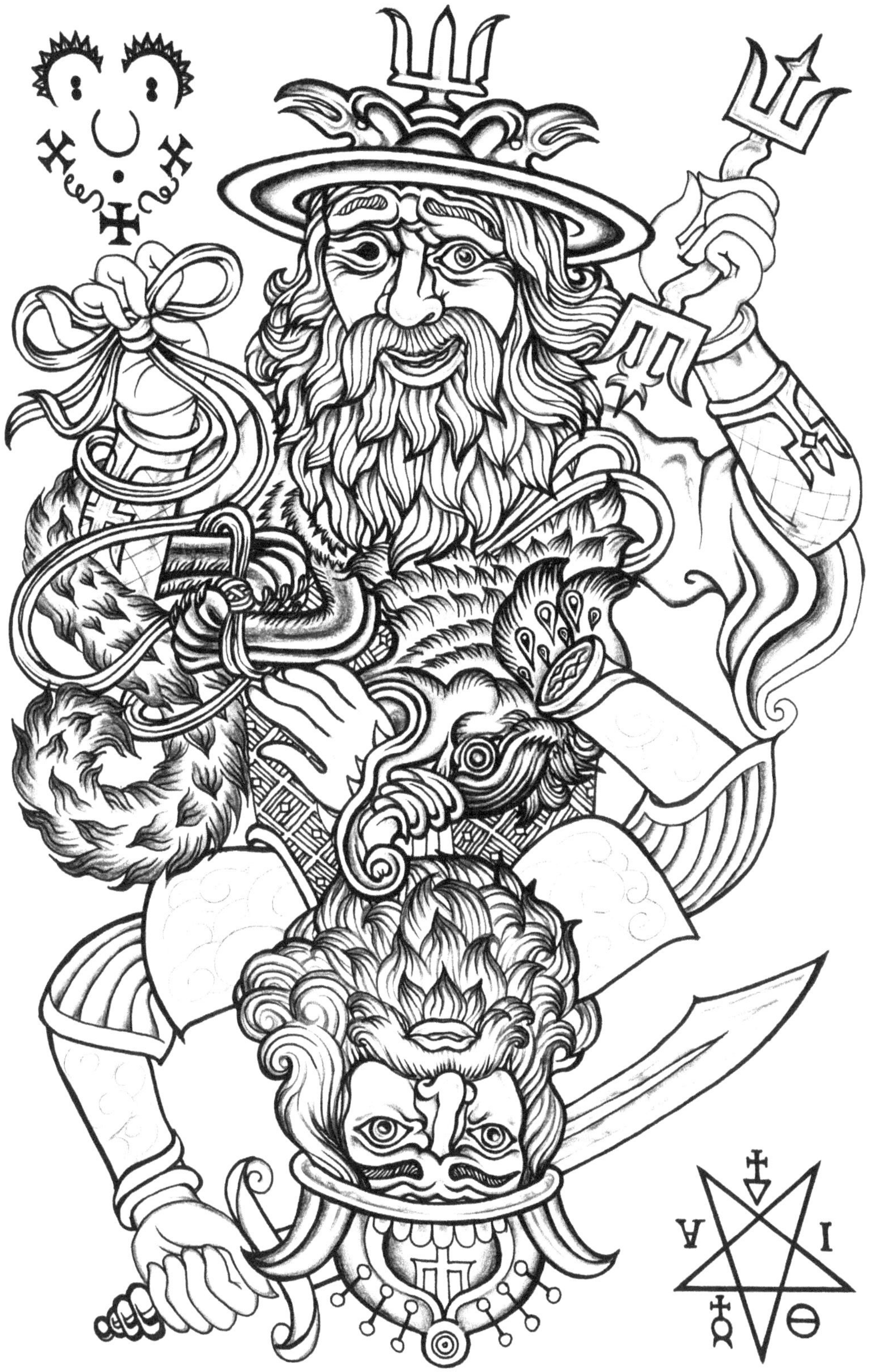

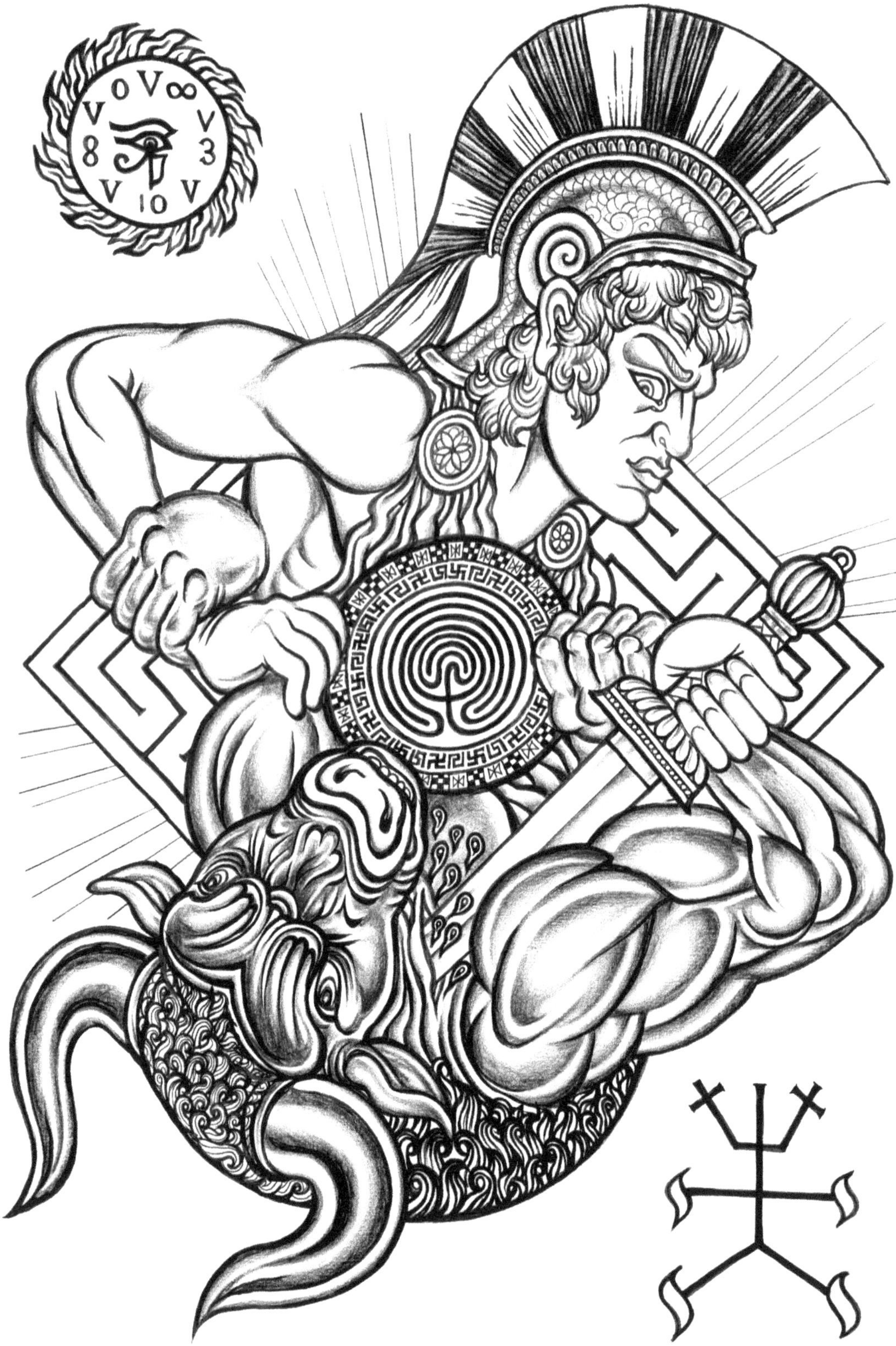
0 V ∞
V V
8 3
V 10 V

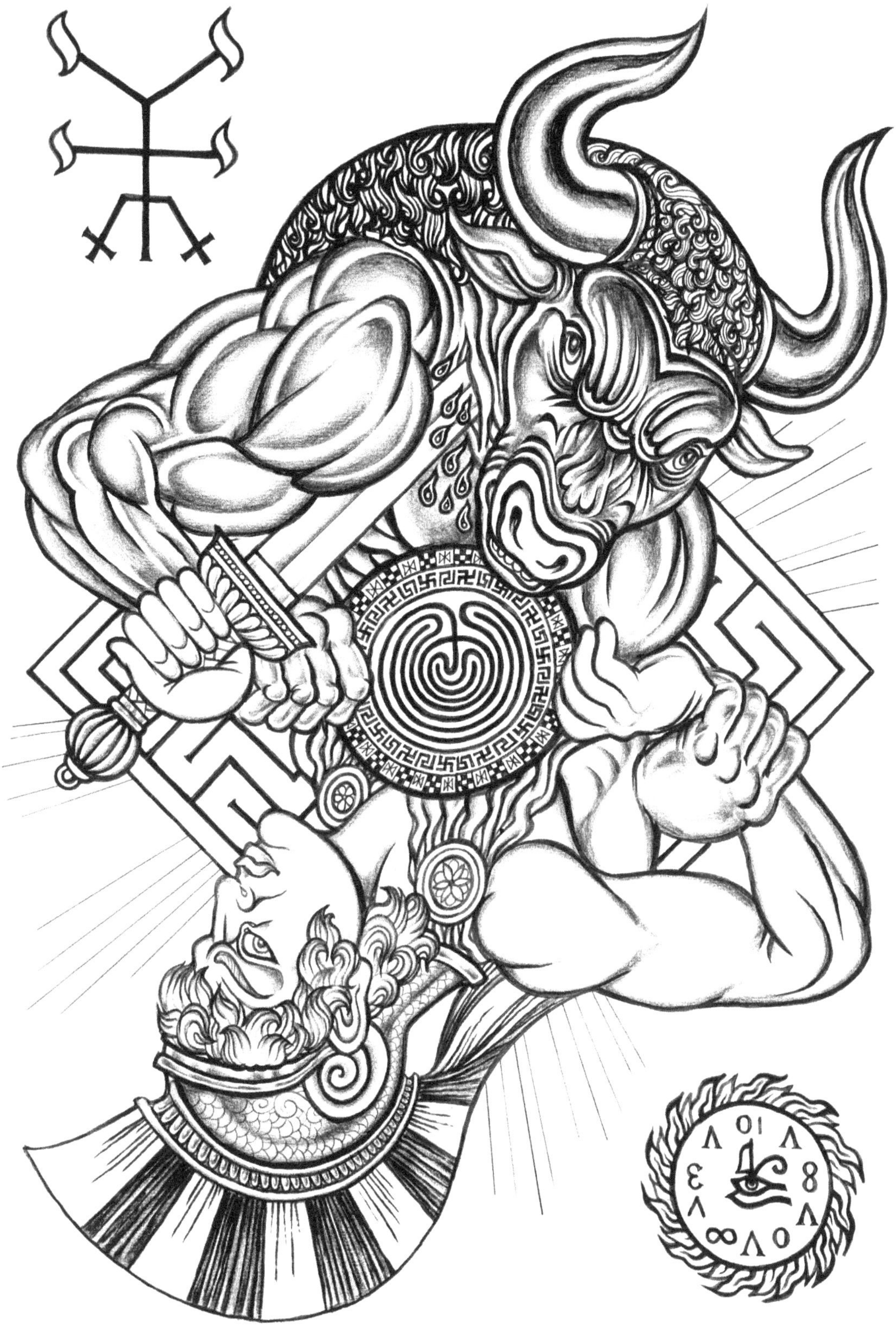

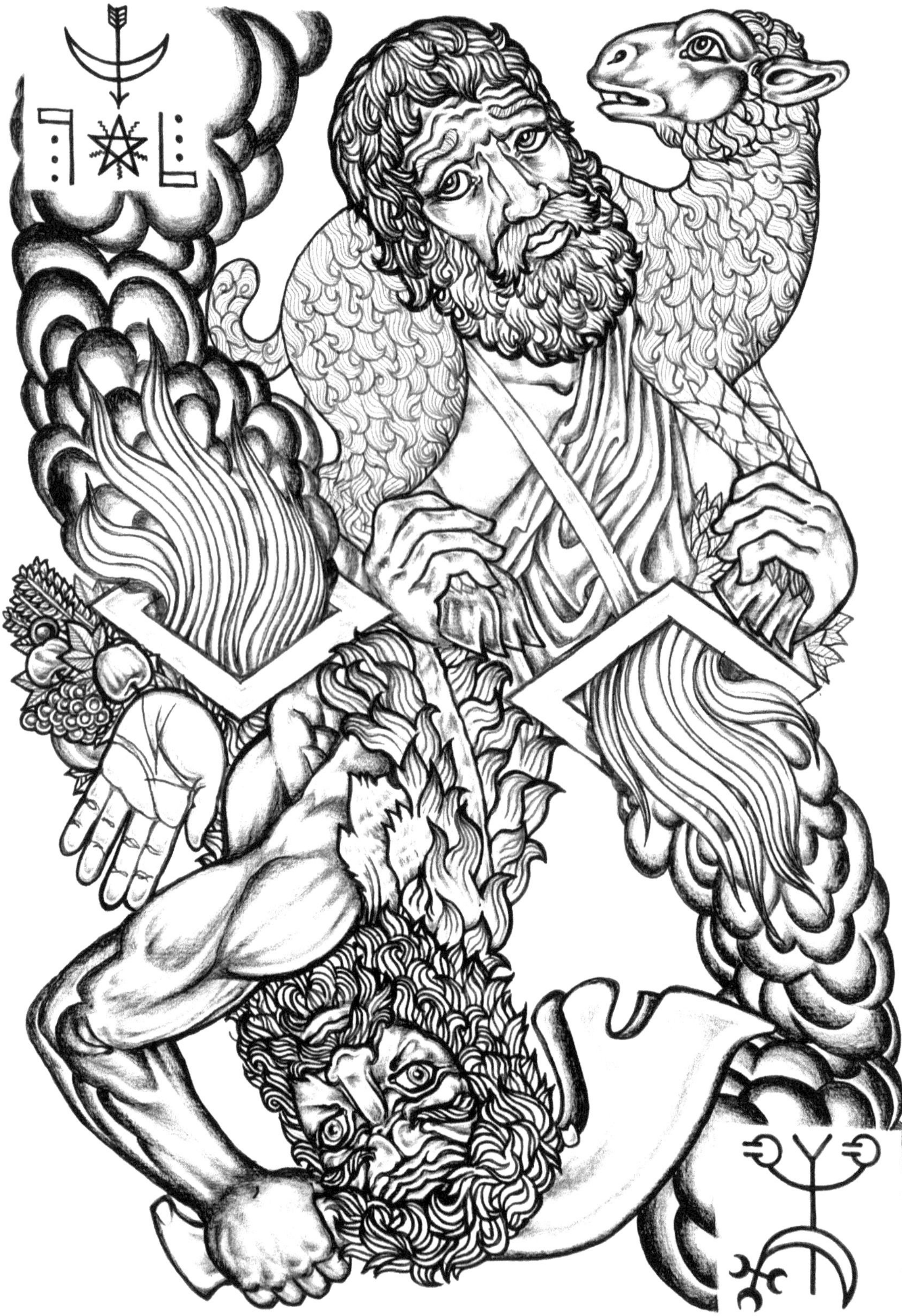

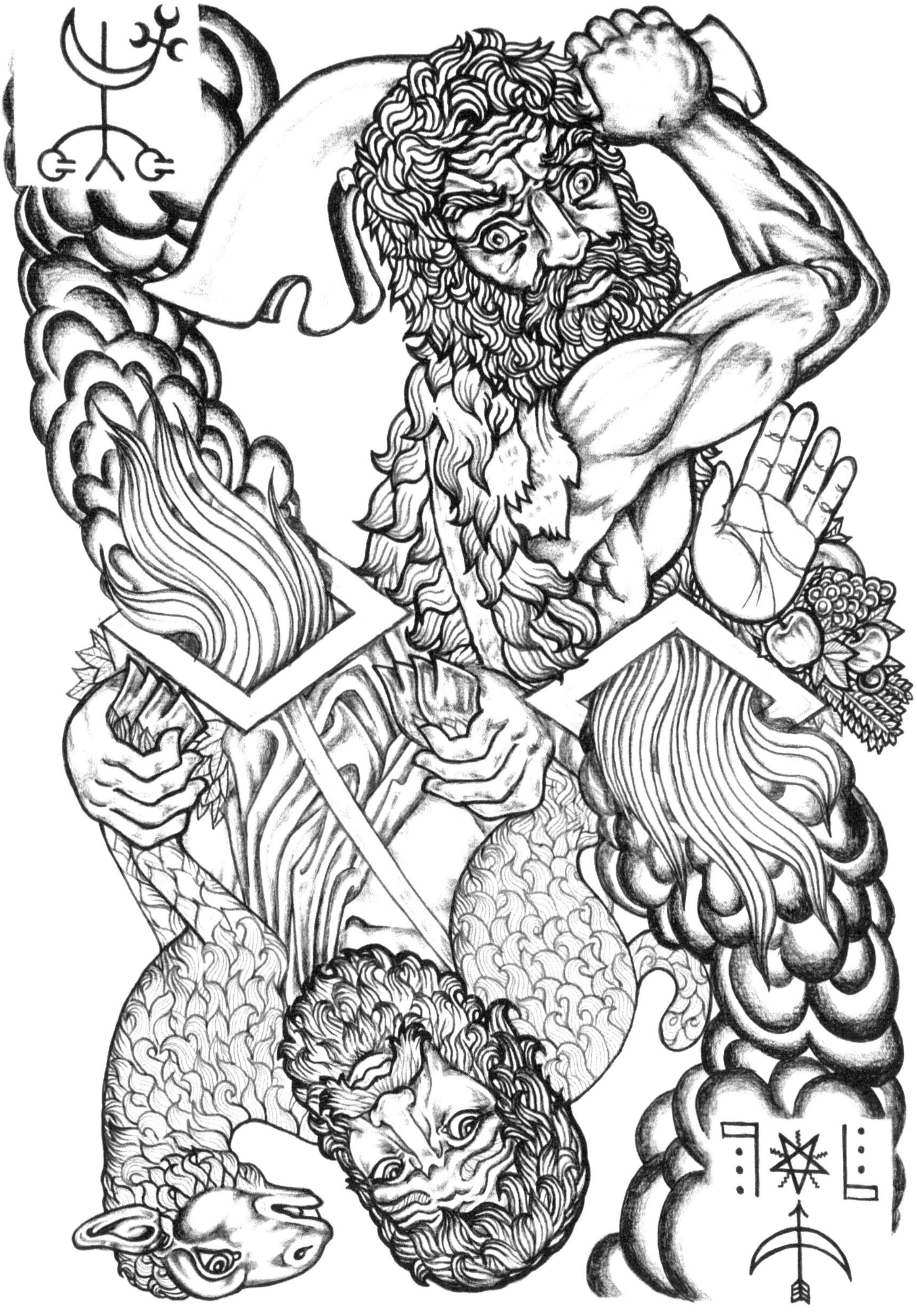

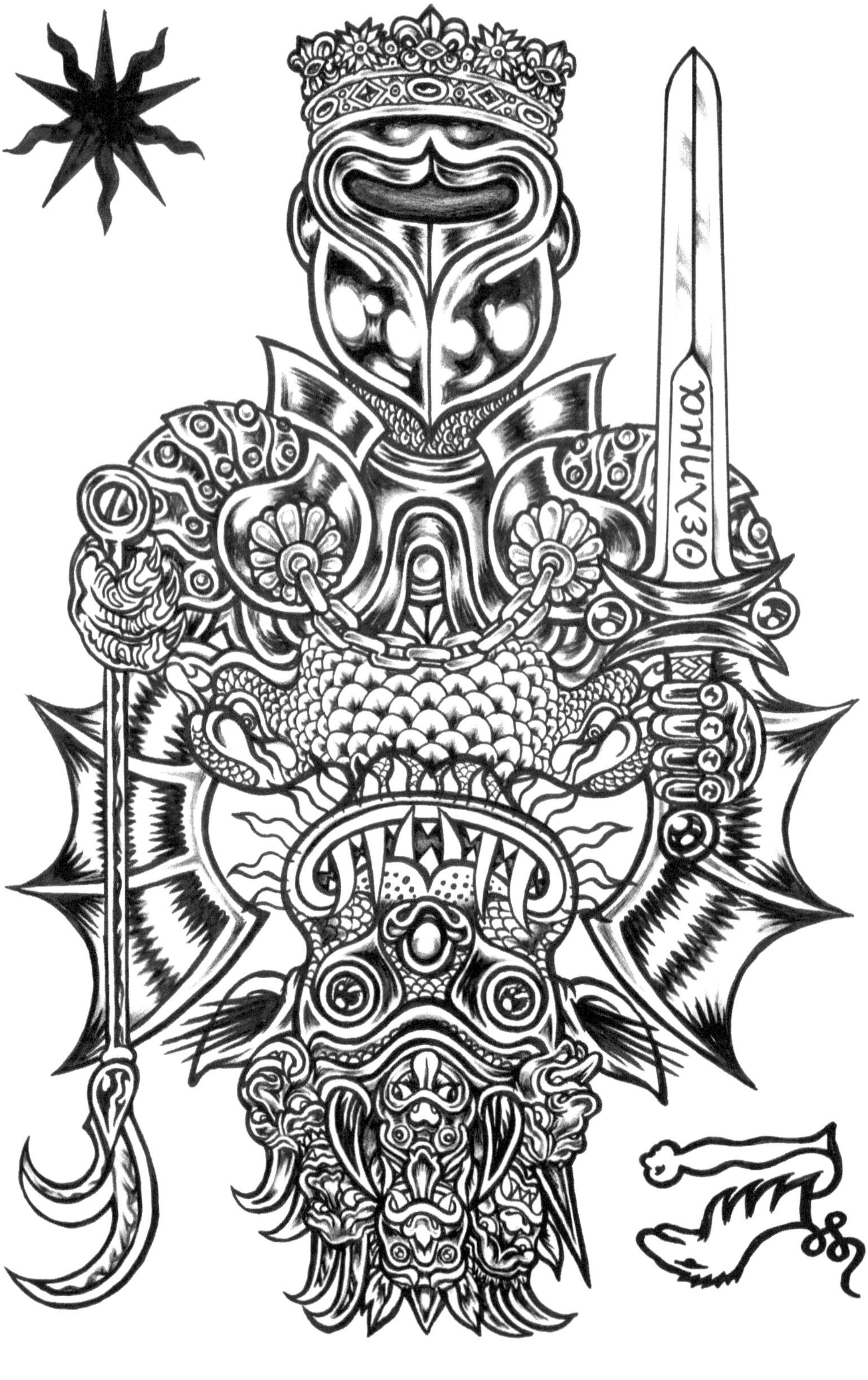

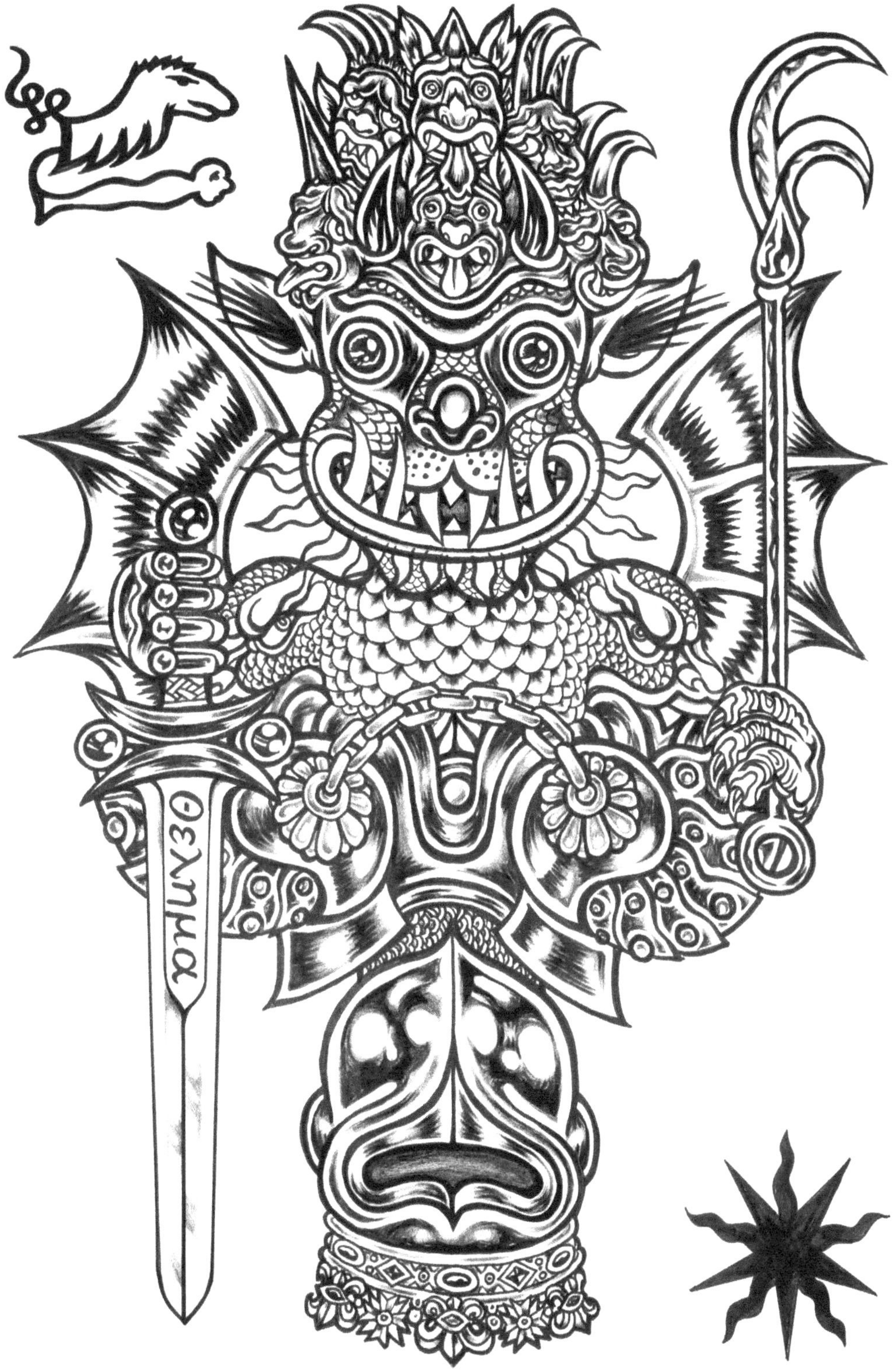
Θελημα

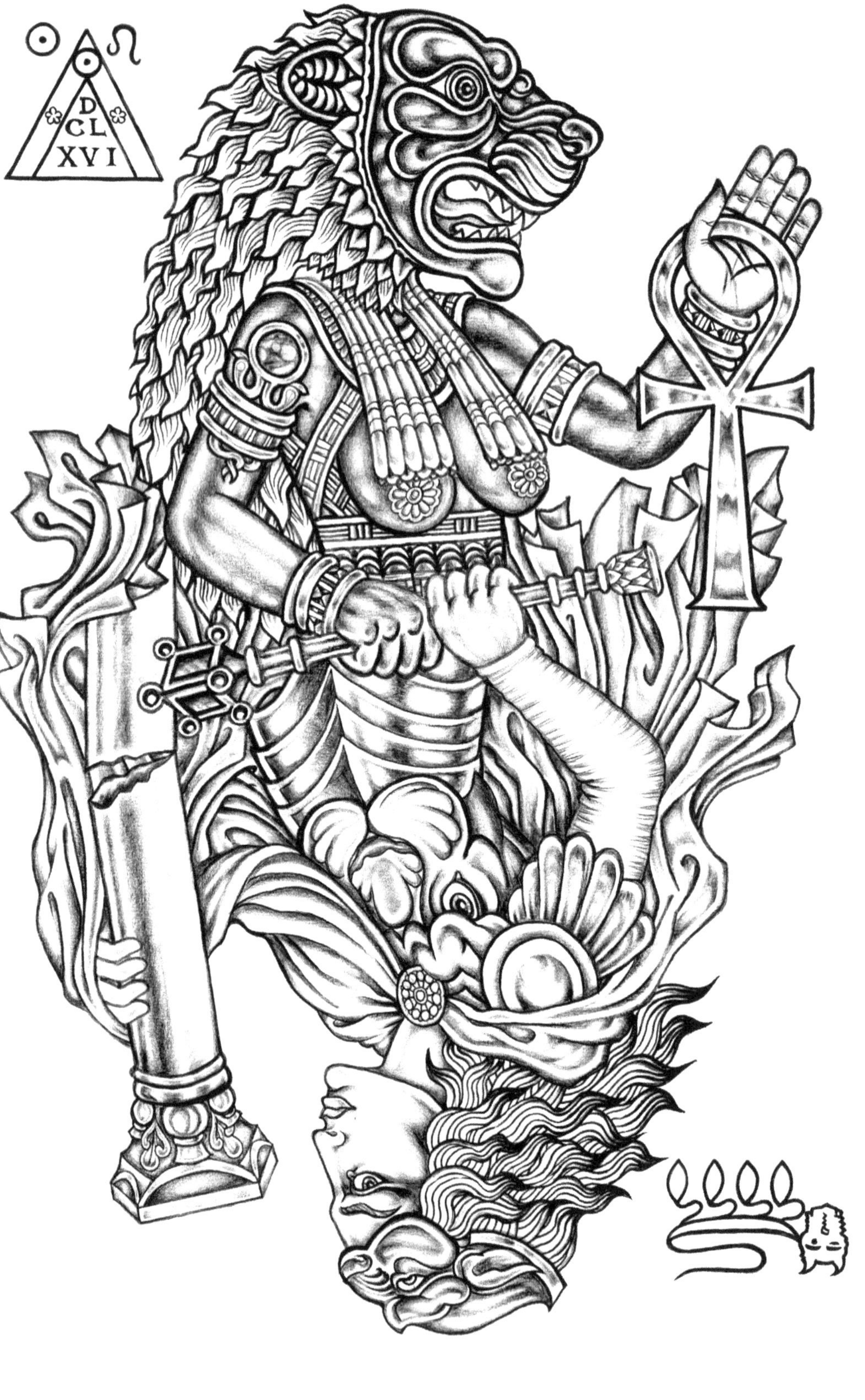
D
CL
XVI

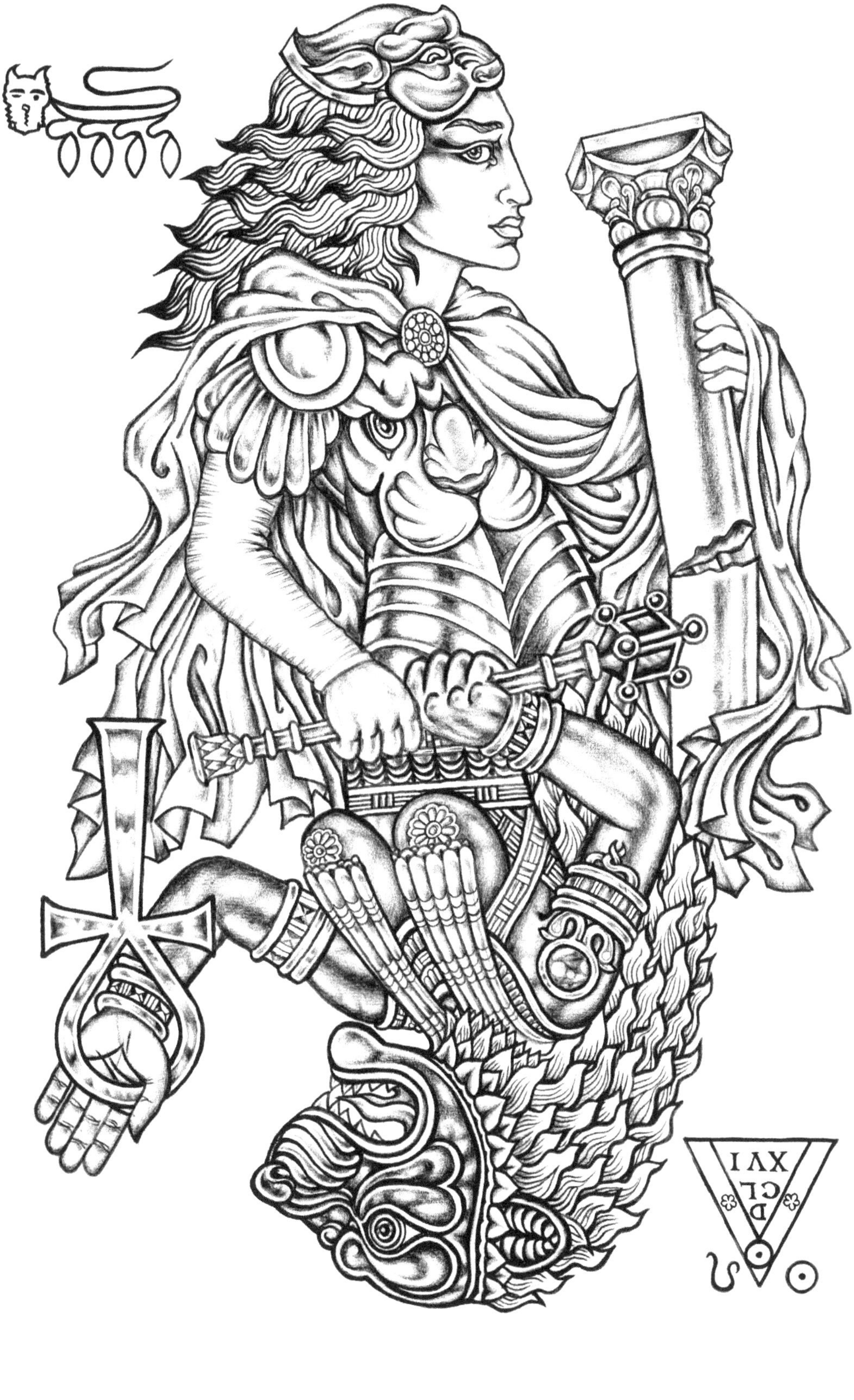

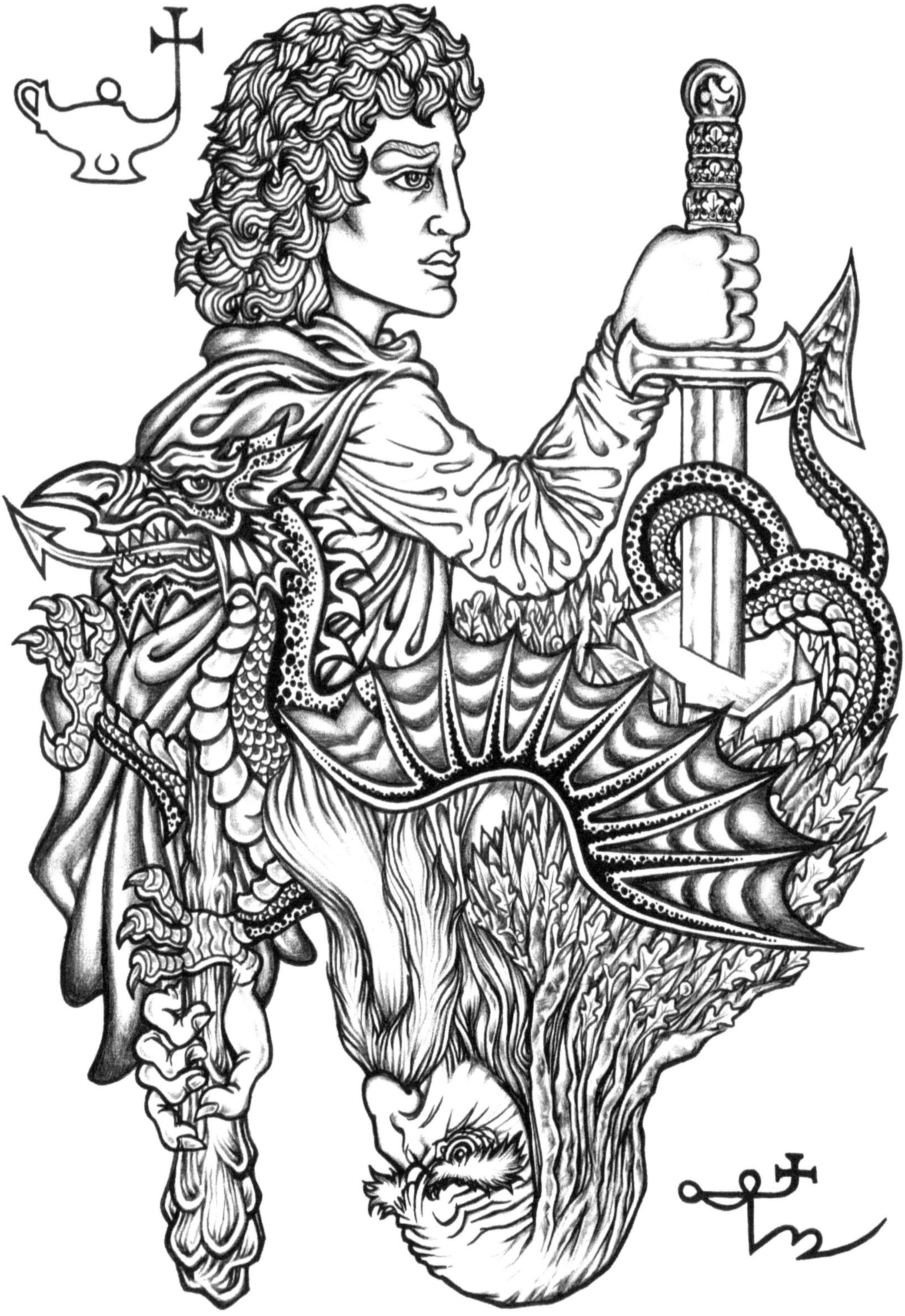

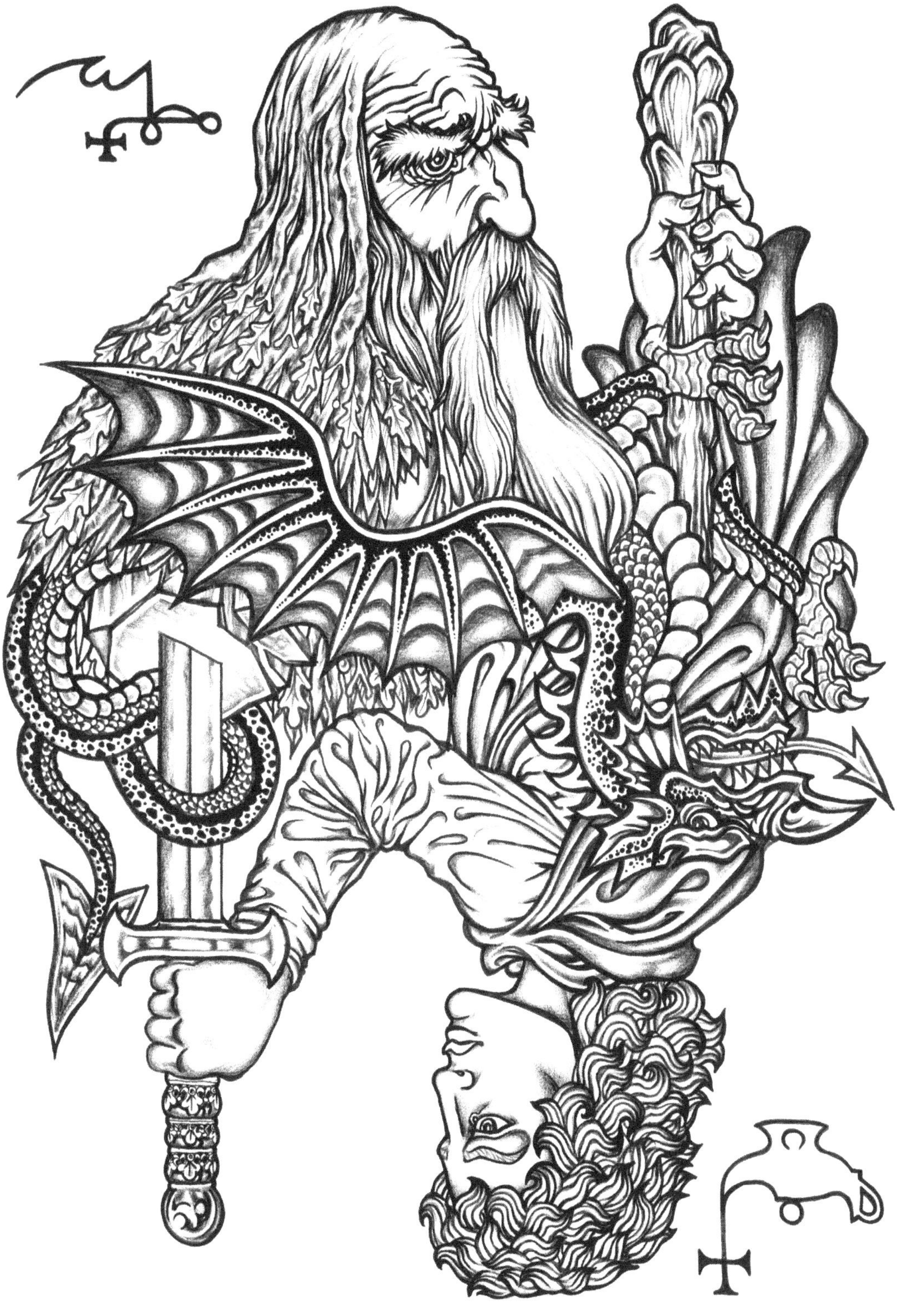

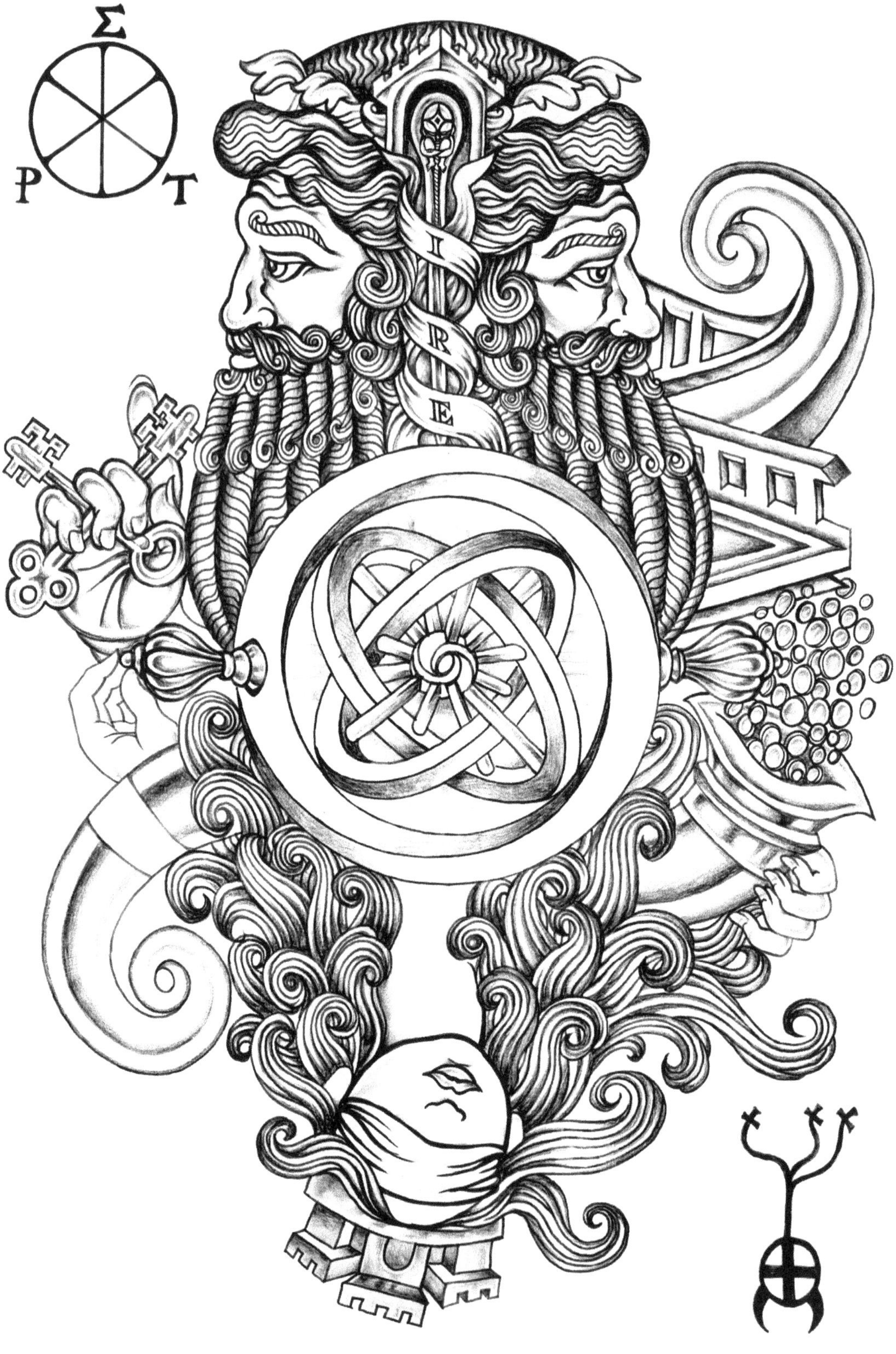
Σ
P
T
I
R
E

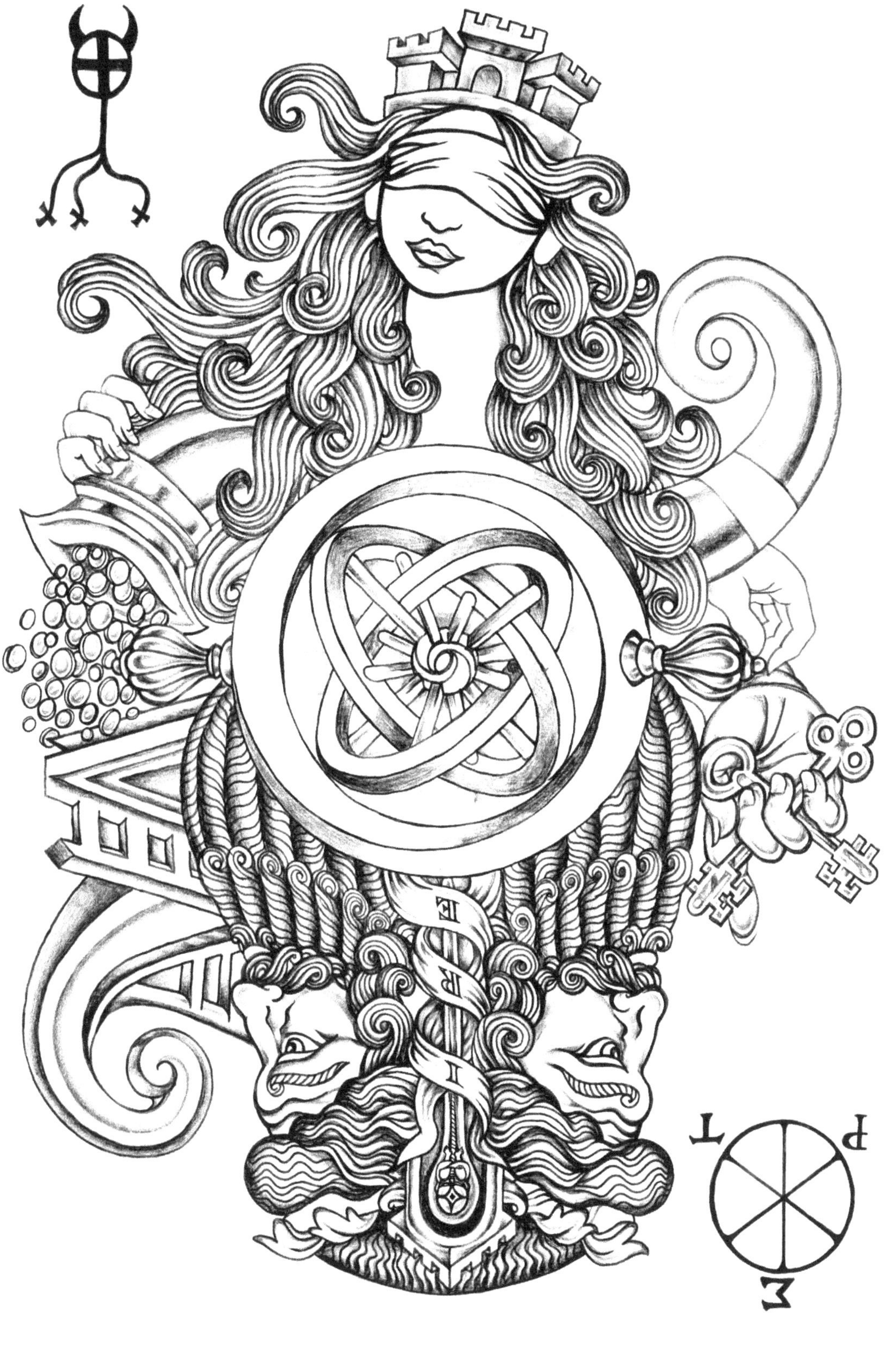

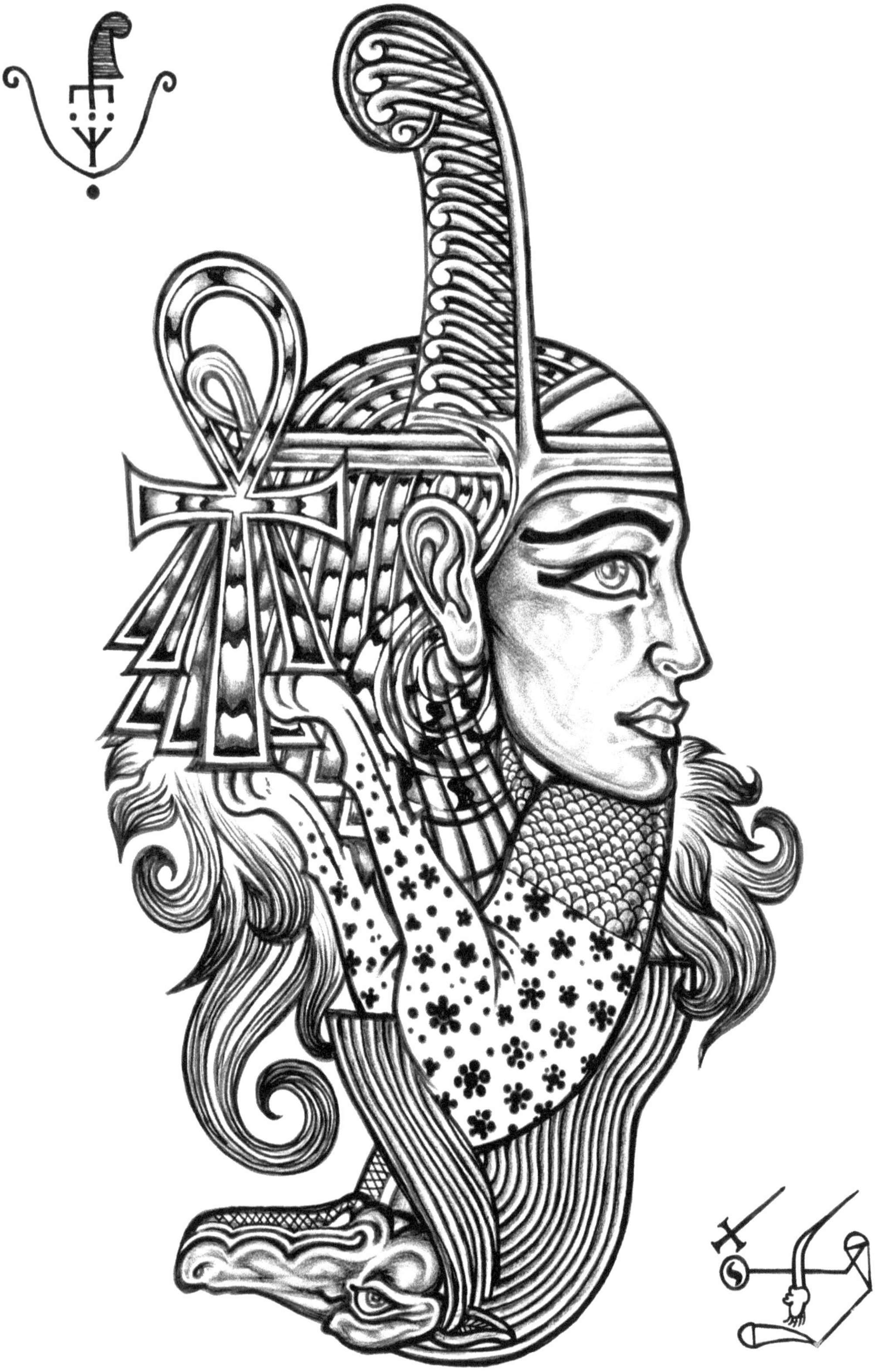

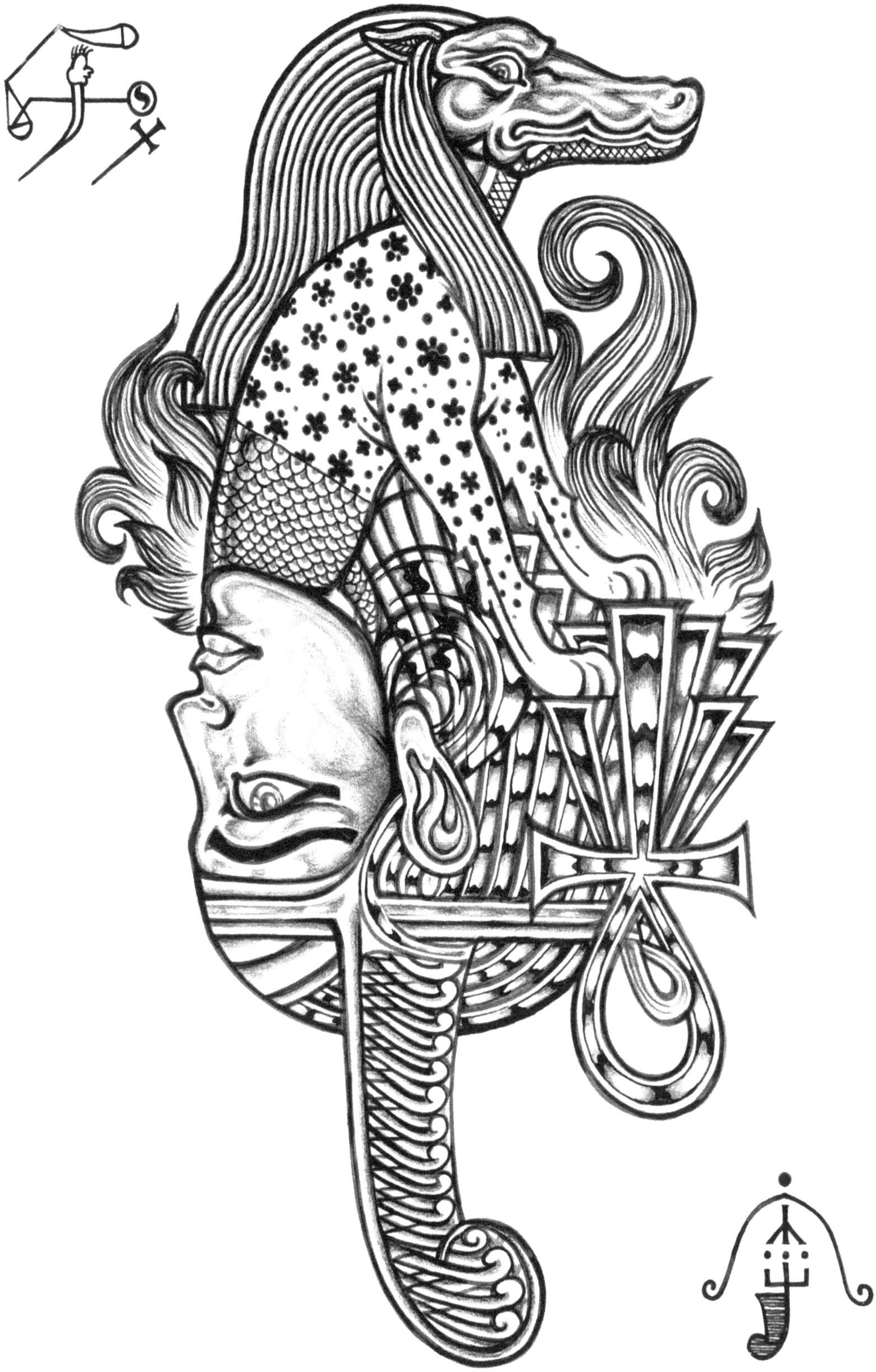

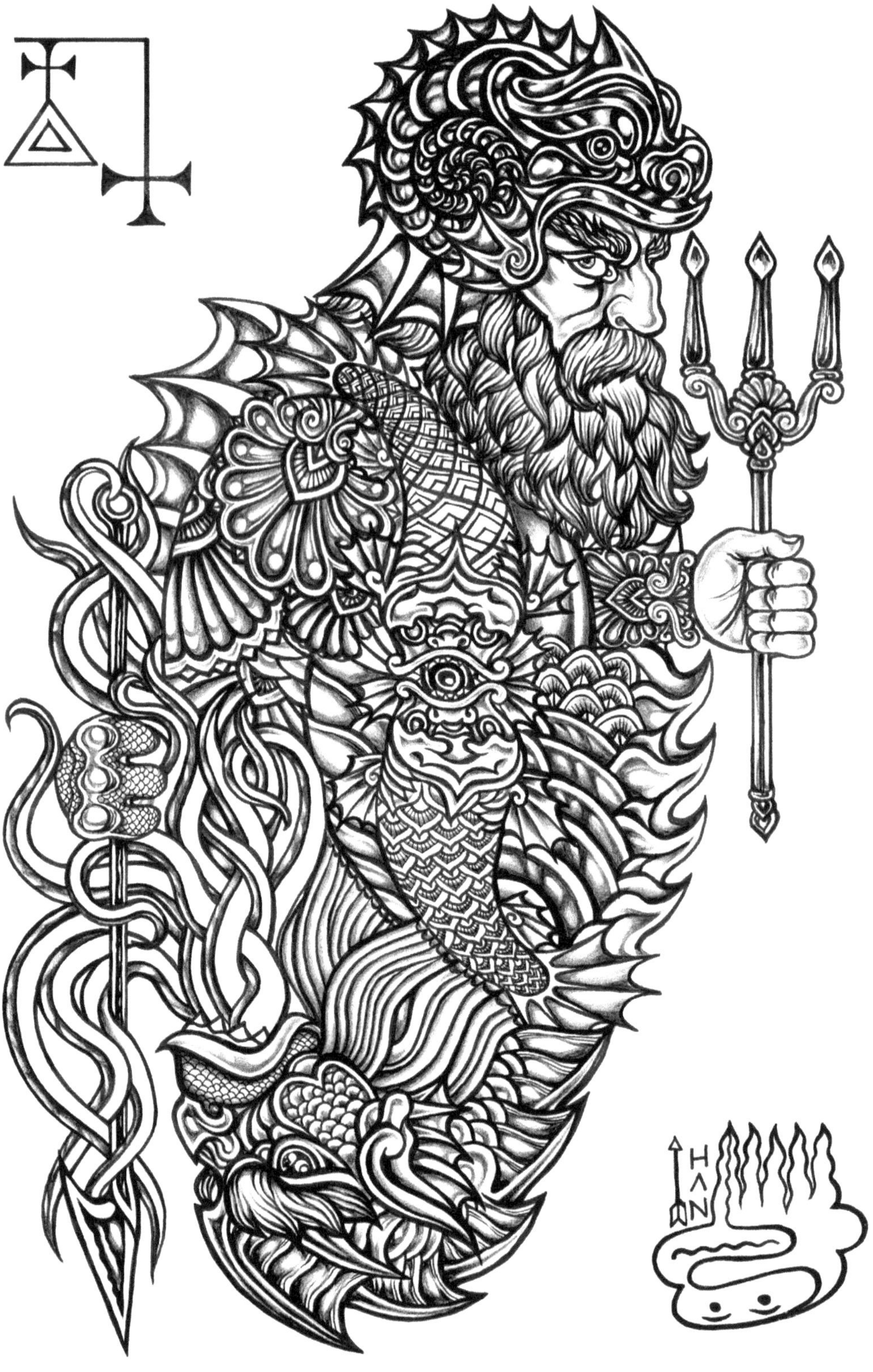
HAN

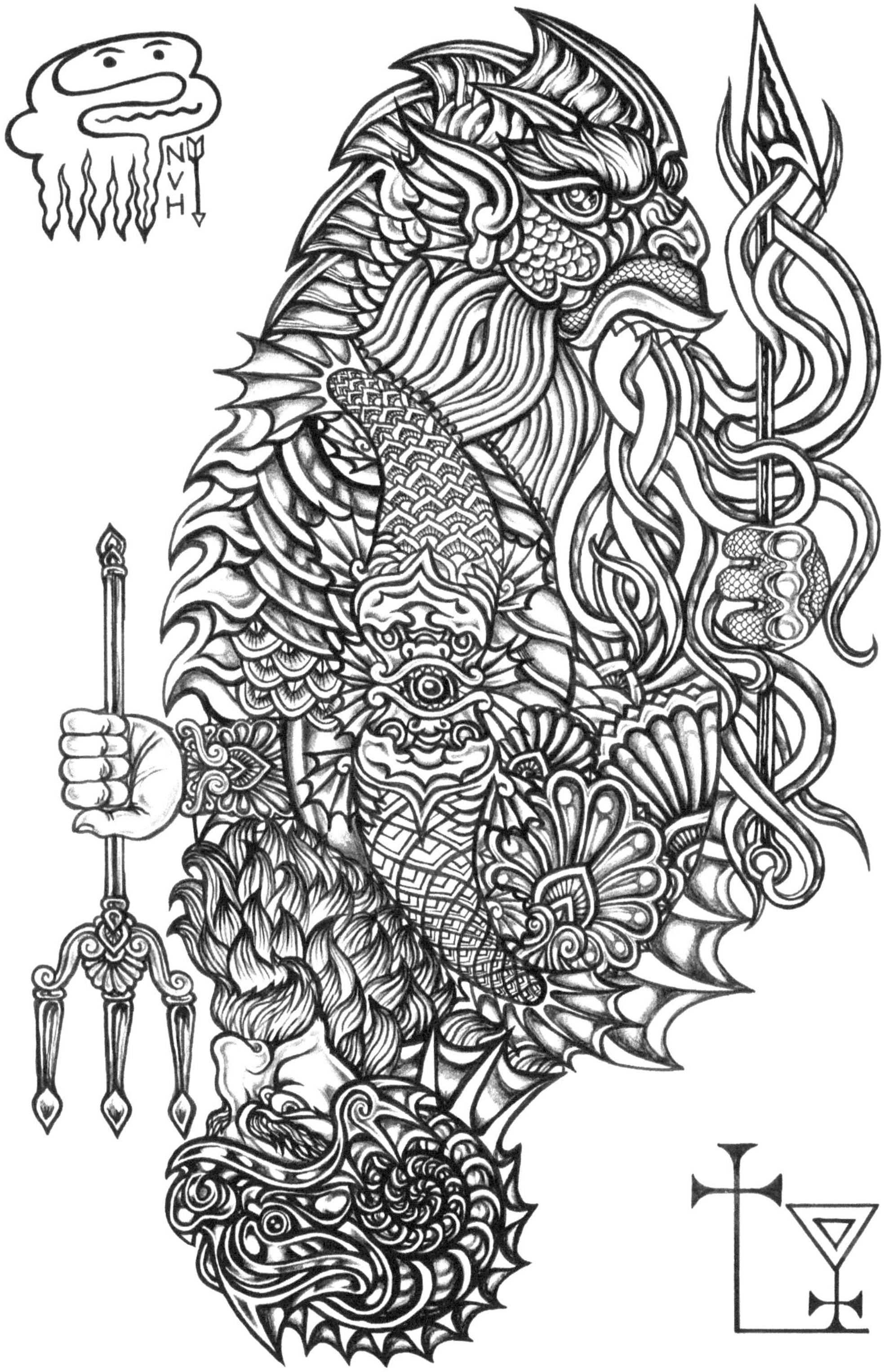

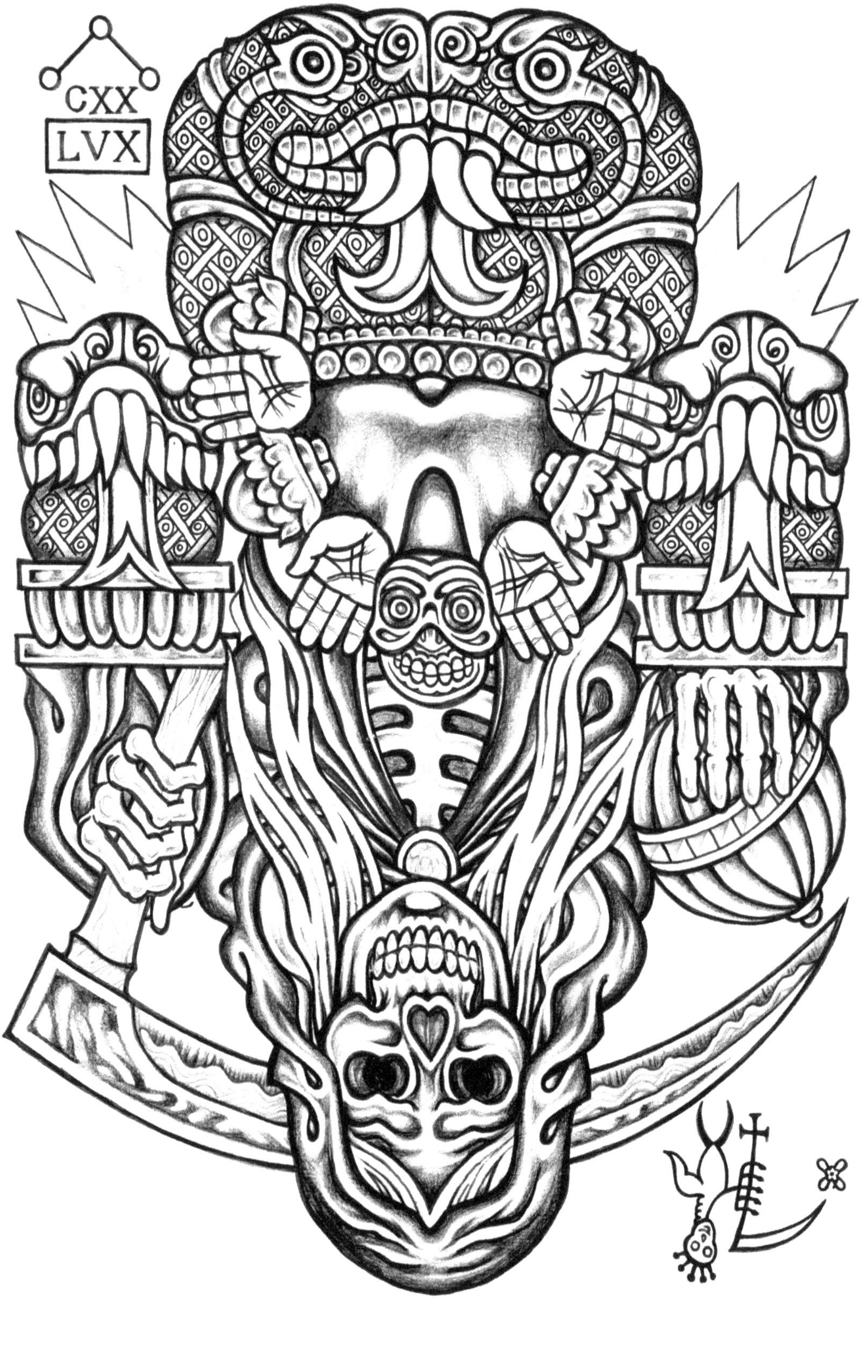
CXX
LVX

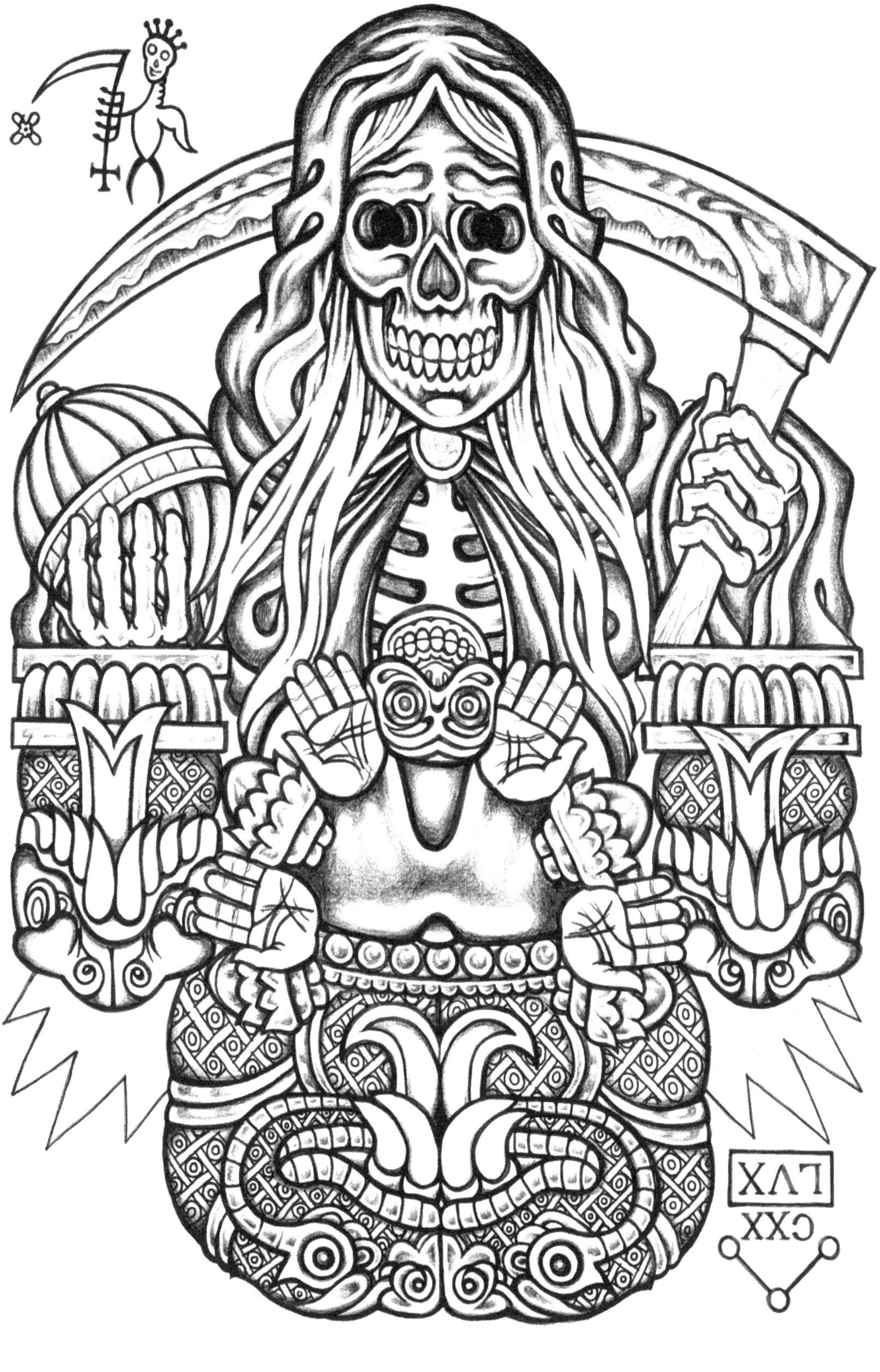

QST
VISITA INTERIORA TERRAE RECTIFICANDO INVENIES OCCULTUM LAPIDEM

VISITA INTERIOR TERRAE RECTIFICANDO INVENIES OCCULTUM LAPIDEM

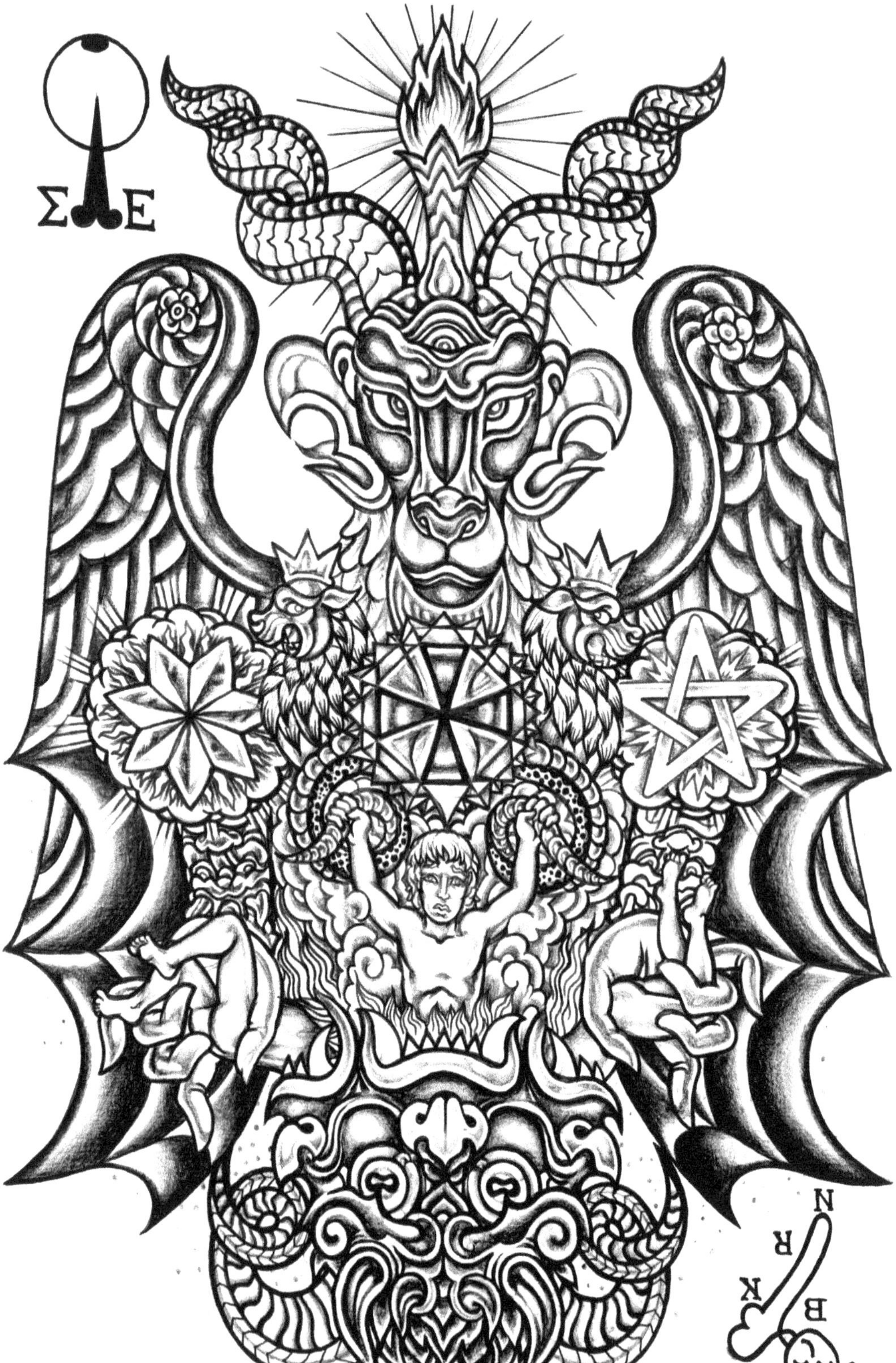

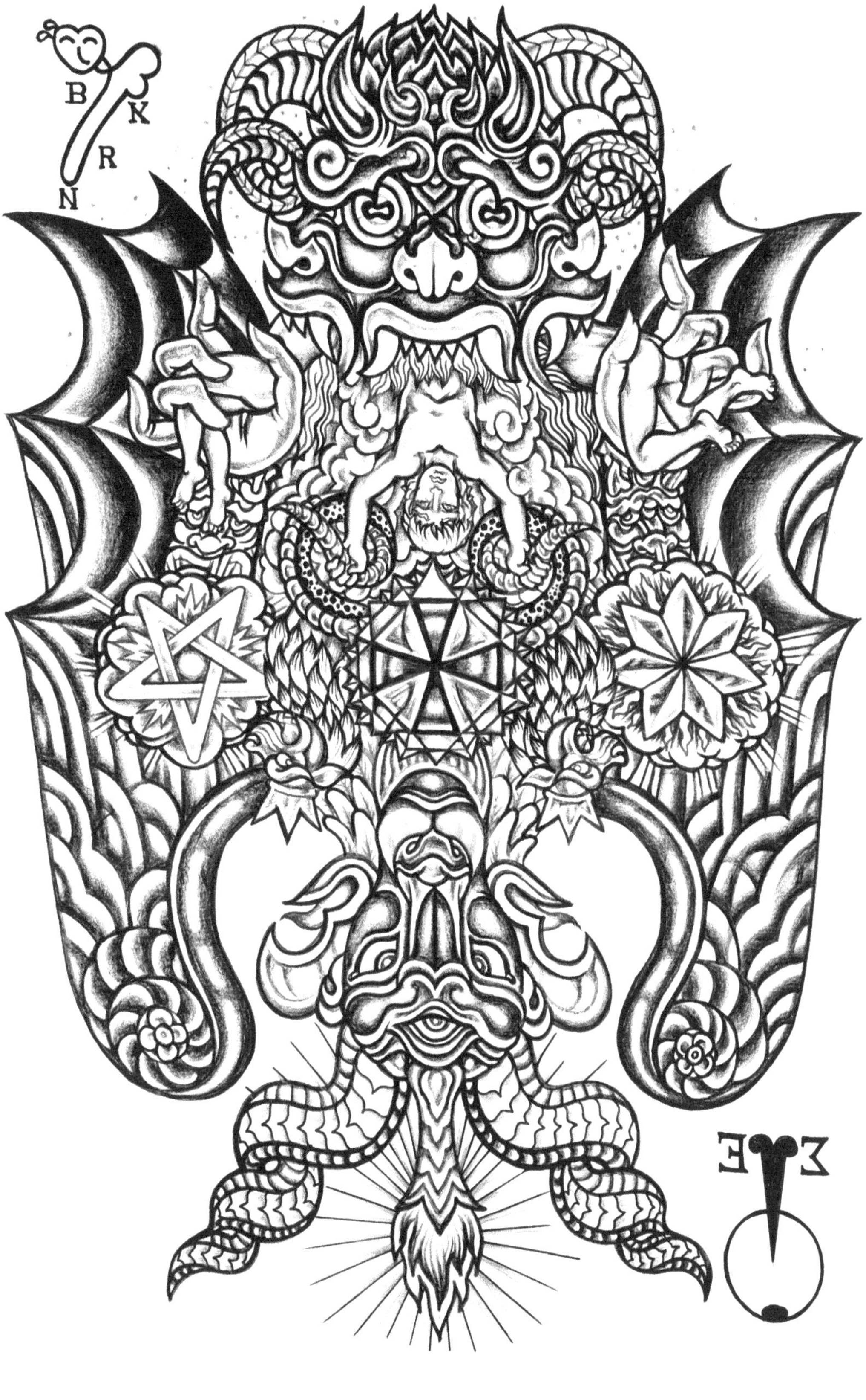
B
K
R
N

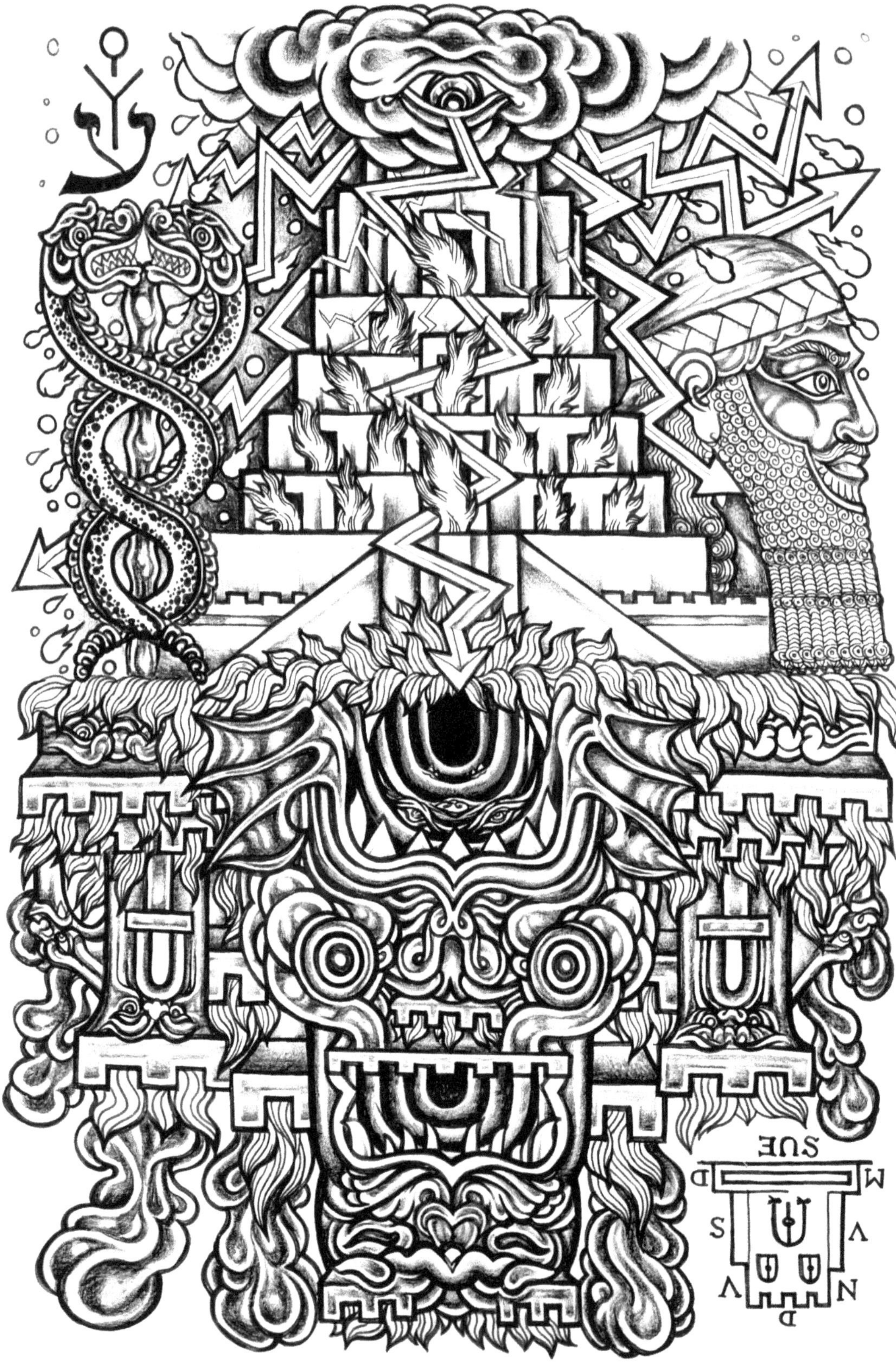

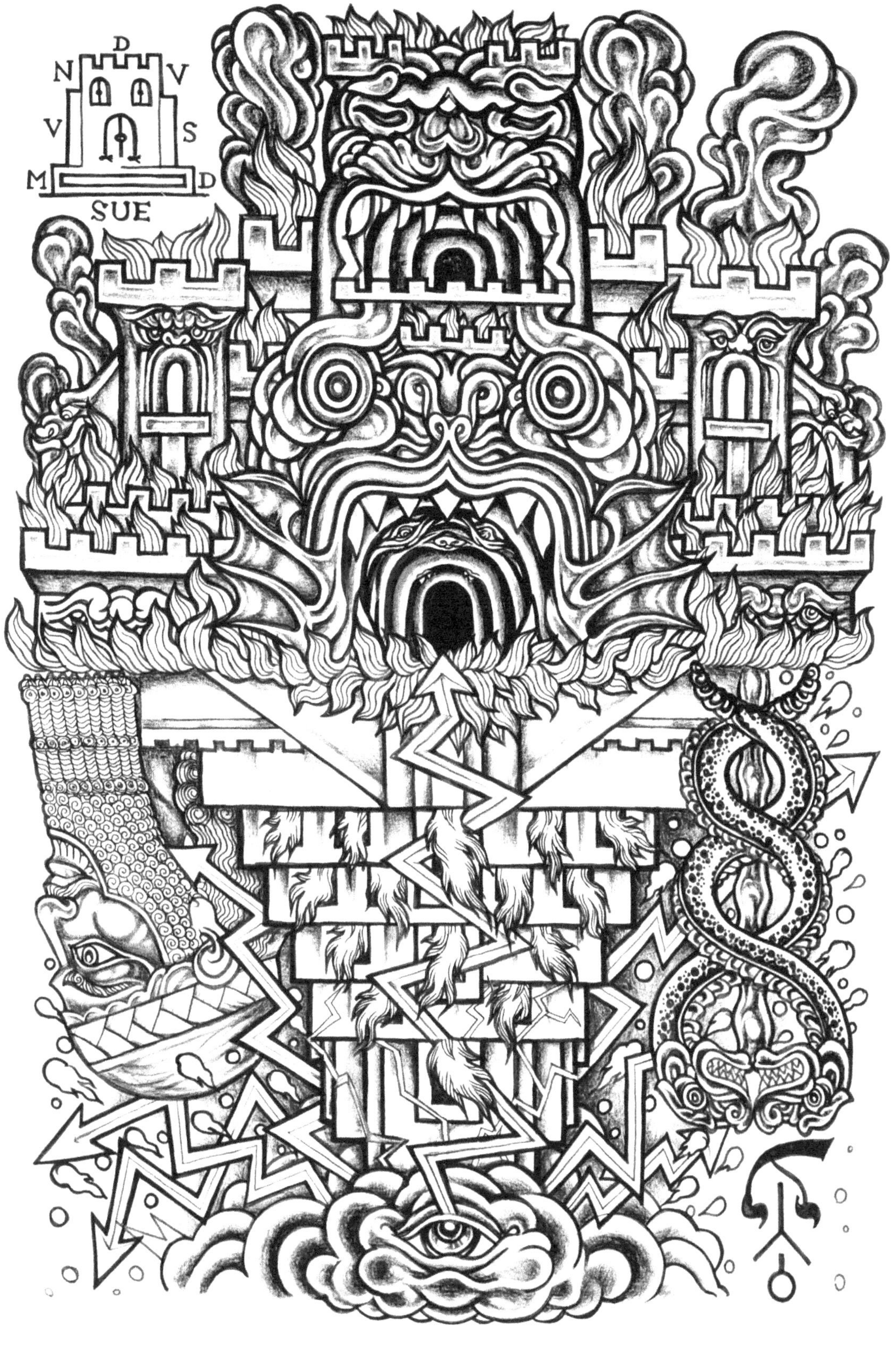
D
N V
V S
M D
SUE

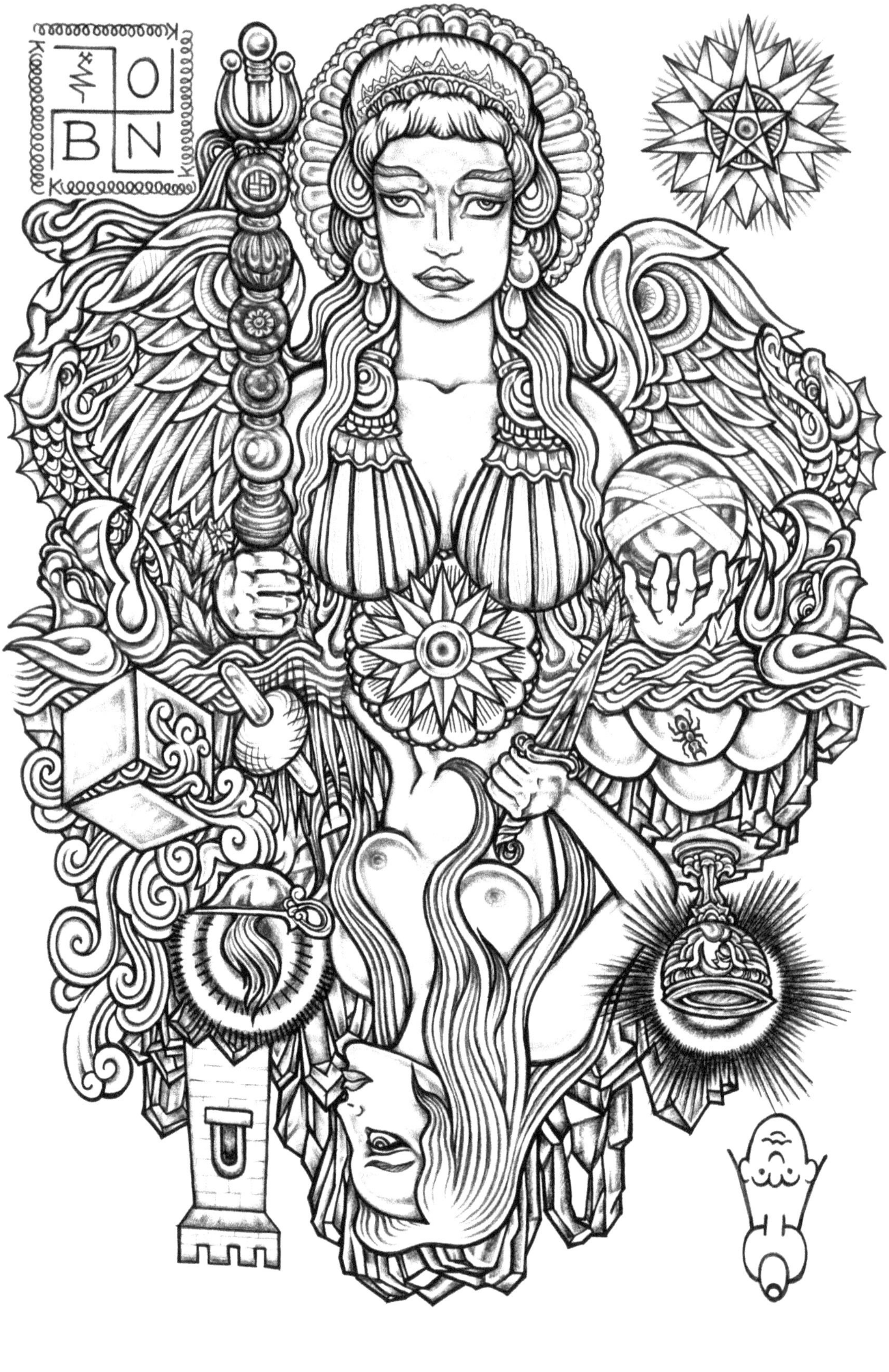
O
B N

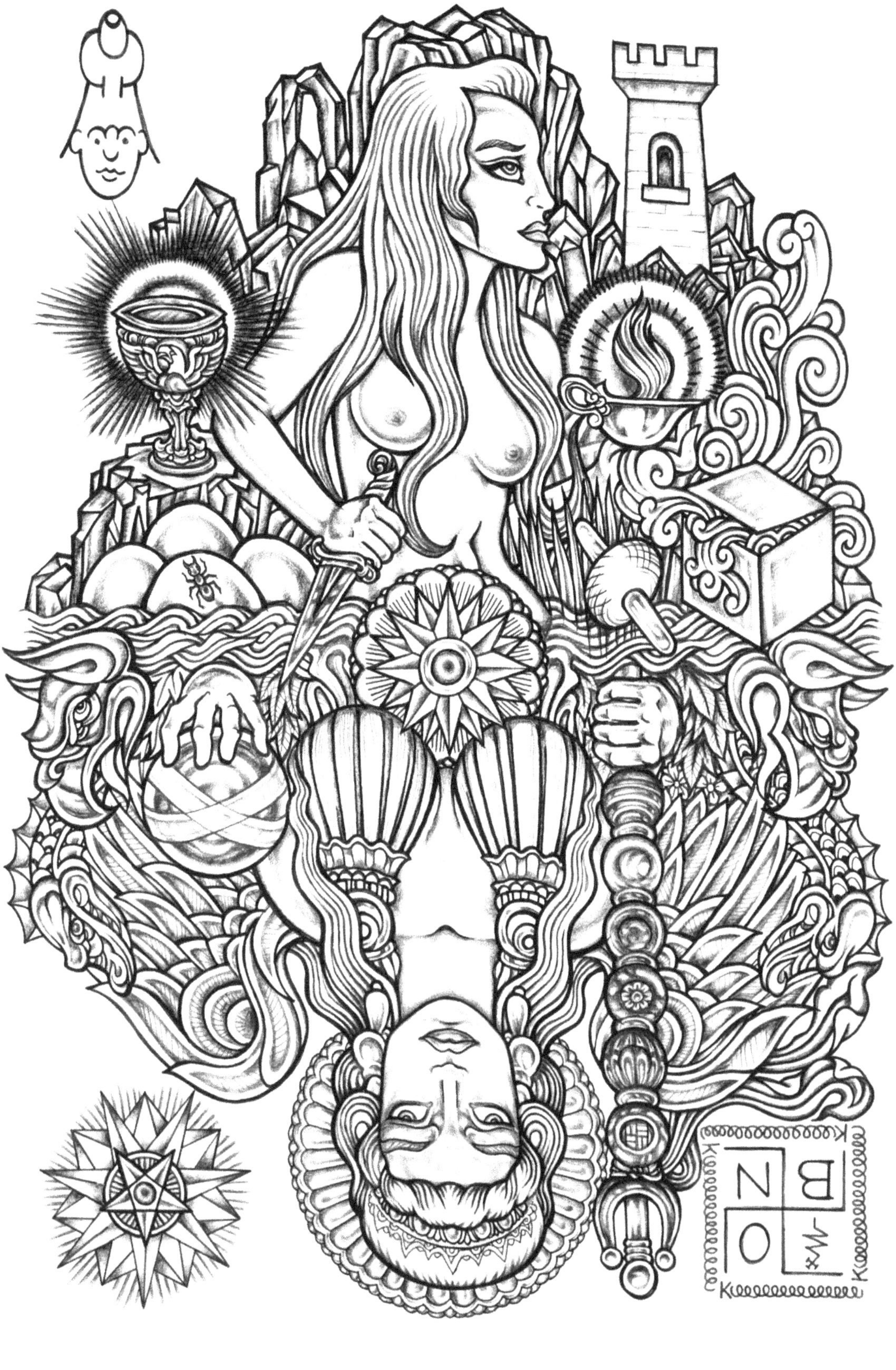
N
B
O

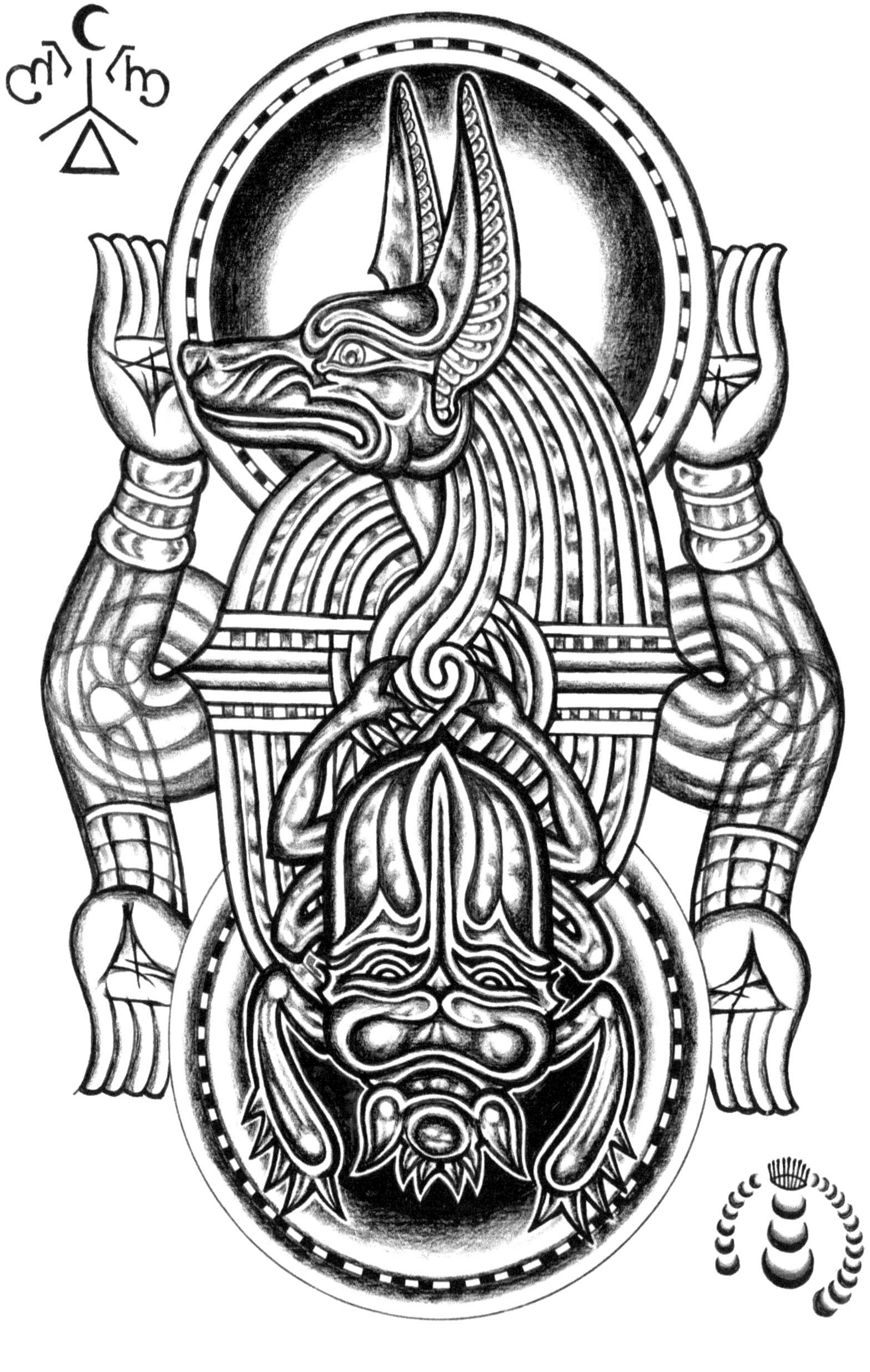

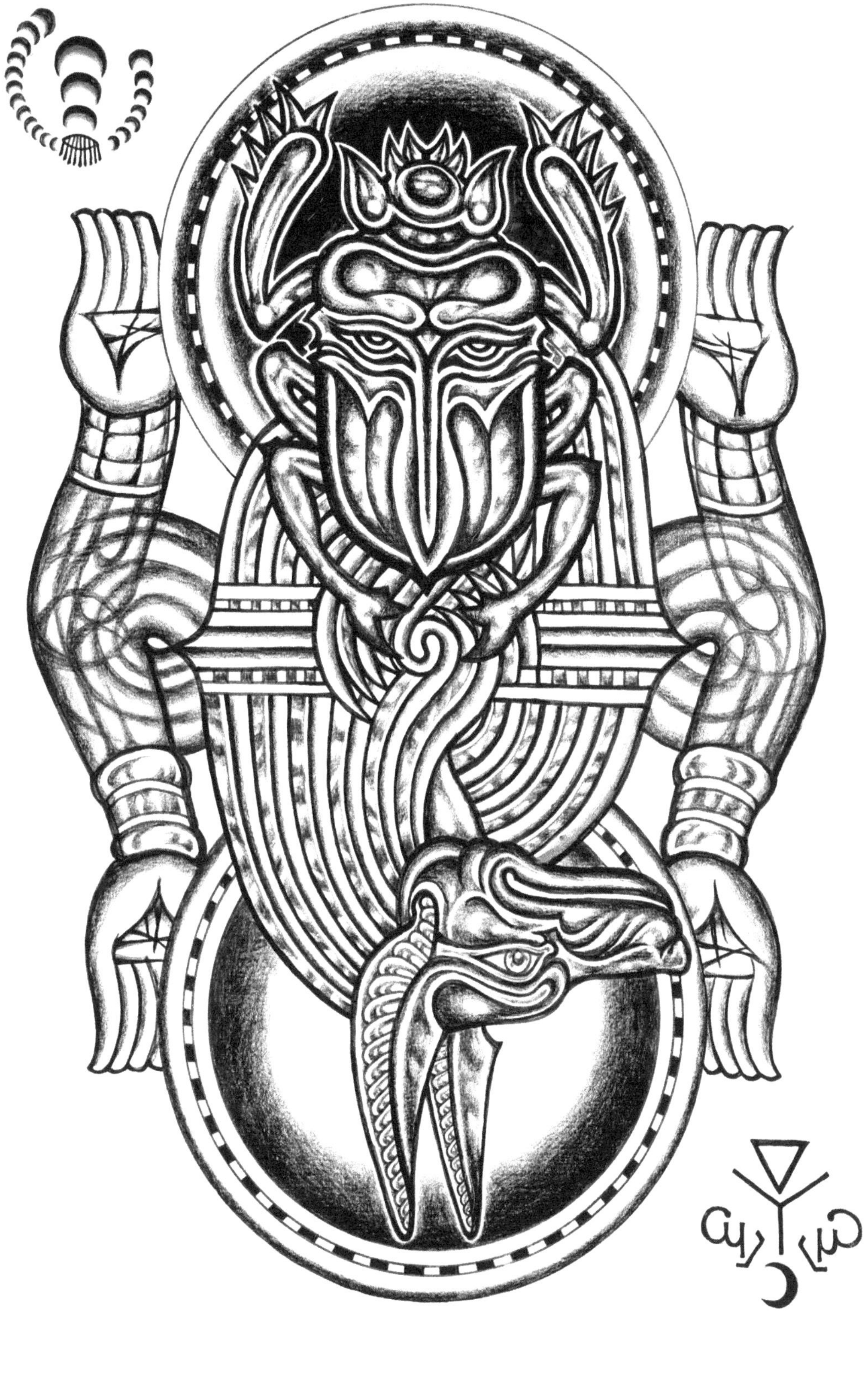

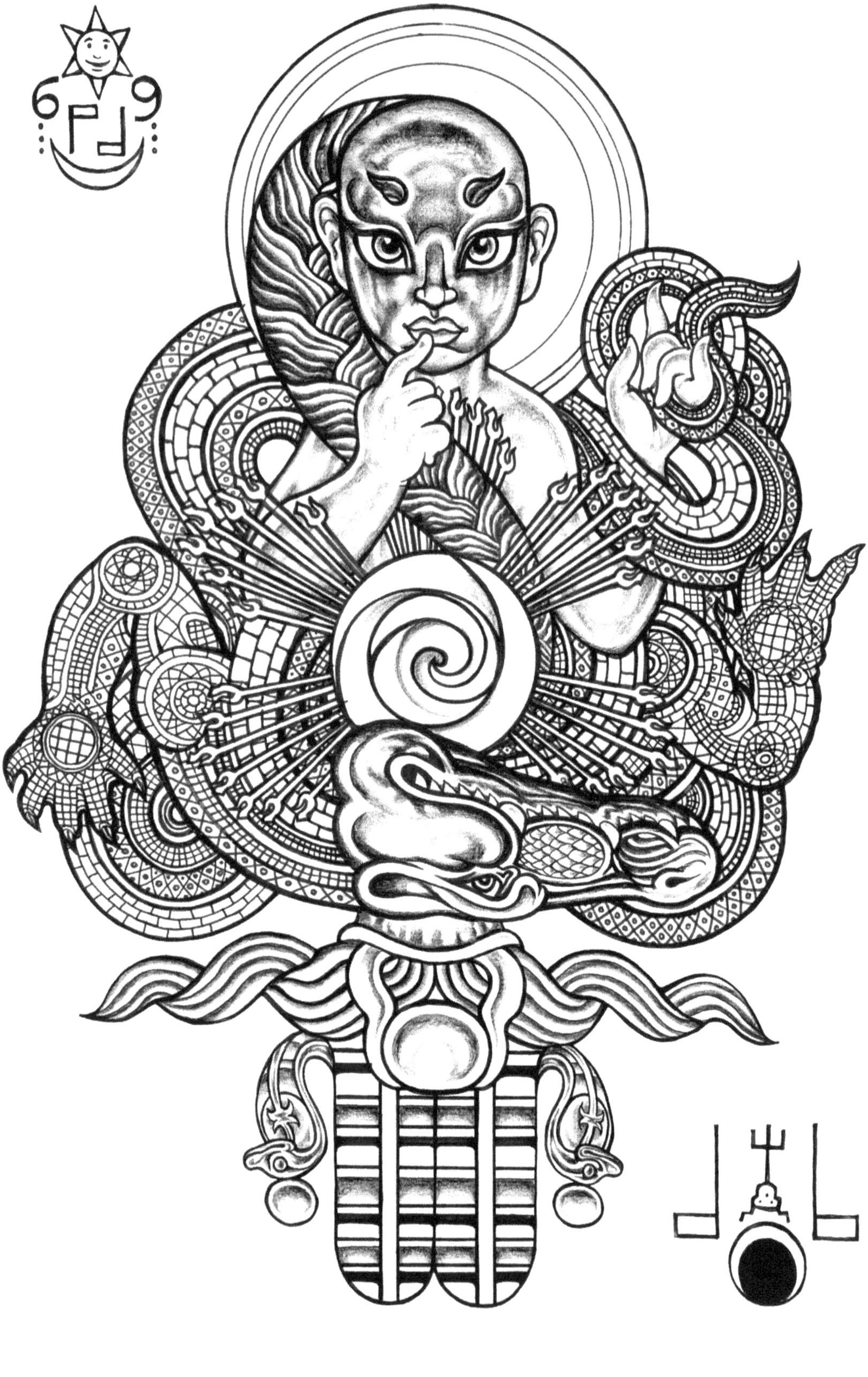

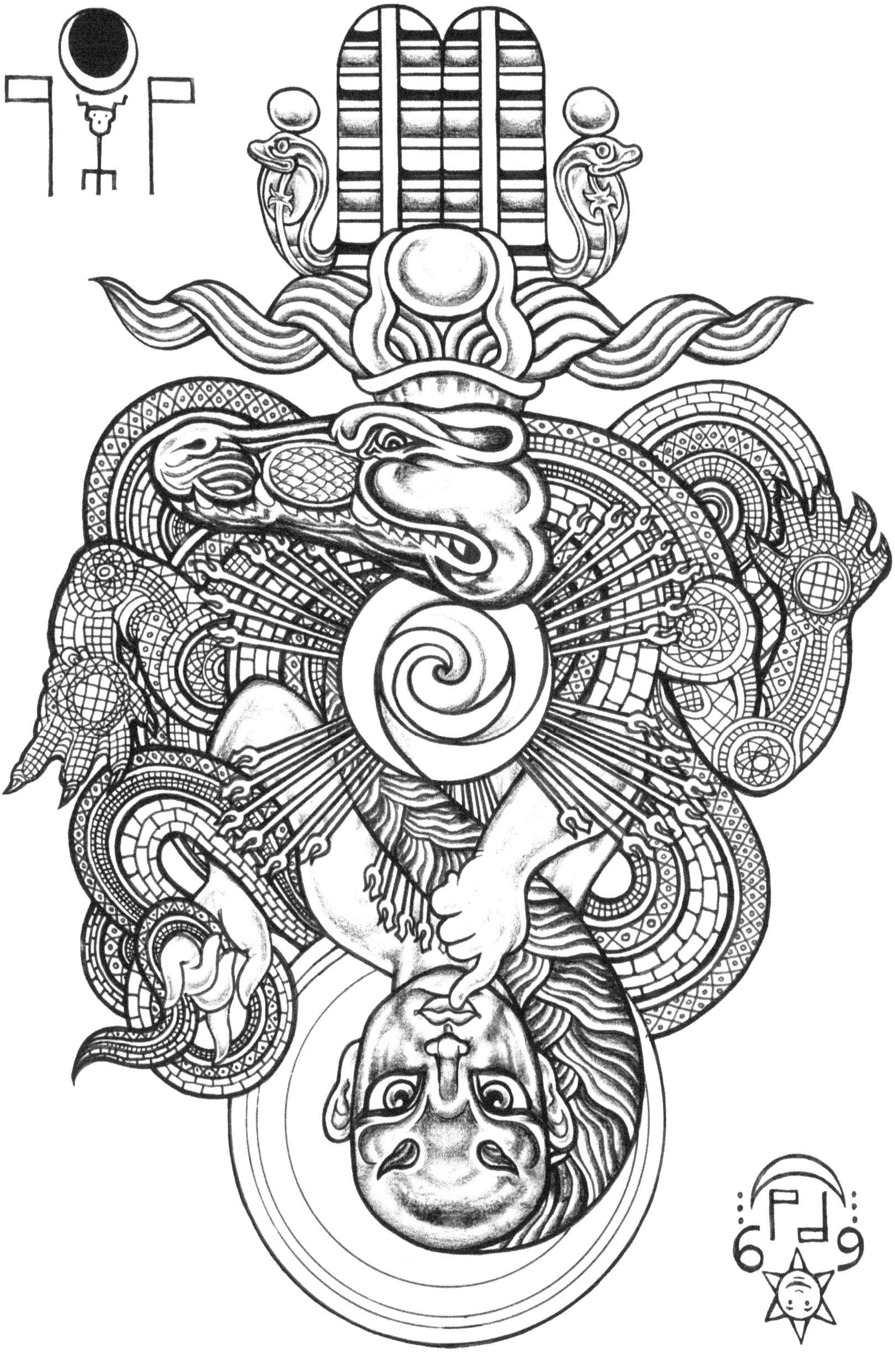

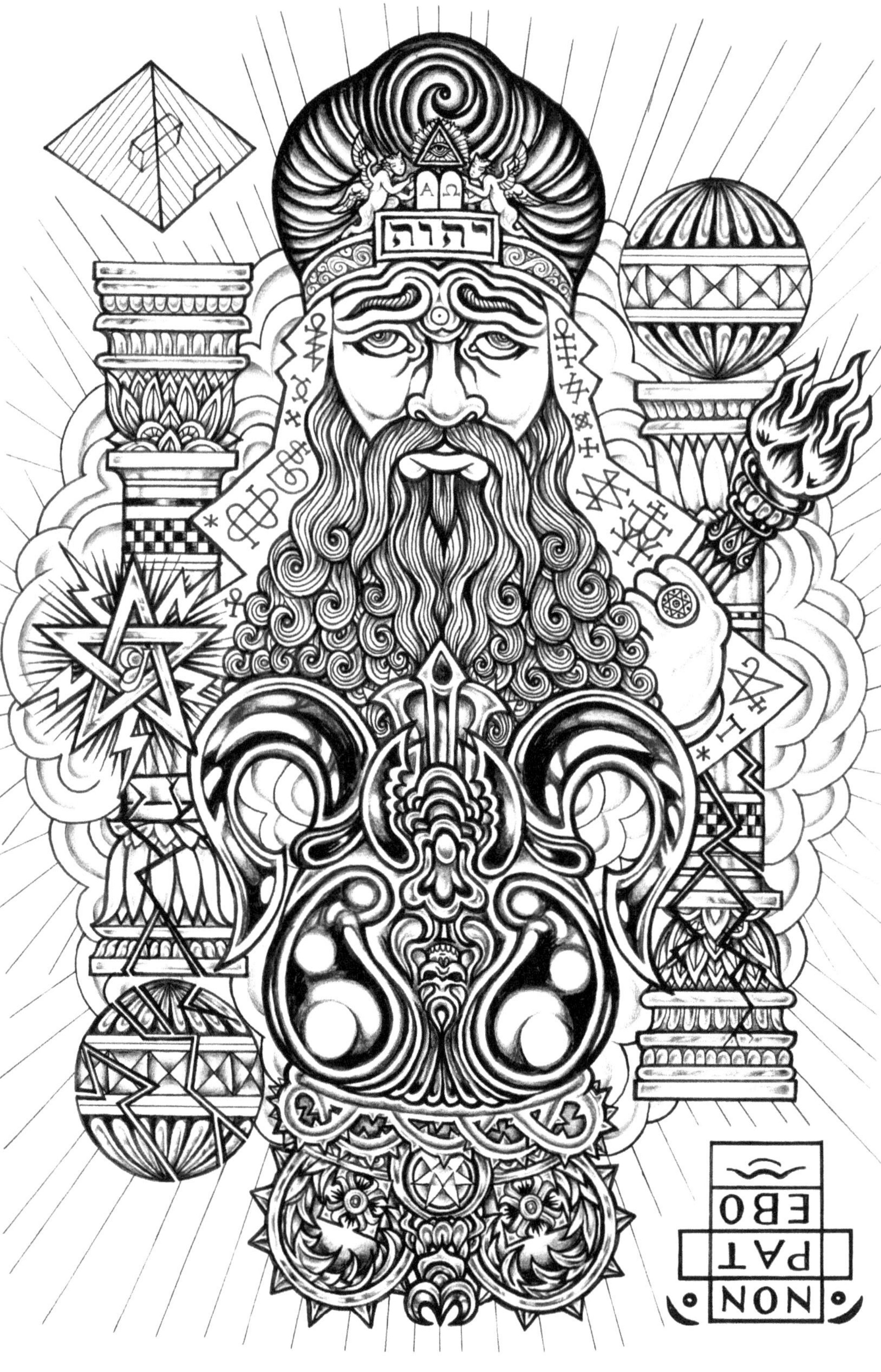
A Ω
יהוה
NON
PAT
EBO

NON
PAT
EBO

Leo

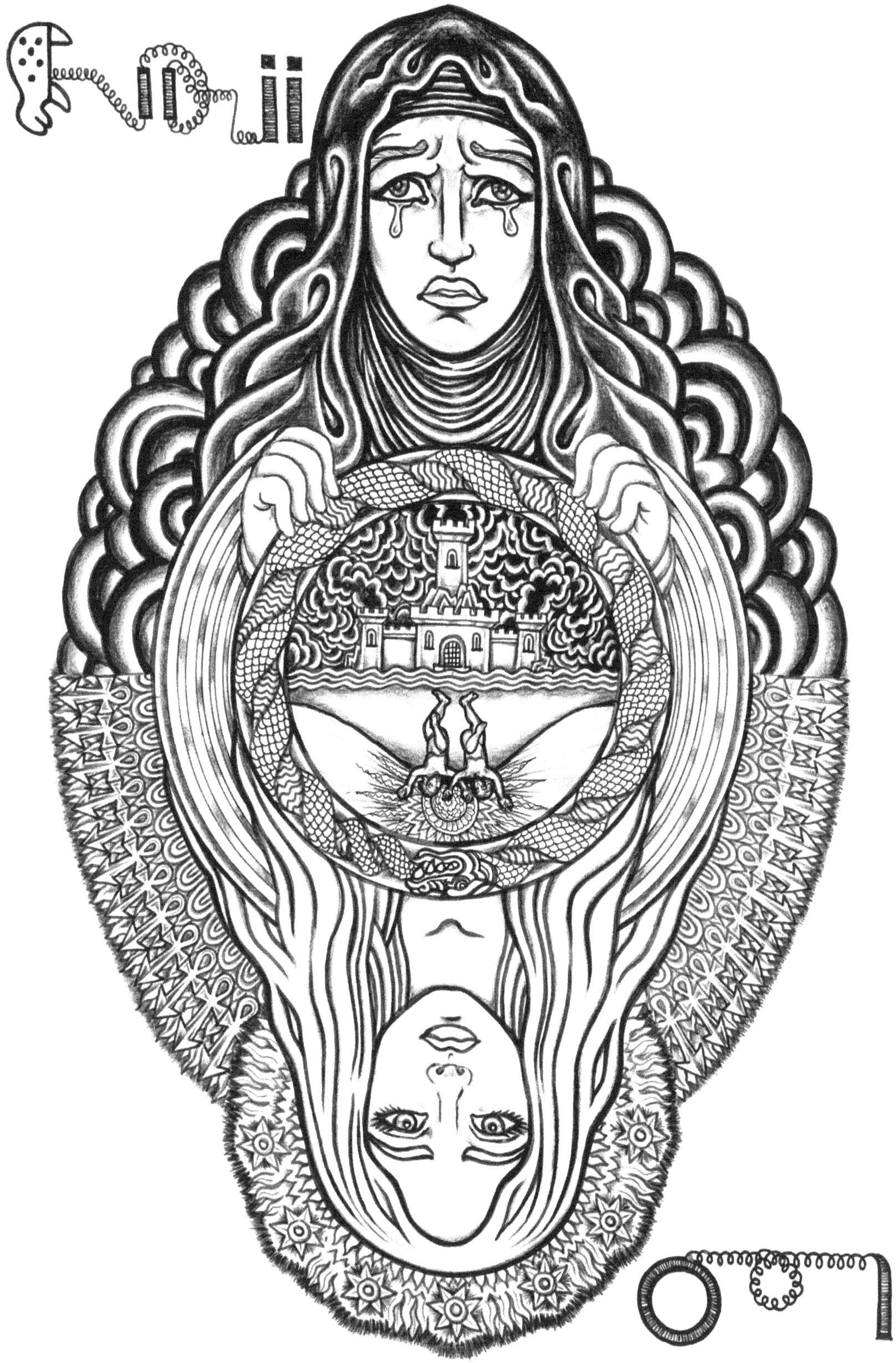